HAL•LEONARD ESSENTIAL SONGS

FOR ORGANS, PIANOS & ELECTRONIC KEYBOARDS

51

The 1950s

T0055353

ISBN 978-0-634-09240-4

7777 W. BLUEMOUND RD. P.O. BOX 13819 MILWAUKEE, WI 53213

Visit Hal Leonard Online at
www.halleonard.com

All Shook Up

Registration 5
Rhythm: Rock

Words and Music by Otis Blackwell
and Elvis Presley

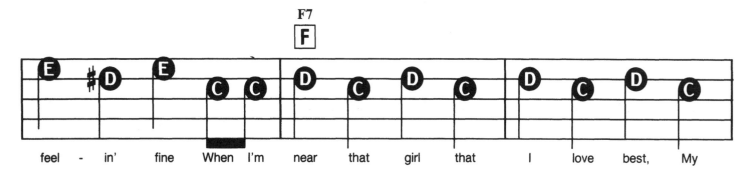

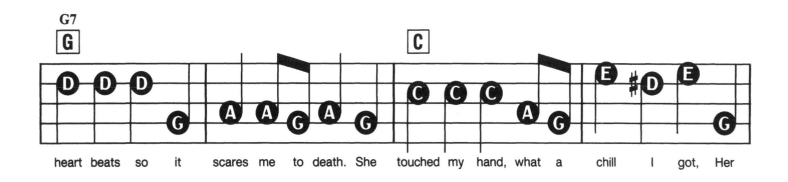

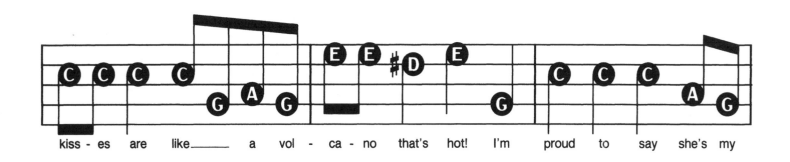

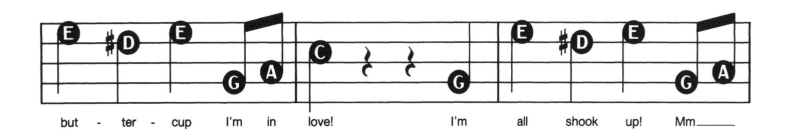

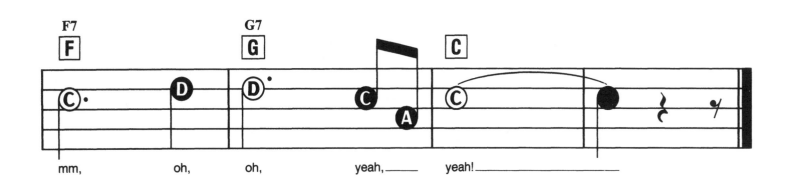

Along Came Jones

Registration 10
Rhythm: Country or Bluegrass

Words and Music by Jerry Leiber
and Mike Stoller

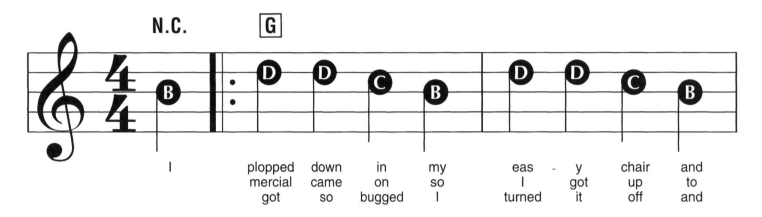

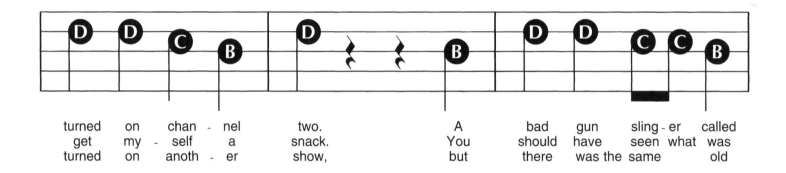

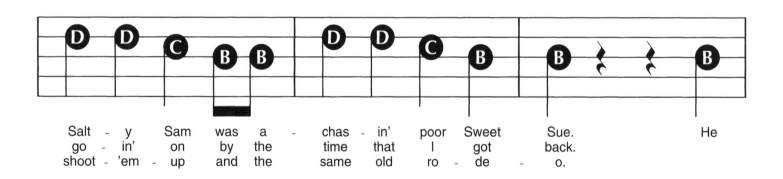

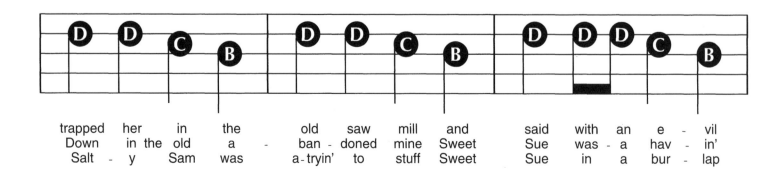

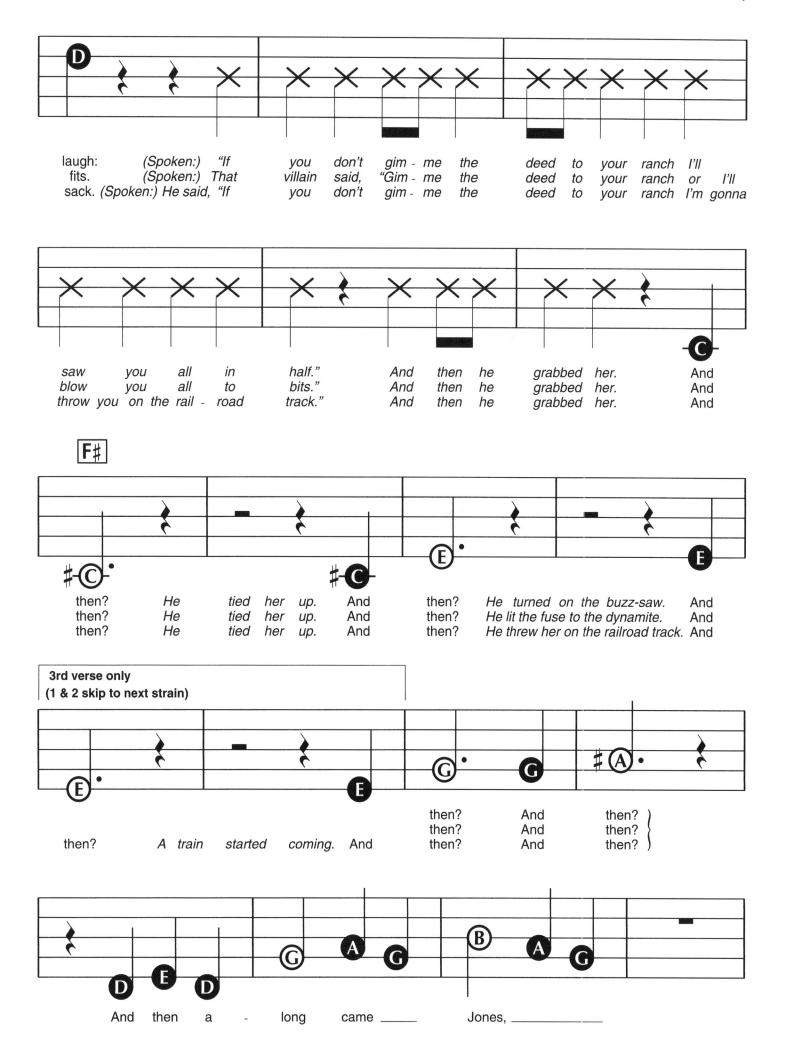

laugh: (Spoken:) "If   you   don't   gim - me   the   deed   to   your   ranch   I'll
fits.   (Spoken:) That   villain said, "Gim - me   the   deed   to   your   ranch   or   I'll
sack. (Spoken:) He said, "If you   don't   gim - me   the   deed   to   your   ranch   I'm gonna

saw   you   all   in   half."   And   then   he   grabbed her.   And
blow   you   all   to   bits."   And   then   he   grabbed her.   And
throw   you   on the rail - road   track." And   then   he   grabbed her.   And

F#

then?   He   tied   her   up.   And   then?   He turned on the buzz-saw.   And
then?   He   tied   her   up.   And   then?   He lit the fuse to the dynamite.   And
then?   He   tied   her   up.   And   then?   He threw her on the railroad track. And

3rd verse only
(1 & 2 skip to next strain)

                                                        then?   And   then? ⎫
                                                        then?   And   then? ⎬
then?   A   train   started   coming. And   then?   And   then? ⎭

And   then   a - long   came _____ Jones, _____

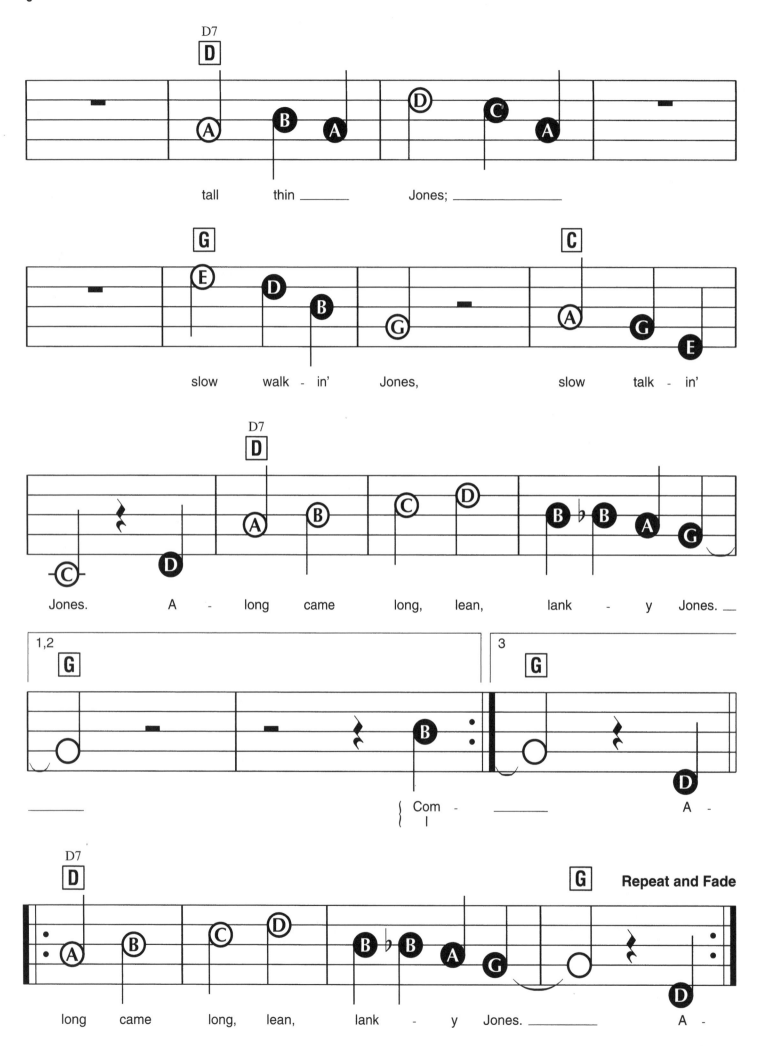

Believe What You Say

Registration 8
Rhythm: Shuffle or Rock

Words and Music by Dorsey Burnette
and Johnny Burnette

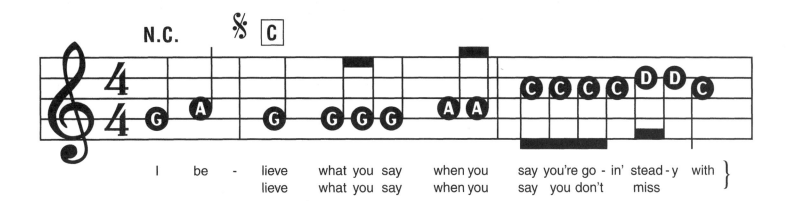

I be - lieve what you say when you say you're go - in' stead - y with
lieve what you say when you say you don't miss

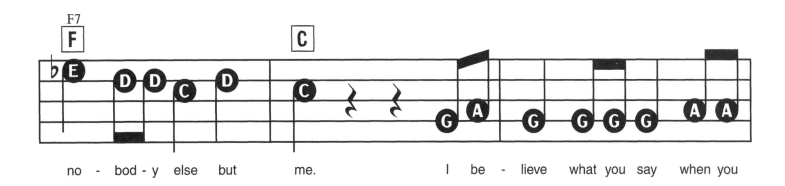

no - bod - y else but me. I be - lieve what you say when you

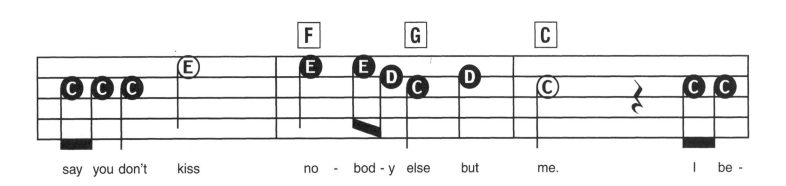

say you don't kiss no - bod - y else but me. I be -

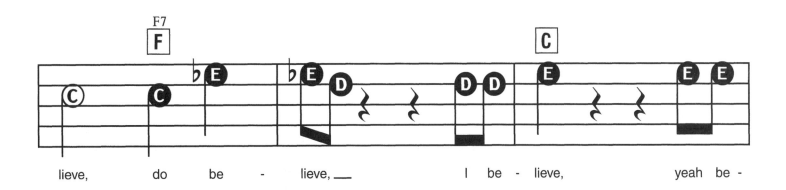

lieve, do be - lieve, ___ I be - lieve, yeah be -

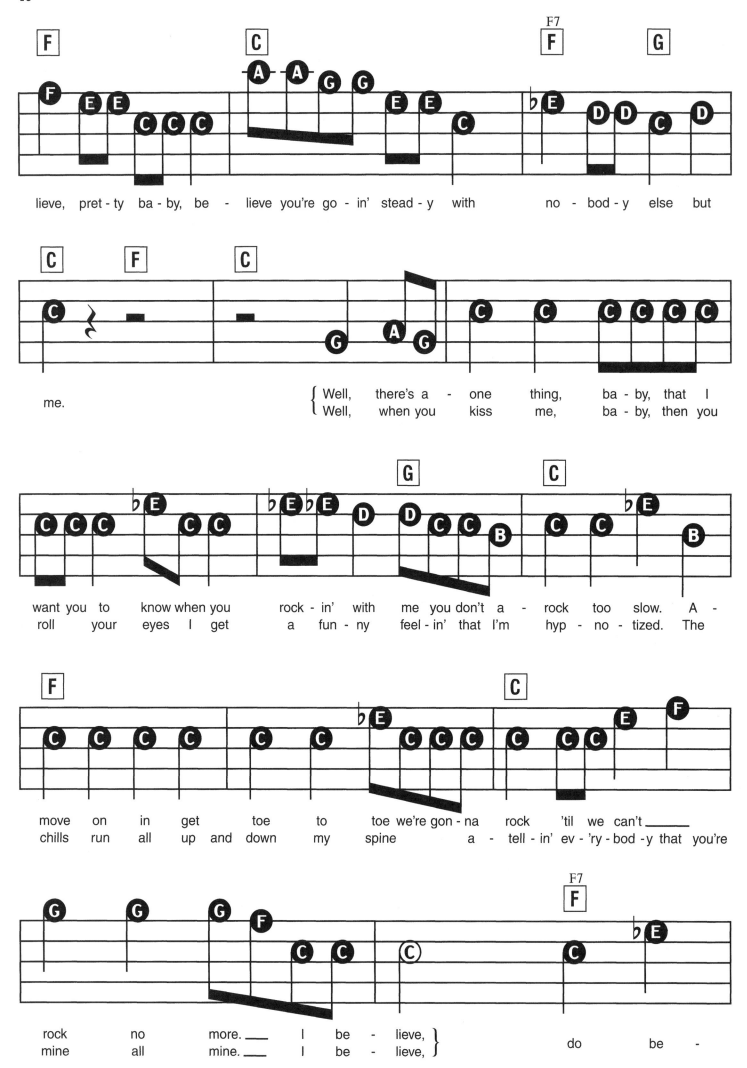

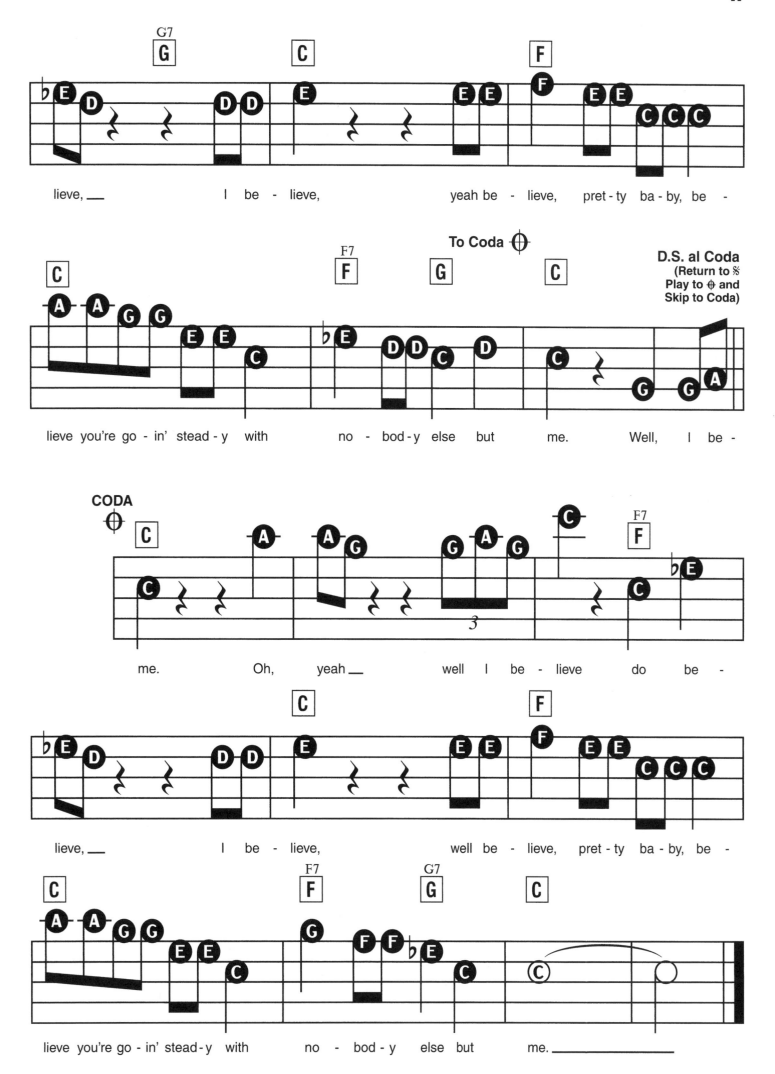

12

Are You Sincere

Registration 1
Rhythm: Fox Trot

*Words and Music by Wayne Walker
and Lucky Moeller*

Are you sin - cere when you say, "I love you?" _____ Are you sin - cere when you say, "I'll be true?" _____ Do you mean ev - 'ry word that my ears have heard? I'd like to know _____ which way to go. _____ Will our love grow? _____ Are you sin-

Copyright © 1957, 1958 UNIVERSAL - CEDARWOOD PUBLISHING
Copyright Renewed
All Rights Controlled and Administered by UNIVERSAL - SONGS OF POLYGRAM INTERNATIONAL, INC.
All Rights Reserved   Used by Permission

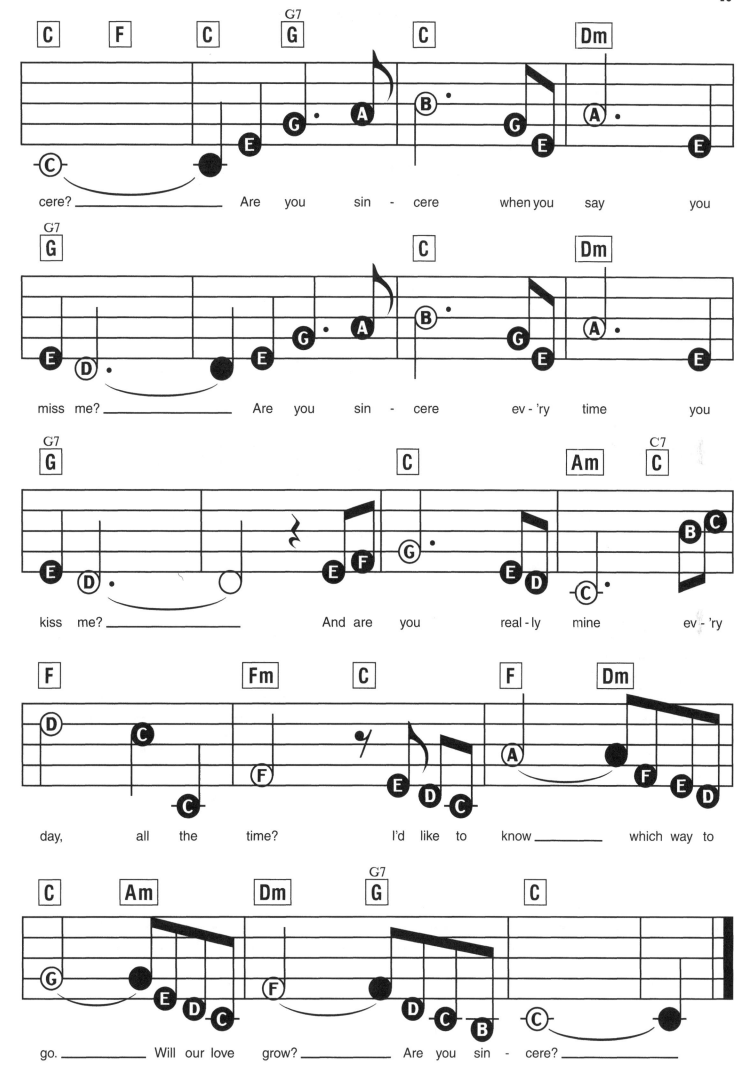

At the Hop

Registration 5
Rhythm: Rock

Words and Music by Arthur Singer,
John Madara and David White

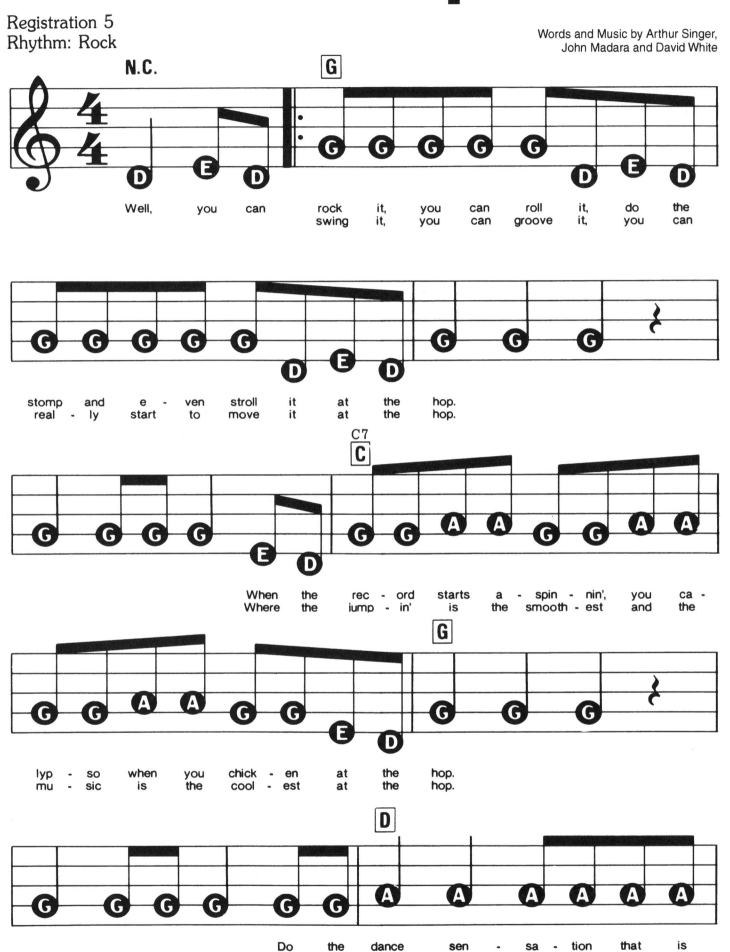

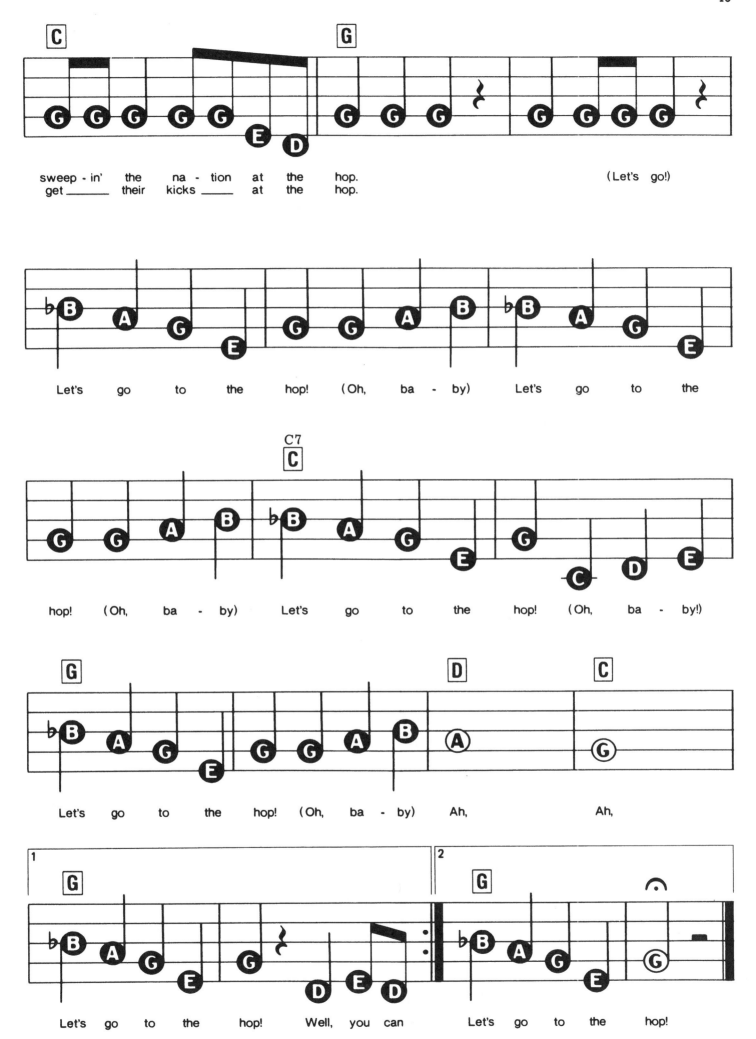

Autumn Leaves

Registration 2
Rhythm: Fox Trot or Swing

English lyric by Johnny Mercer
French lyric by Jacques Prevert
Music by Joseph Kosma

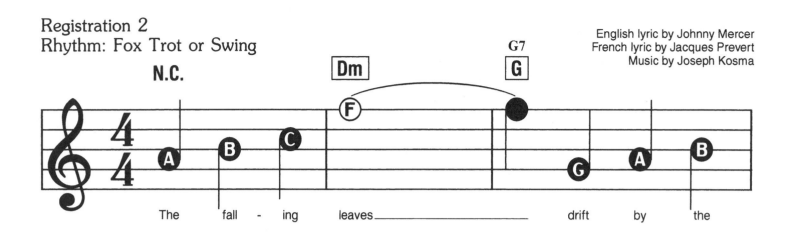

The fall - ing leaves_____ drift by the

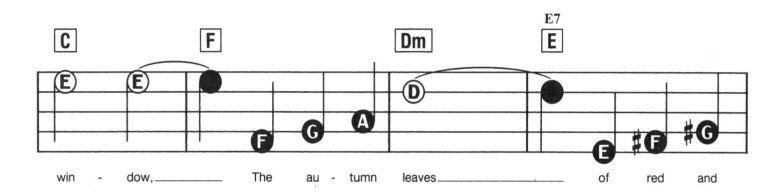

win - dow,_____ The au - tumn leaves_____ of red and

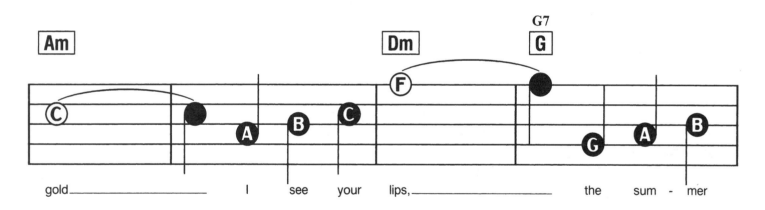

gold_____ I see your lips,_____ the sum - mer

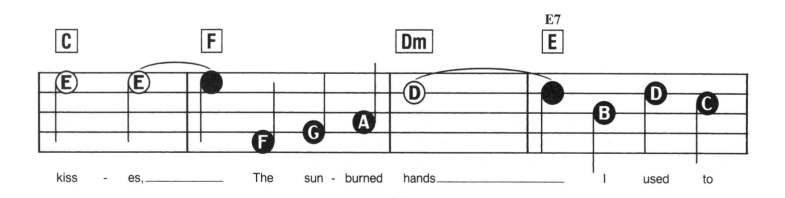

kiss - es,_____ The sun - burned hands_____ I used to

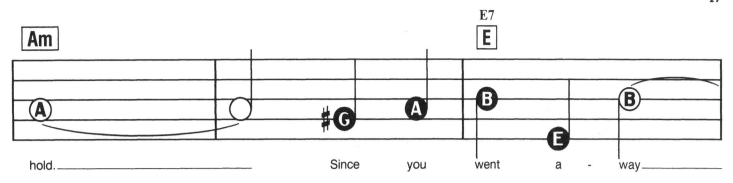

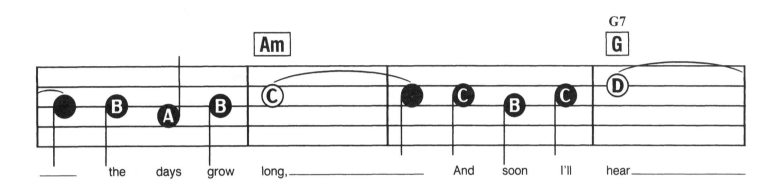

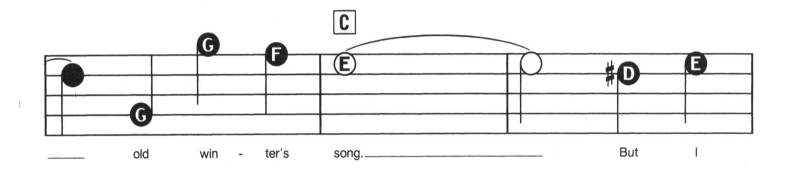

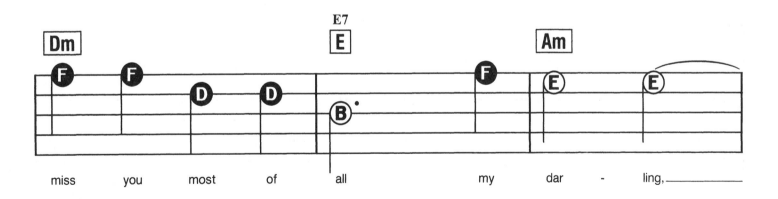

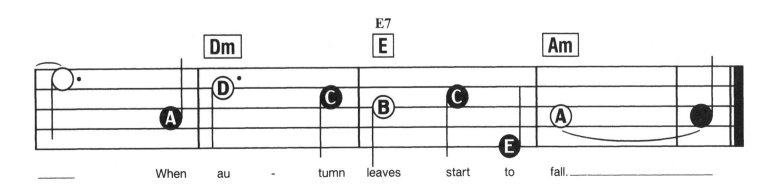

The Big Hurt

Registration 4
Rhythm: Beguine or Latin

Words and Music by
Wayne Shanklin

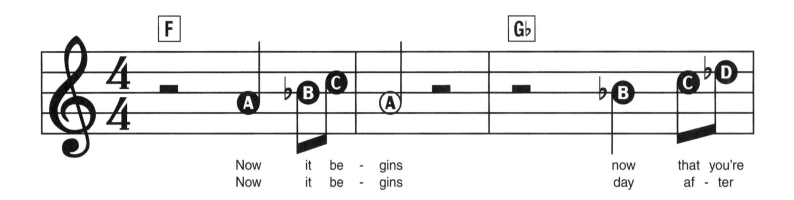

Now it be - gins now that you're
Now it be - gins day af - ter

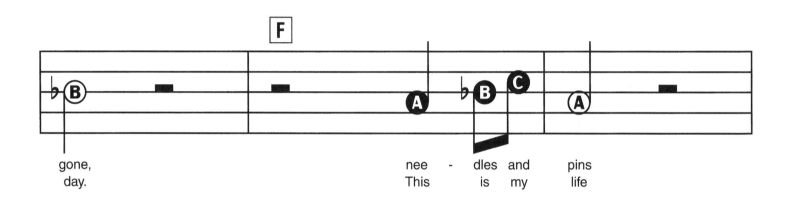

gone,
day.

nee - dles and pins
This is my life

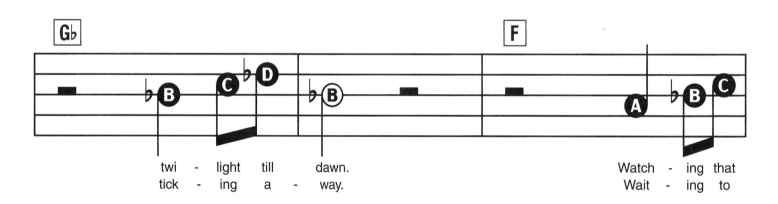

twi - light till dawn.
tick - ing a - way.

Watch - ing that
Wait - ing to

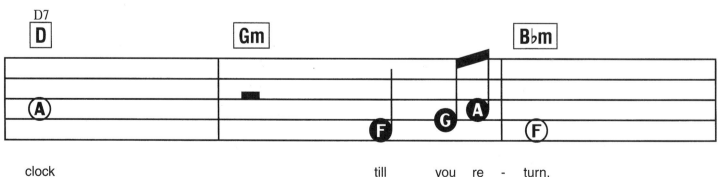

clock
hear

till you re - turn,
foot - steps that say

19

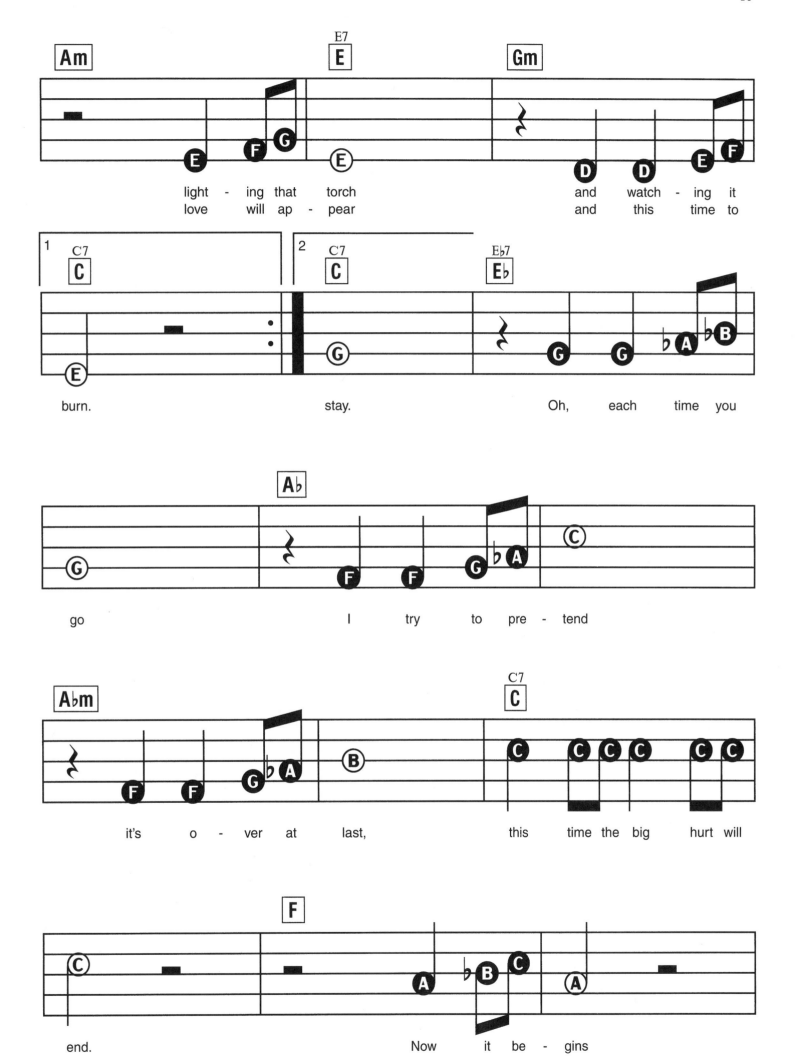

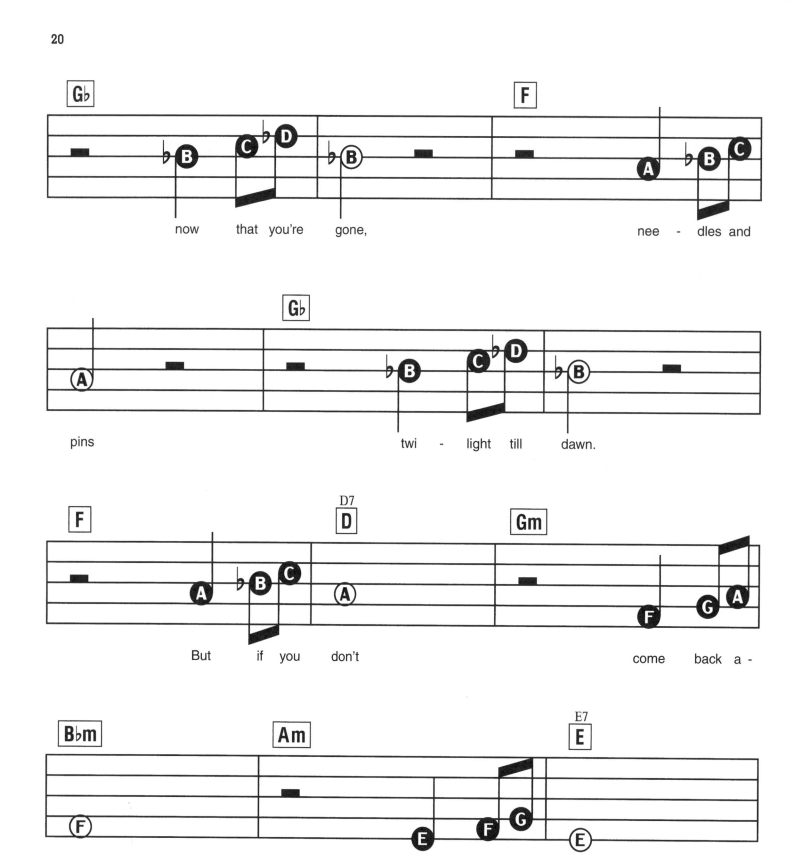

now that you're gone, nee - dles and

pins twi - light till dawn.

But if you don't come back a -

gain, I won - der when,

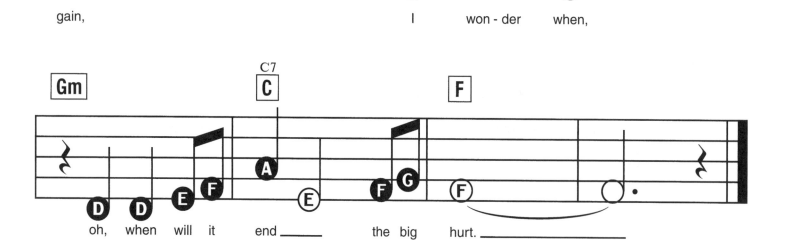

oh, when will it end ____ the big hurt. ____

Bird Dog

Registration 7
Rhythm: Rock

Words and Music by
Boudleaux Bryant

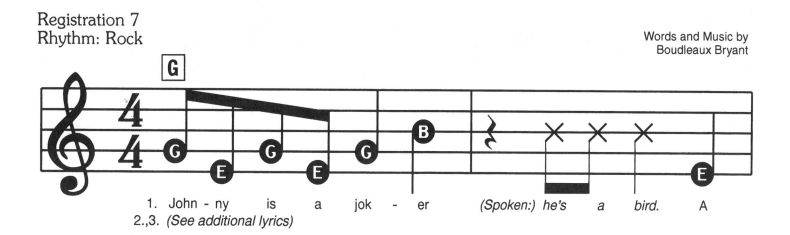

1. John - ny is a jok - er (Spoken:) he's a bird. A
2.,3. *(See additional lyrics)*

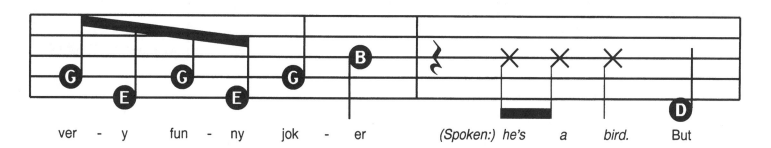

ver - y fun - ny jok - er (Spoken:) he's a bird. But

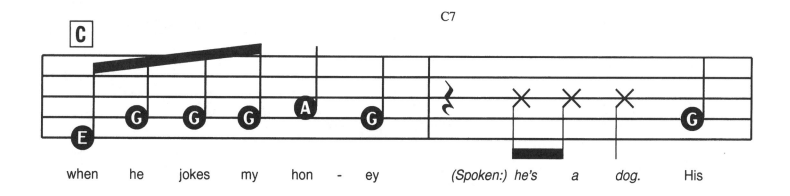

when he jokes my hon - ey (Spoken:) he's a dog. His

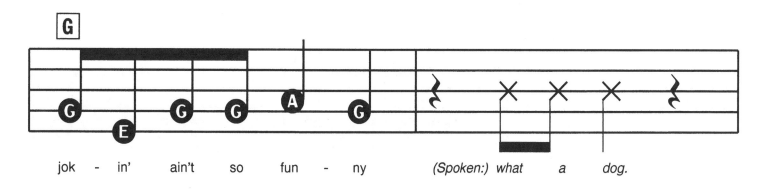

jok - in' ain't so fun - ny (Spoken:) what a dog.

22

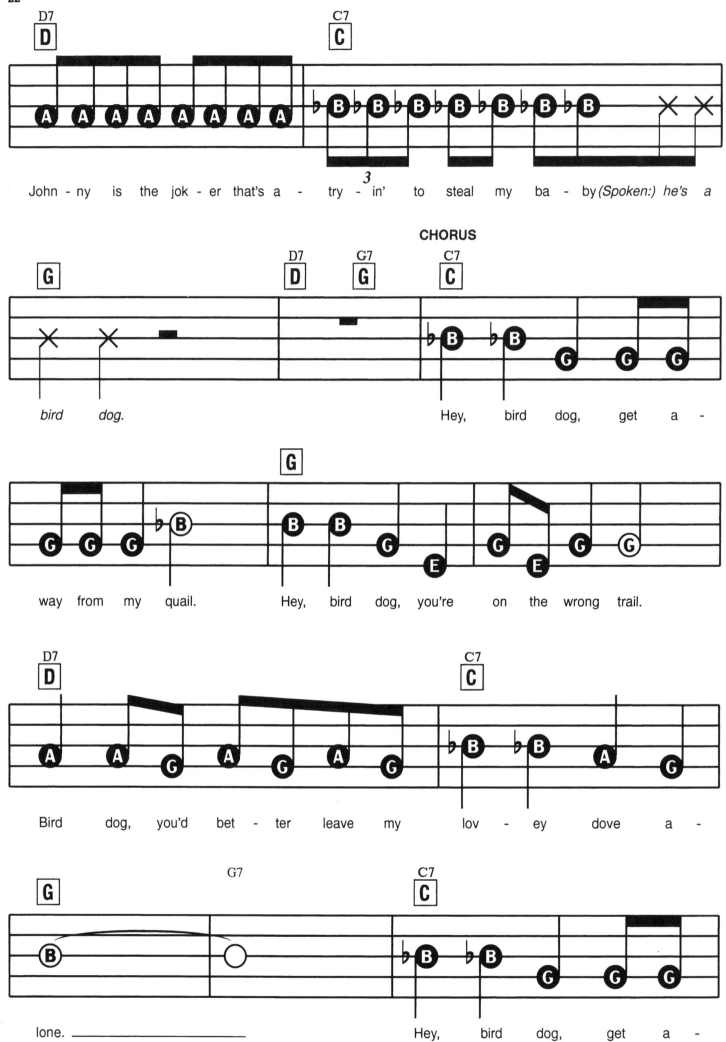

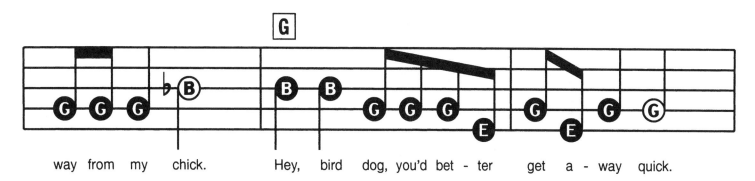

way from my chick. Hey, bird dog, you'd bet - ter get a - way quick.

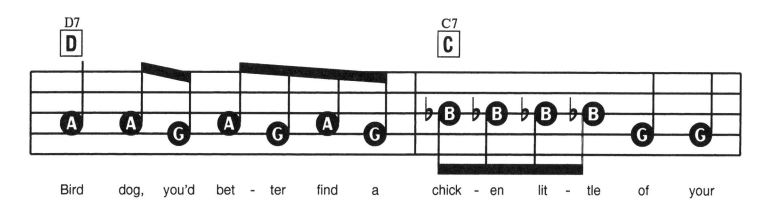

Bird dog, you'd bet - ter find a chick - en lit - tle of your

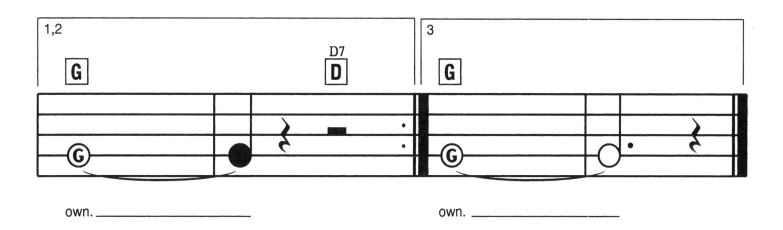

own. _____   own. _____

Additional Lyrics

2. Johnny sings a love song *(Like a bird)*
He sings the sweetest love song *(You ever heard)*
But when he sings to my gal *(What a howl)*
To me he's just a wolf dog *(On the prowl)*
Johnny wants to fly away and puppy love my baby *(He's a bird dog)*
To Chorus

3. Johnny kissed the teacher *(He's a bird)*
He tiptoed up to reach her *(He's a bird)*
Well, he's the teacher's pet now *(He's a dog)*
What he wants he can get now *(What a dog)*
He even made the teacher let him sit next to my baby. *(He's a bird dog)*
To Chorus

Blueberry Hill

Registration 2
Rhythm: Fox Trot or Swing

Words and Music by Al Lewis,
Larry Stock and Vincent Rose

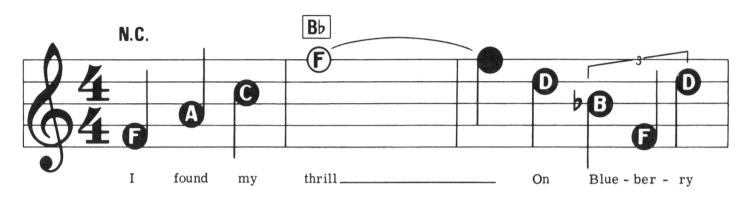

I found my thrill _____ On Blue - ber - ry

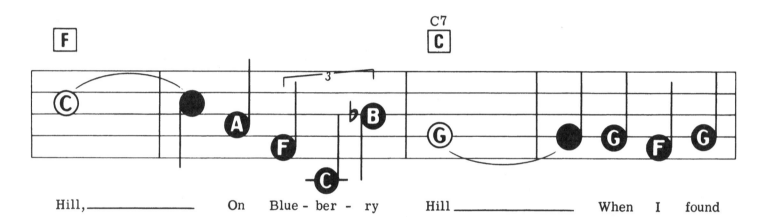

Hill, _____ On Blue - ber - ry Hill _____ When I found

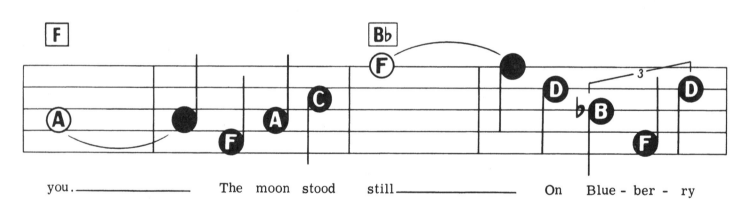

you. _____ The moon stood still _____ On Blue - ber - ry

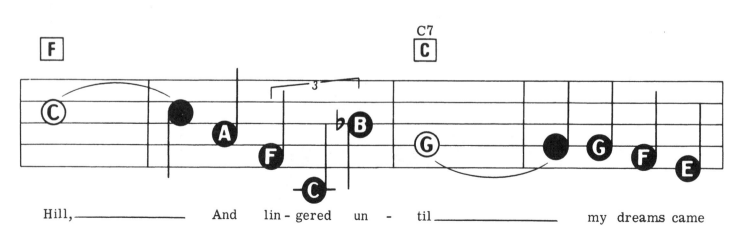

Hill, _____ And lin - gered un - til _____ my dreams came

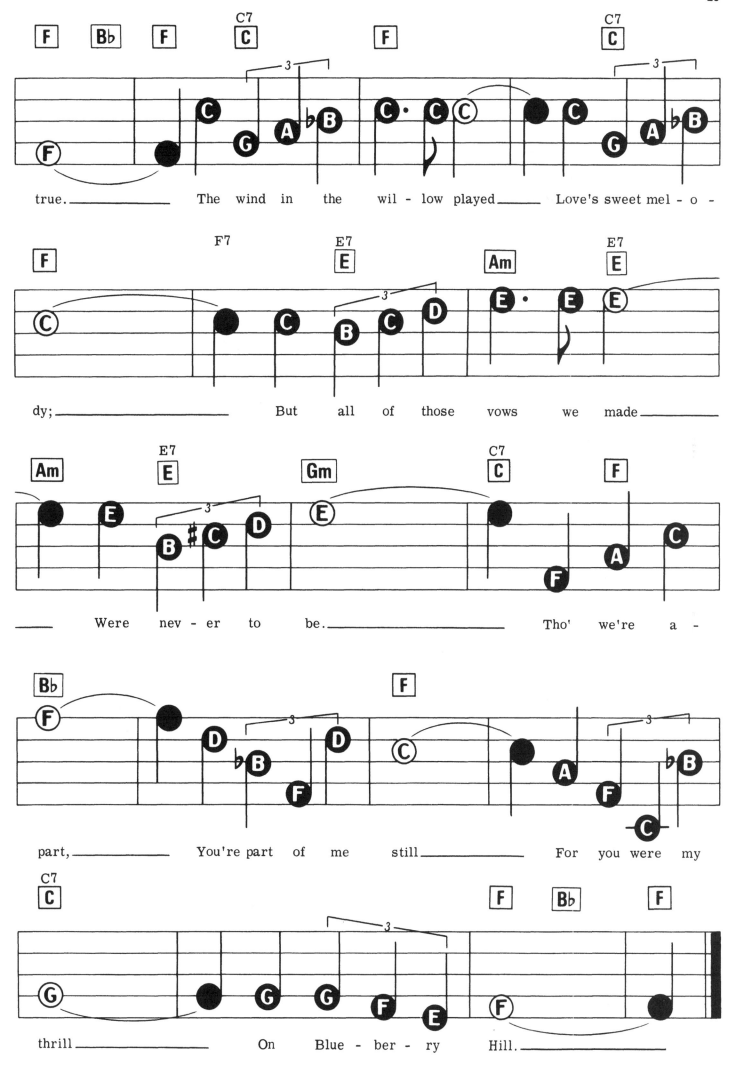

Bony Moronie

Registration 4
Rhythm: Fox Trot or Rock

Words and Music by
Larry Williams

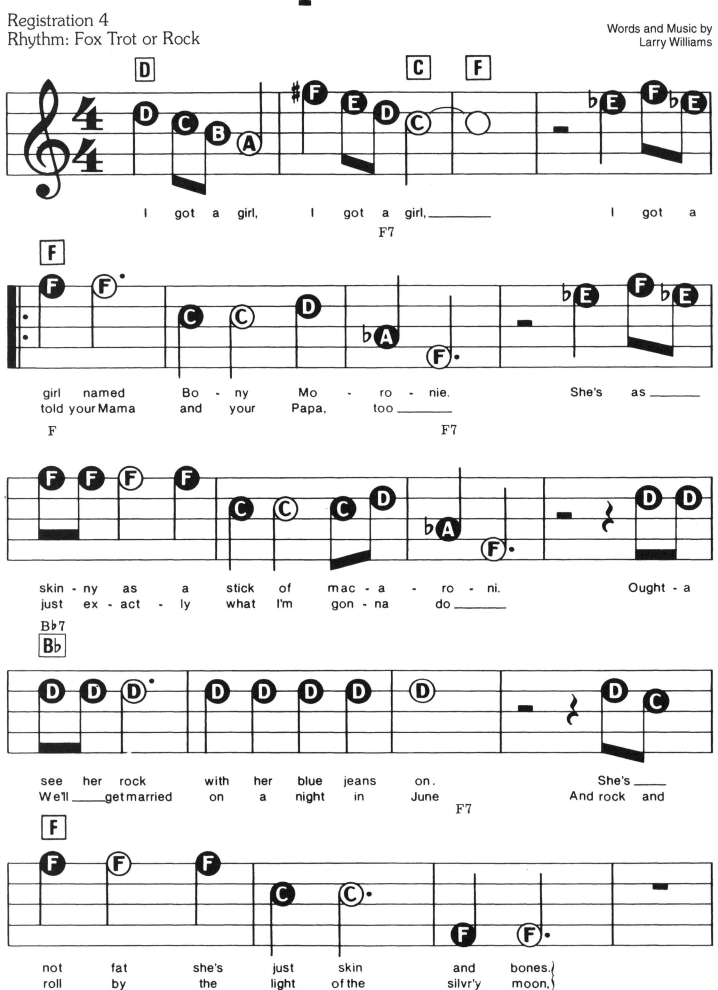

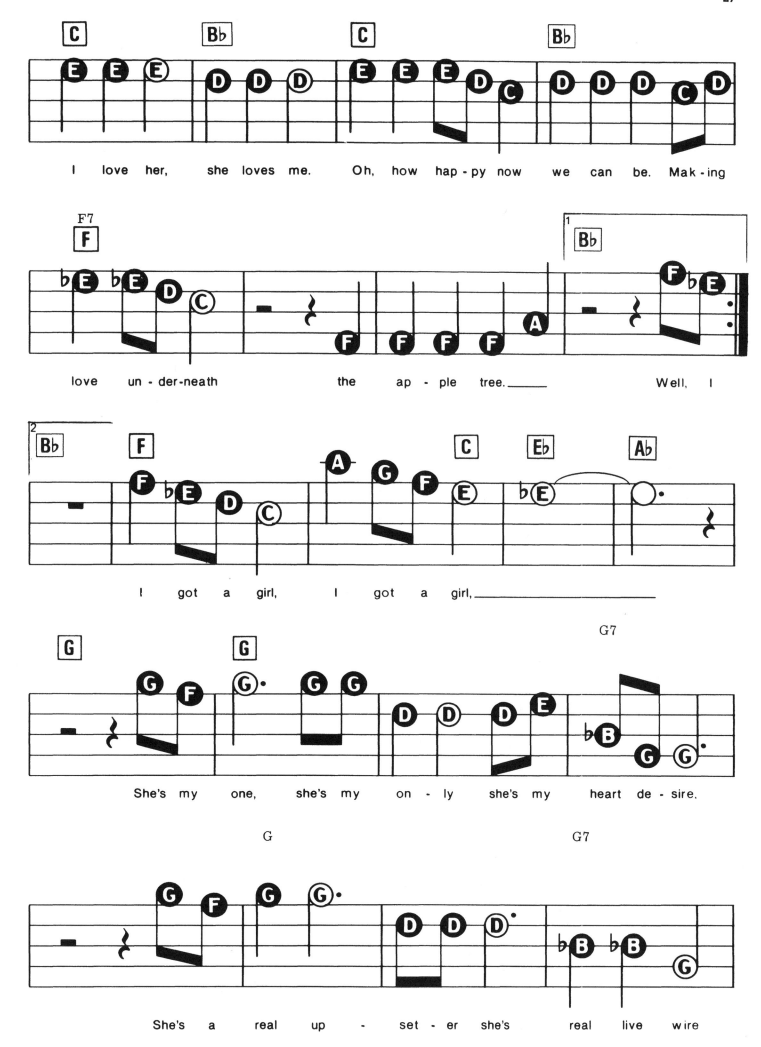

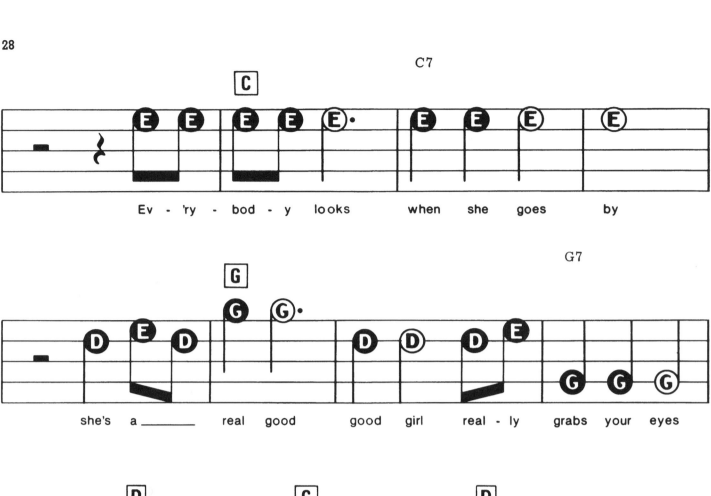

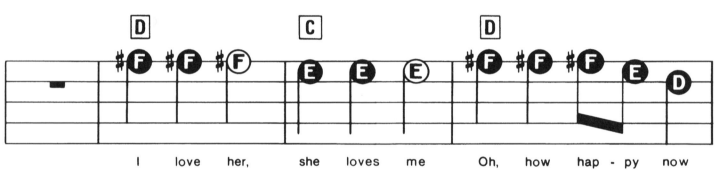

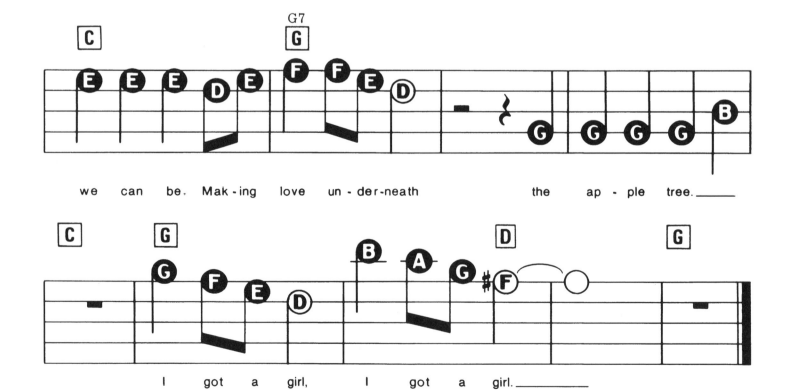

Breathless

Registration 8
Rhythm: Rock

Words and Music by
Otis Blackwell

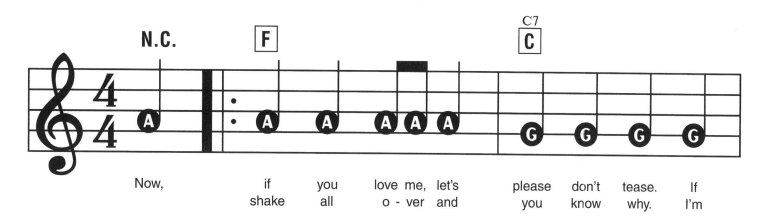

Now,
if you love me, let's please don't tease. If
shake all o - ver and you know why. I'm

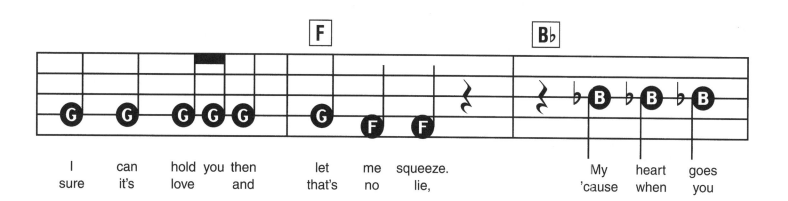

I can hold you then let me squeeze. My heart goes
sure it's love and that's no lie, 'cause when you

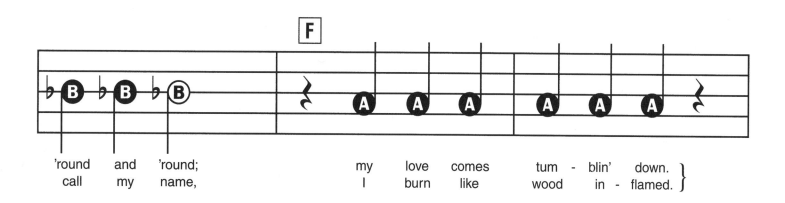

'round and 'round; my love comes tum - blin' down.
call my name, I burn like wood in - flamed.

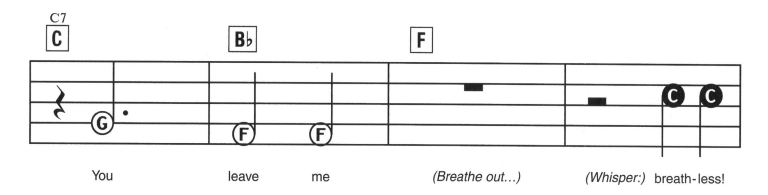

You leave me (Breathe out...) (Whisper:) breath-less!

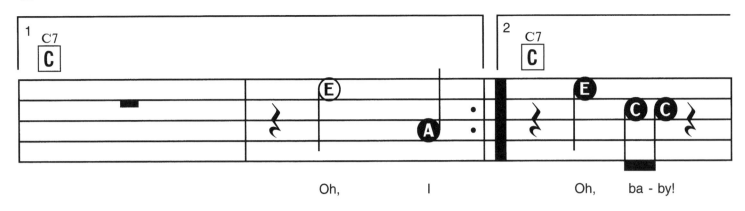

Oh,   I   Oh,   ba - by!

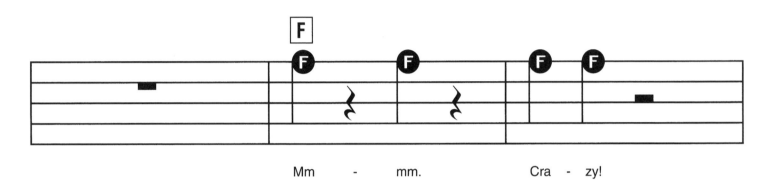

Mm - mm.   Cra - zy!

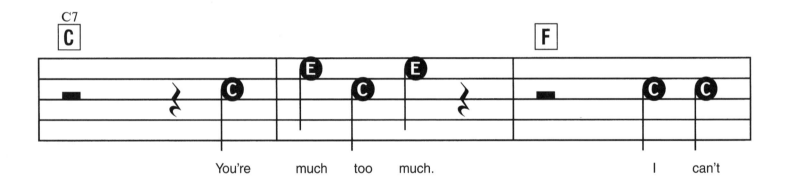

You're much too much.   I can't

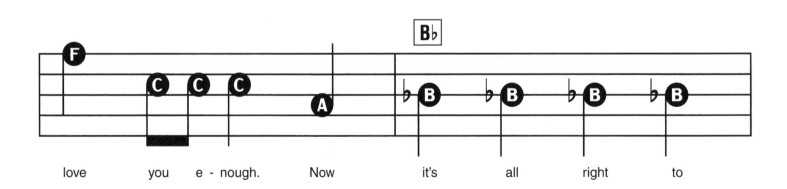

love you e - nough. Now   it's   all   right to

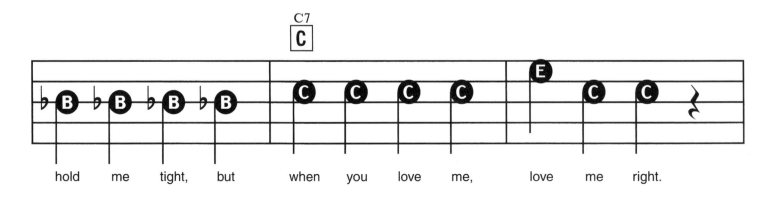

hold me tight, but   when you love me,   love me right.

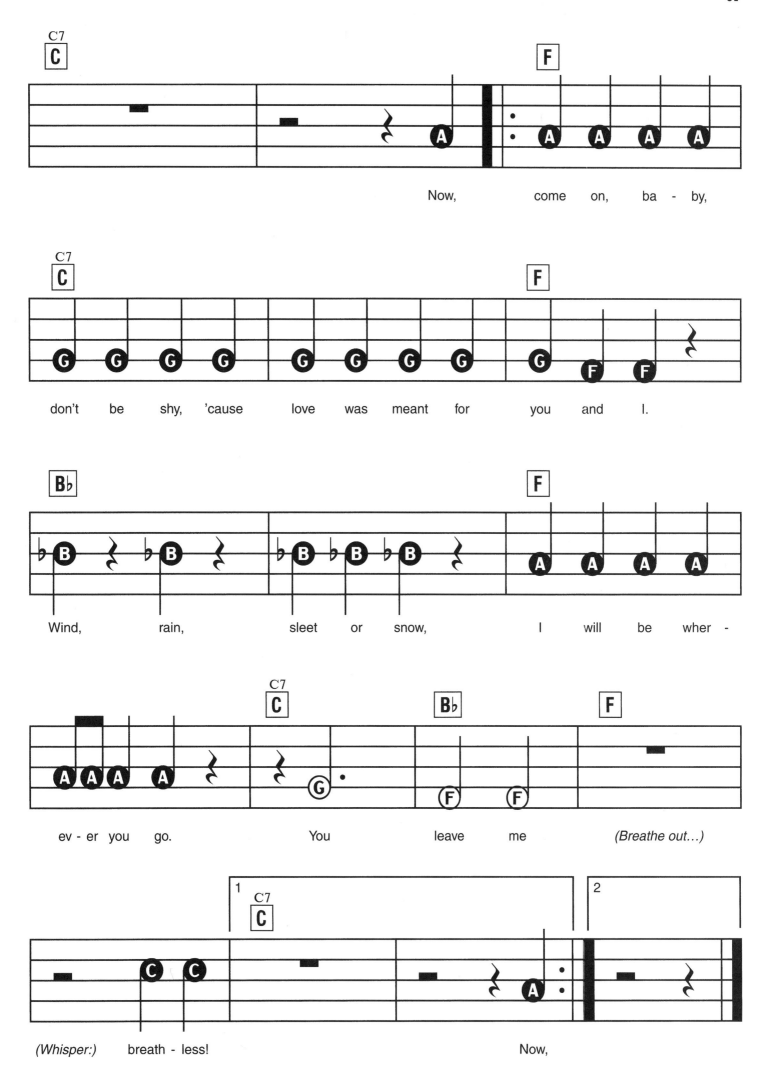

Born to Be with You

Registration 8
Rhythm: Country or Fox Trot

Words and Music by
Don Robertson

By _____ your side, _____
Won - drous - ly, _____
Do _____ I find _____

sat - is - fied _____
love _____ can see. _____
peace _____ of mind? _____

through _____ and through _____ 'cause I was
So _____ I knew _____ that I was
Yes, _____ I do! _____ 'Cause I was

born to be with _____ you. _____
born to be with _____ you. _____
born to be with _____ you. _____

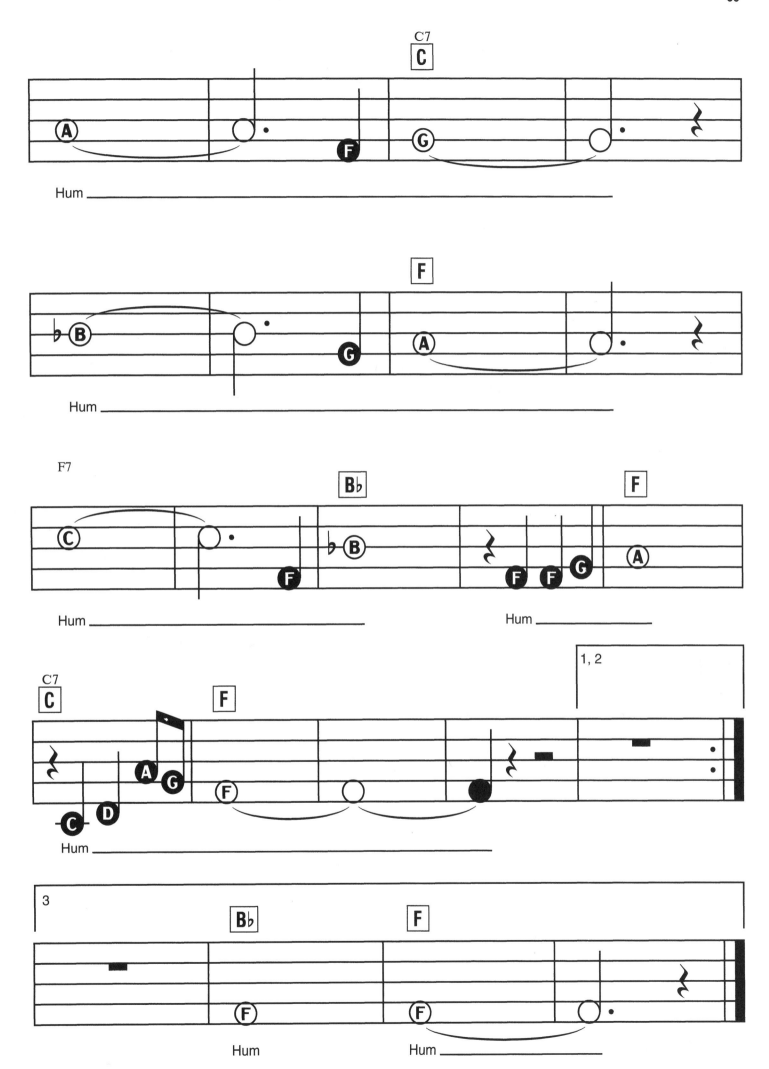

Bye Bye Love

Registration 4
Rhythm: Fox Trot or Swing

Words and Music by Felice Bryant
and Boudleaux Bryant

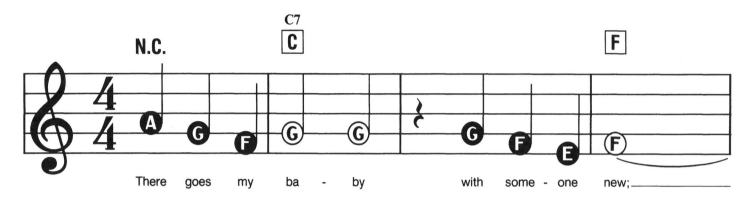

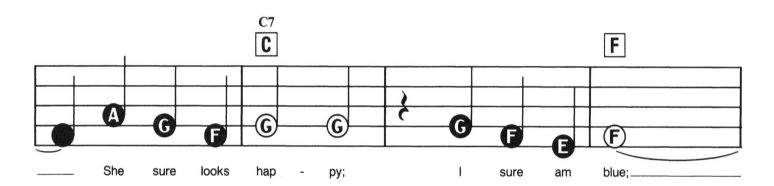

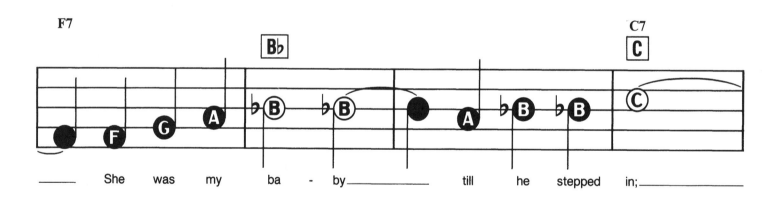

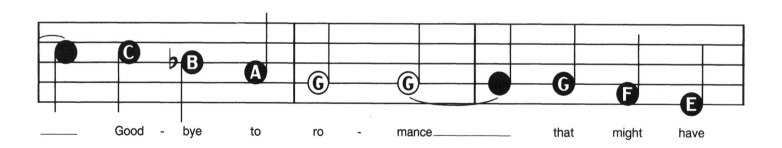

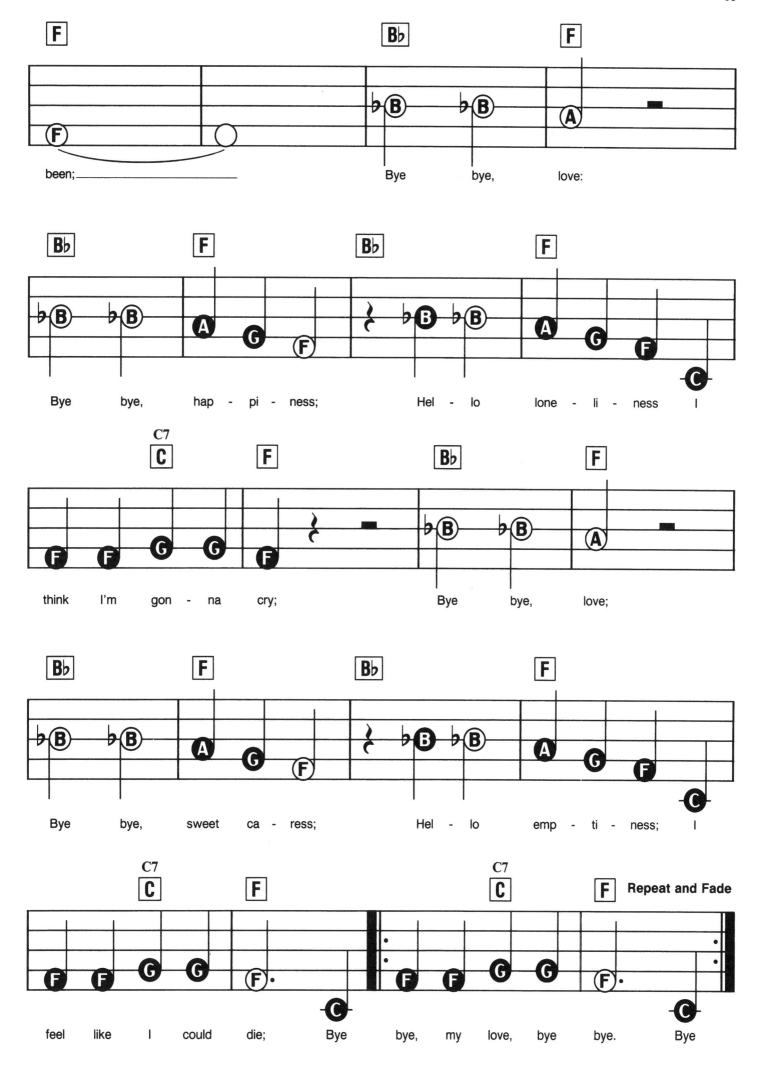

Catch a Falling Star

Registration 7
Rhythm: Bossa Nova or Latin

Words and Music by Paul Vance
and Lee Pockriss

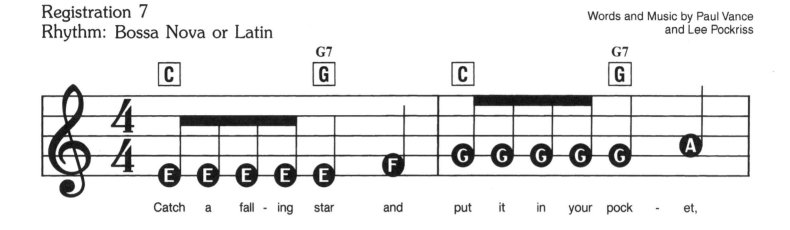

Catch a fall - ing star and put it in your pock - et,

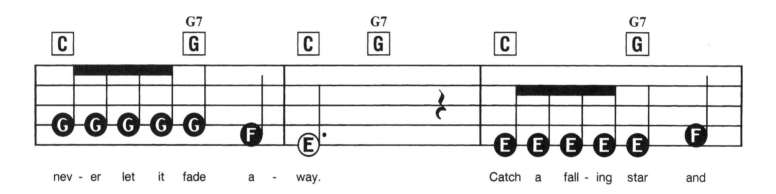

nev - er let it fade a - way. Catch a fall - ing star and

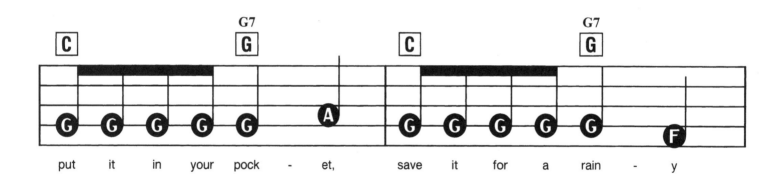

put it in your pock - et, save it for a rain - y

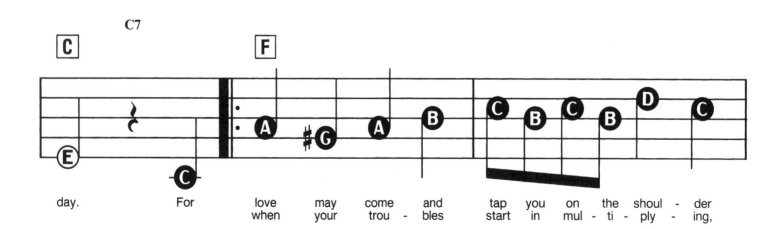

day. For love may come and tap you on the shoul - der
when your trou - bles start in mul - ti - ply - ing,

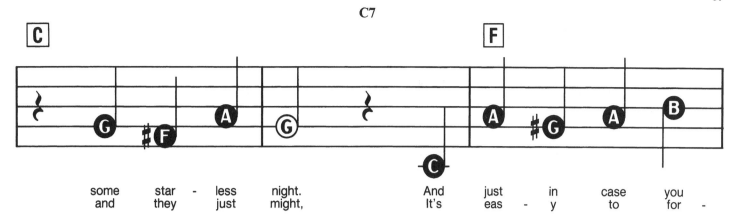

some star - less night.
and they just might,

And just in case you
It's eas - y to for -

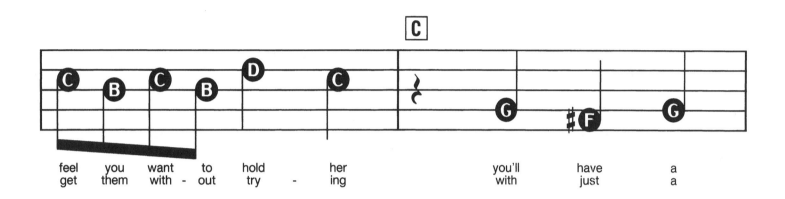

feel you want to hold her
get them with - out try - ing

you'll have a
with just a

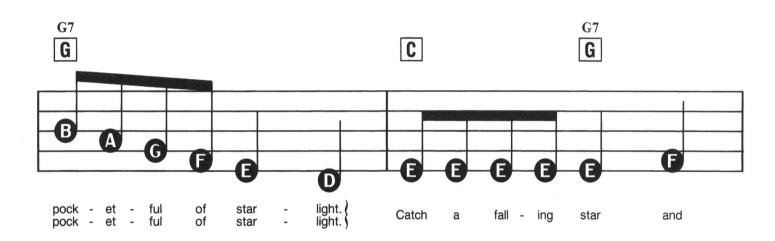

pock - et - ful of star - light.
pock - et - ful of star - light.

Catch a fall - ing star and

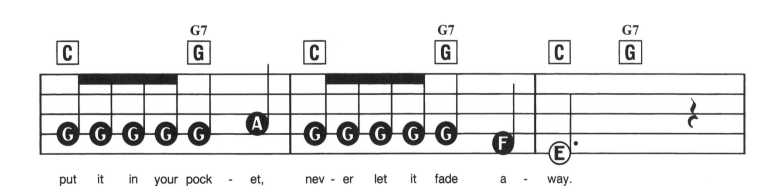

put it in your pock - et, nev - er let it fade a - way.

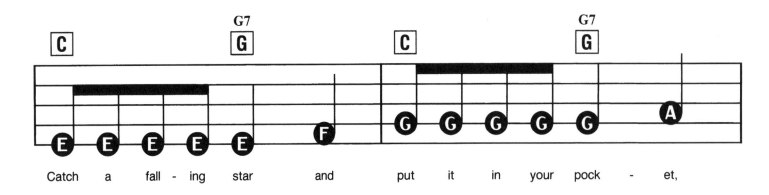

Catch a fall - ing star and put it in your pock - et,

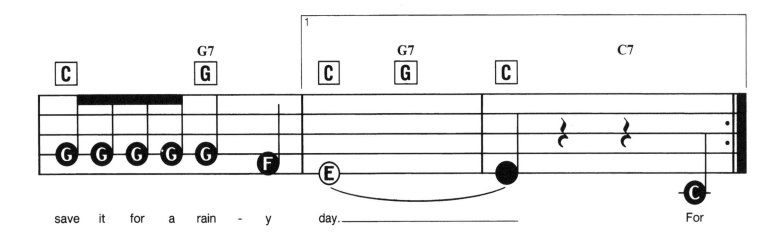

save it for a rain - y day. _____ For

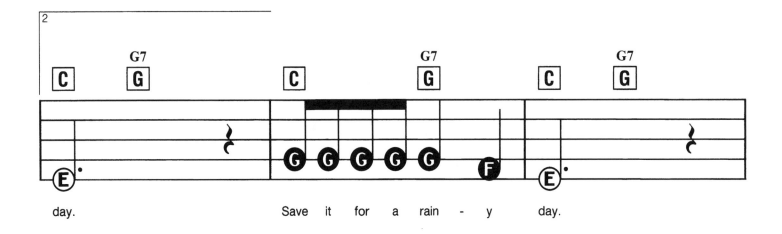

day. Save it for a rain - y day.

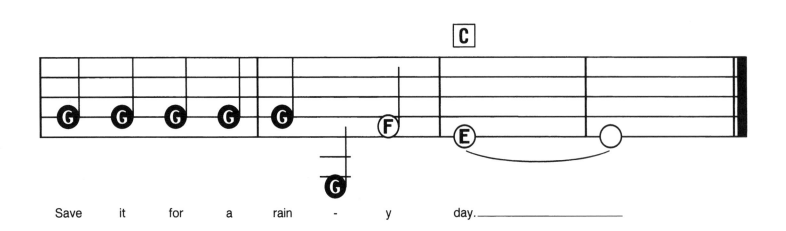

Save it for a rain - y day. _____

Changing Partners

Registration 2
Rhythm: Waltz

Words by Joe Darion
Music by Larry Coleman

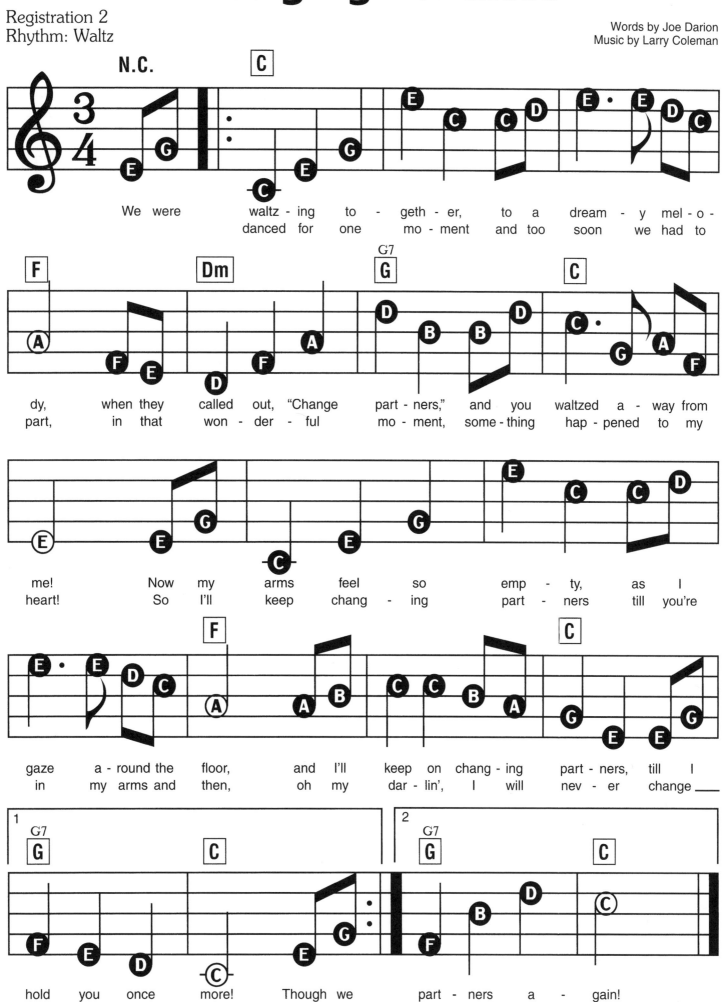

Chanson D'Amour
(The Ra-Da-Da-Da-Da Song)

Registration 7
Rhythm: Swing or Jazz

Words and Music by
Wayne Shanklin

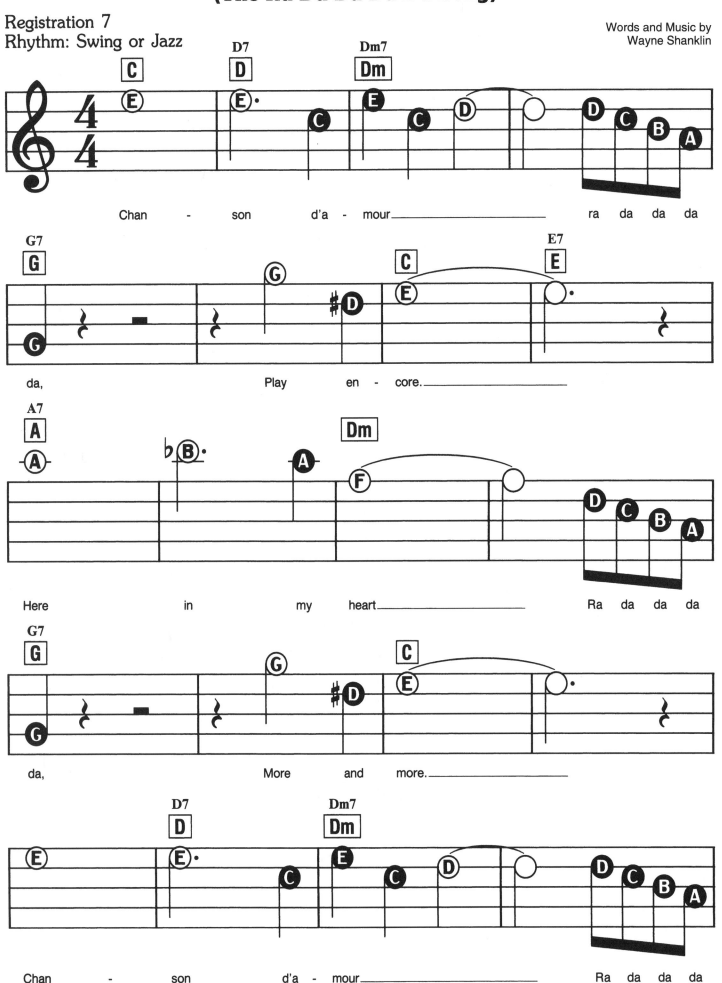

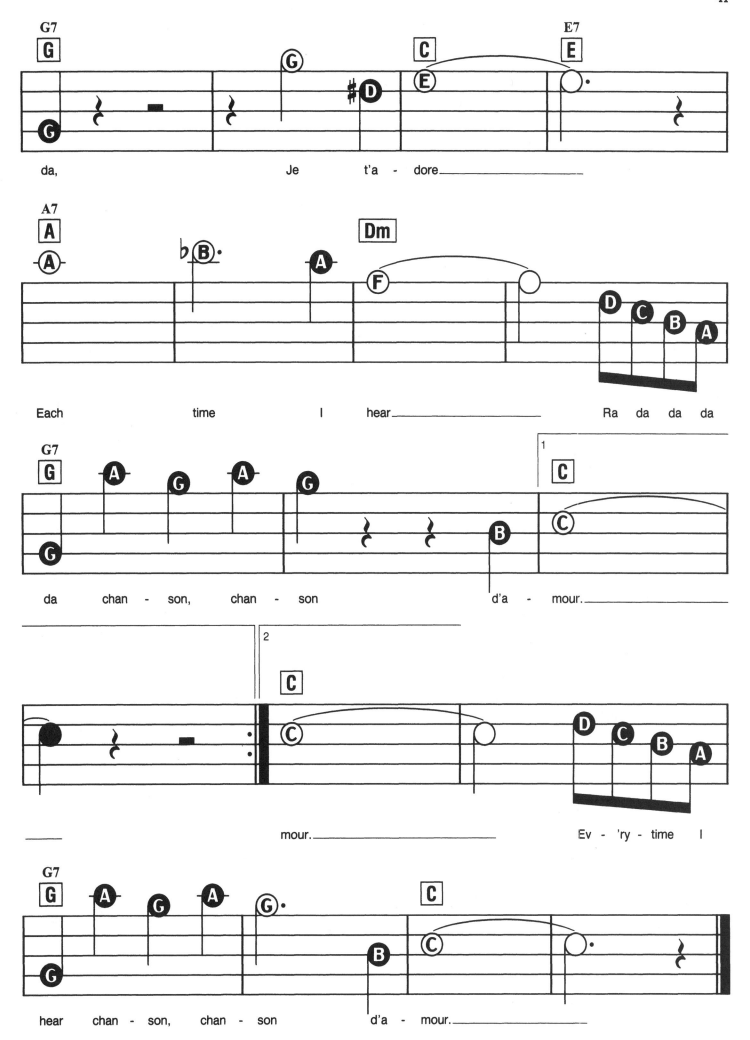

Chantilly Lace

Registration 8
Rhythm: Rock'n'Roll or Rock

Words and Music by
J.P. Richardson

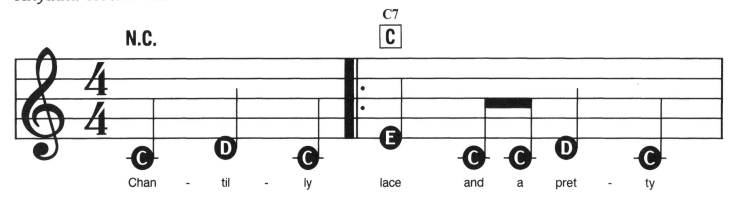

Chan - til - ly lace and a pret - ty

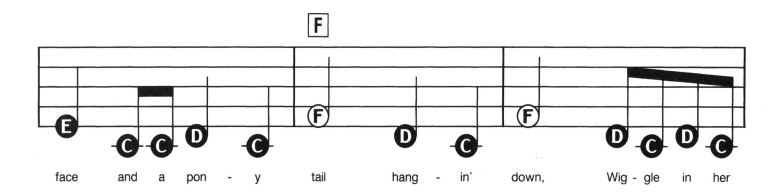

face and a pon - y tail hang - in' down, Wig - gle in her

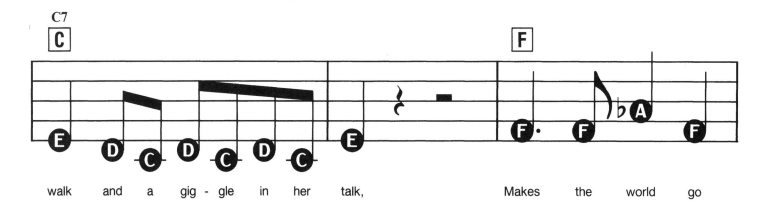

walk and a gig - gle in her talk, Makes the world go

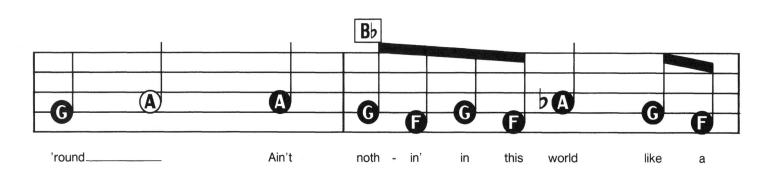

'round_____ Ain't noth - in' in this world like a

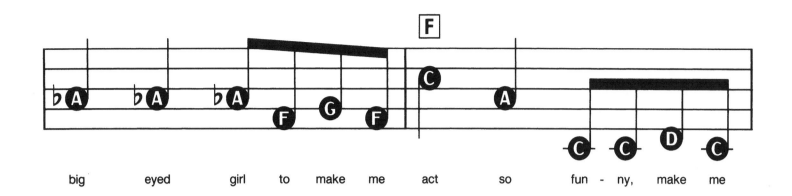

big   eyed   girl   to   make   me   act   so   fun - ny,   make   me

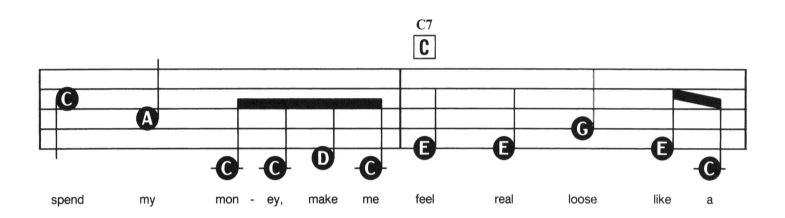

spend   my   mon - ey,   make   me   feel   real   loose   like   a

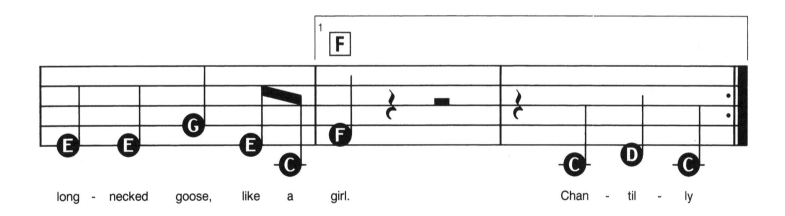

long - necked   goose,   like   a   girl.   Chan - til - ly

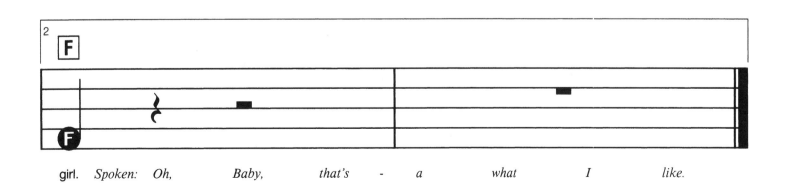

girl. *Spoken: Oh,   Baby,   that's - a   what   I   like.*

Cinco Robles
(Five Oaks)

Registration 4
Rhythm: Waltz

Words by Larry Sullivan
Music by Dorothy Wright

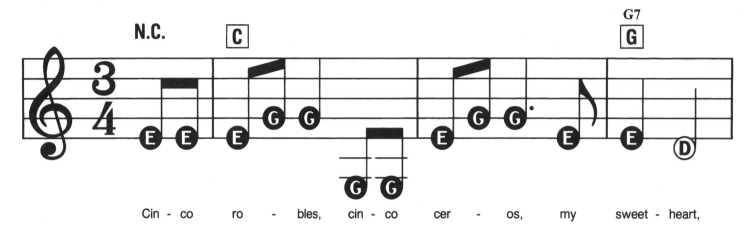

Cin - co ro - bles, cin - co cer - os, my sweet - heart,

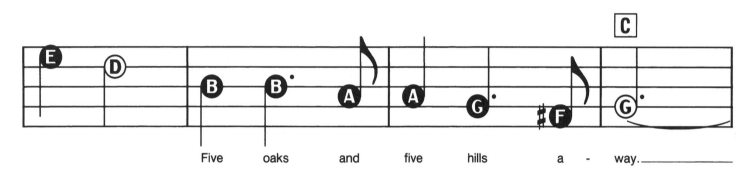

Five oaks and five hills a - way._____

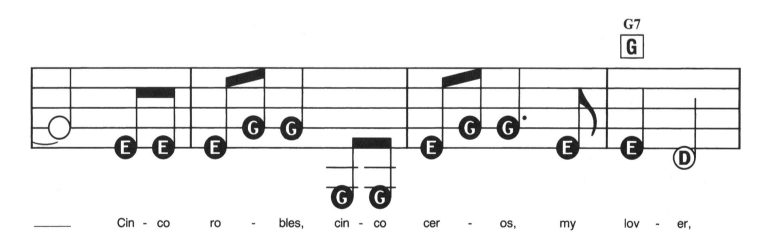

_____ Cin - co ro - bles, cin - co cer - os, my lov - er,

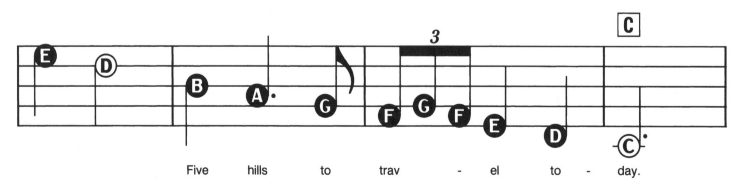

Five hills to trav - el to - day.

45

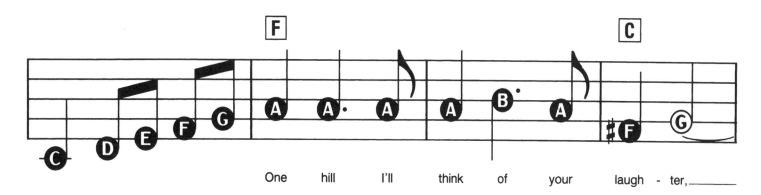

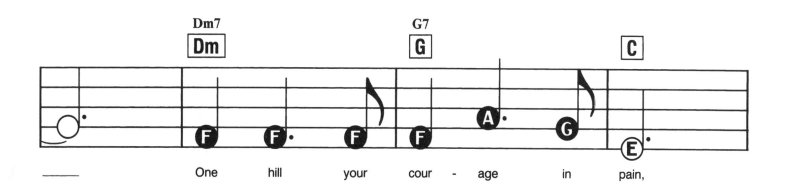

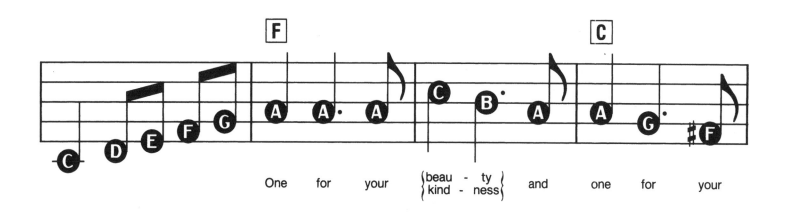

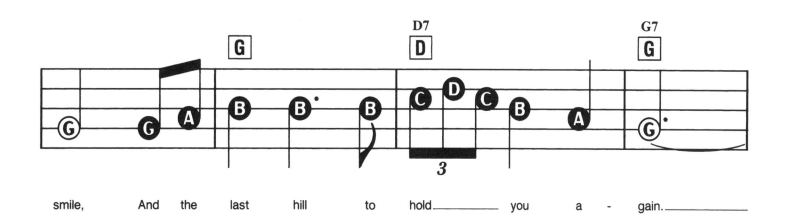

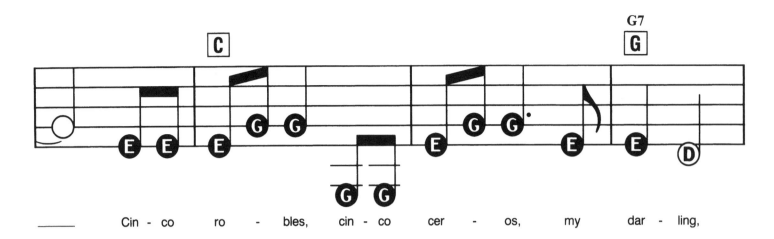

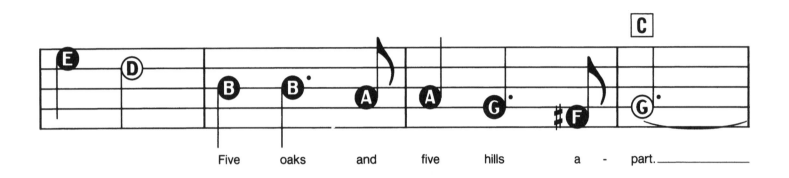

Cin - co ro - bles, cin - co cer - os, my dar - ling,

Five oaks and five hills a - part._____

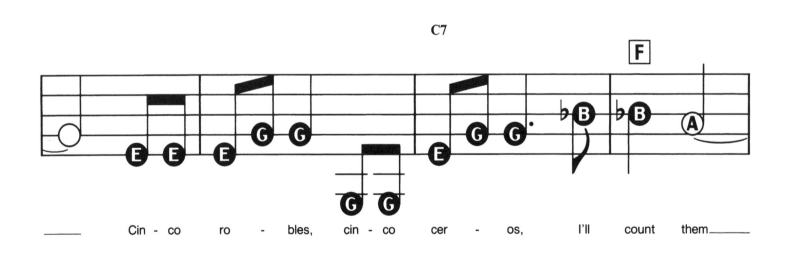

Cin - co ro - bles, cin - co cer - os, I'll count them_____

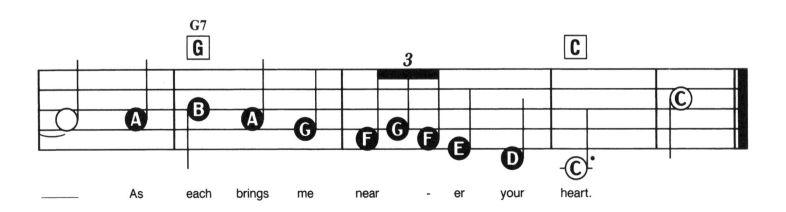

As each brings me near - er your heart.

Dance with Me Henry
(The Wallflower)

Registration 7
Rhythm: Rock or 8 Beat

Words and Music by Hank Ballard,
Etta James and Johnny Otis

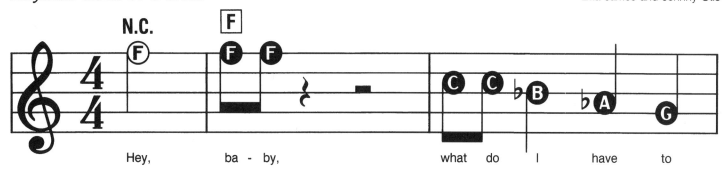

Hey, ba - by, what do I have to

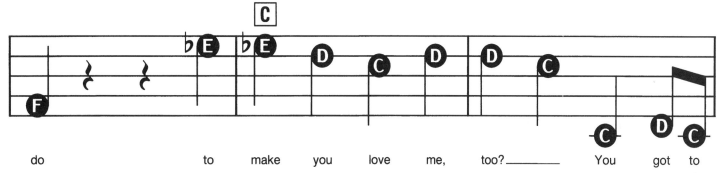

do to make you love me, too? You got to

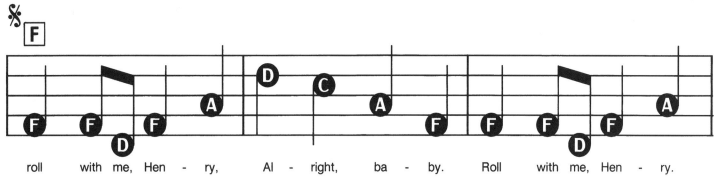

roll with me, Hen - ry, Al - right, ba - by. Roll with me, Hen - ry.

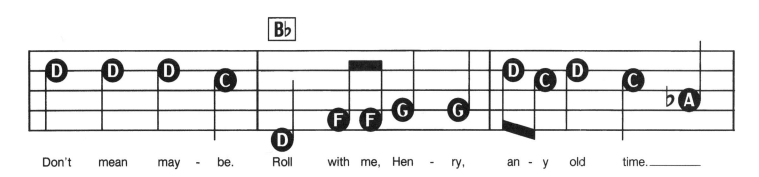

Don't mean may - be. Roll with me, Hen - ry, an - y old time.

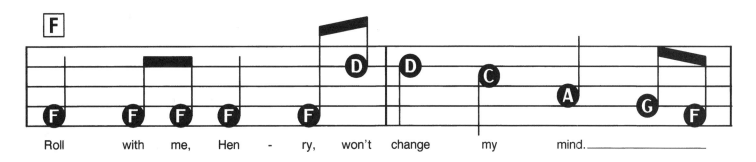

Roll with me, Hen - ry, won't change my mind.

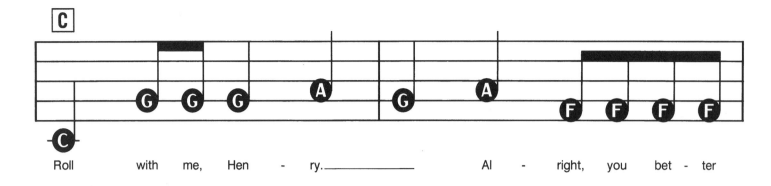

Roll with me, Hen - ry._____ Al - right, you bet - ter

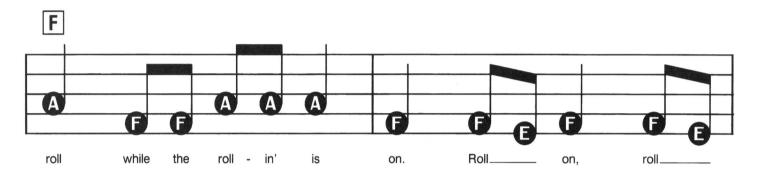

roll while the roll - in' is on. Roll_____ on, roll_____

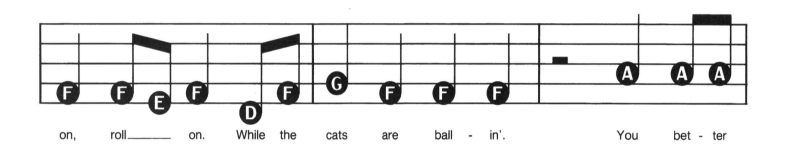

on, roll_____ on. While the cats are ball - in'. You bet - ter

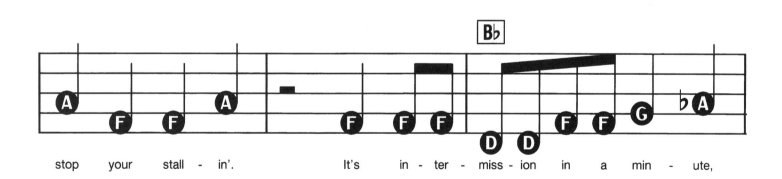

stop your stall - in'. It's in - ter - miss - ion in a min - ute,

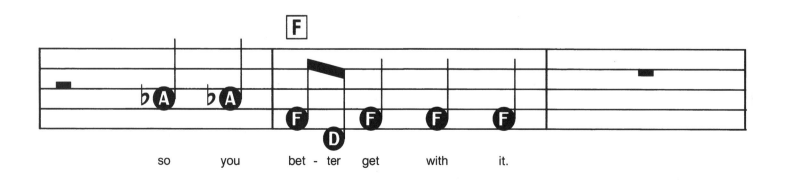

so you bet - ter get with it.

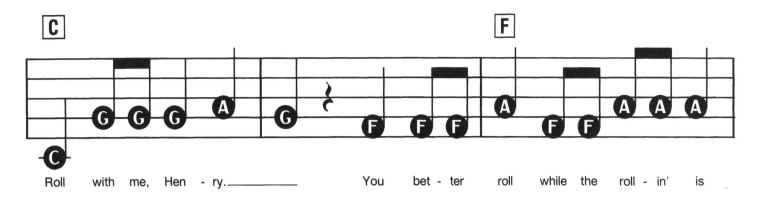

Roll with me, Hen - ry.＿＿＿ You bet - ter roll while the roll - in' is

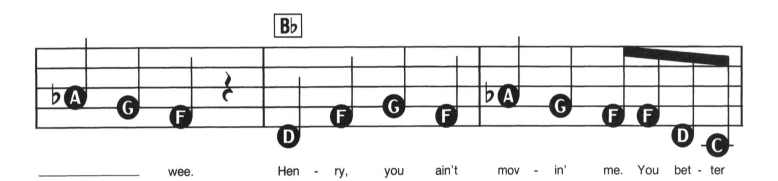

on, roll＿ on, roll＿ on, roll＿ on. Ah ooh＿ ah ooh＿ ooh＿

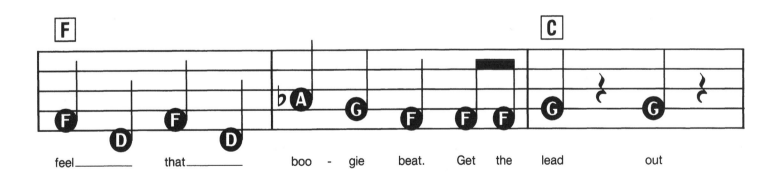

＿＿＿ wee. Hen - ry, you ain't mov - in' me. You bet - ter

feel＿ that＿ boo - gie beat. Get the lead out

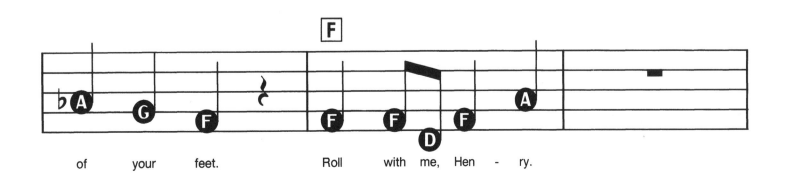

of your feet. Roll with me, Hen - ry.

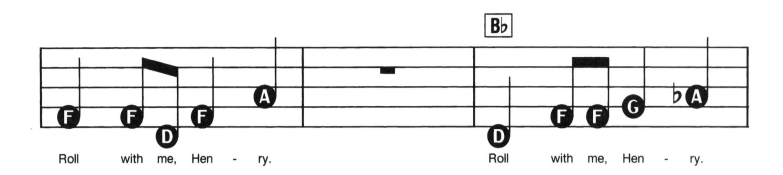

Roll with me, Hen - ry. Roll with me, Hen - ry.

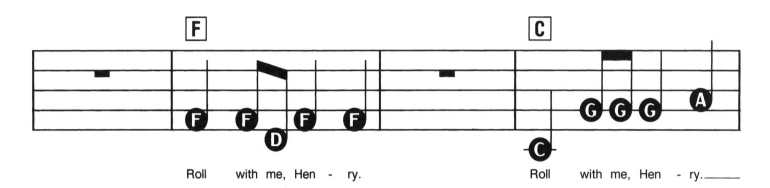

Roll with me, Hen - ry. Roll with me, Hen - ry.____

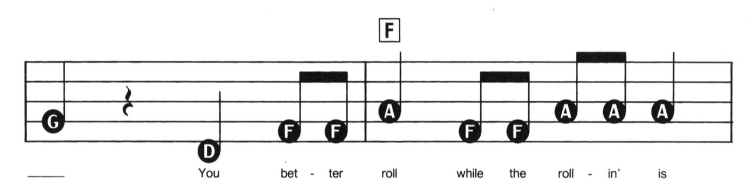

____ You bet - ter roll while the roll - in' is

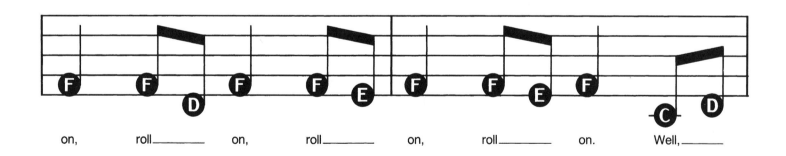

on, roll____ on, roll____ on, roll____ on. Well,____

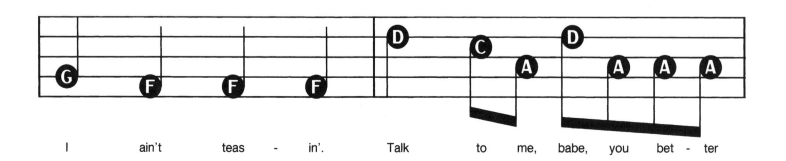

I ain't teas - in'. Talk to me, babe, you bet - ter

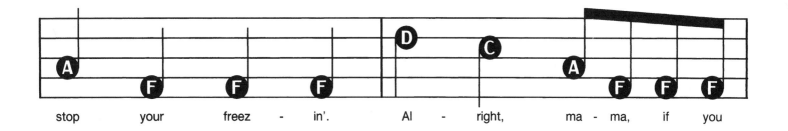

stop your freez - in'. Al - right, ma - ma, if you

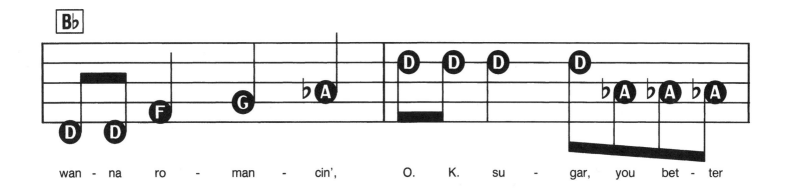

wan - na ro - man - cin', O. K. su - gar, you bet - ter

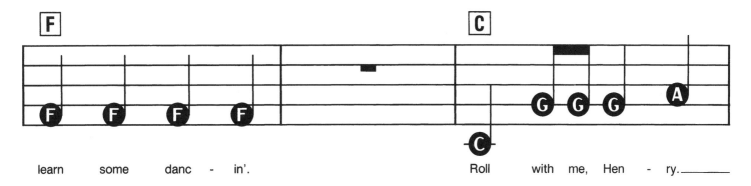

learn some danc - in'. Roll with me, Hen - ry.____

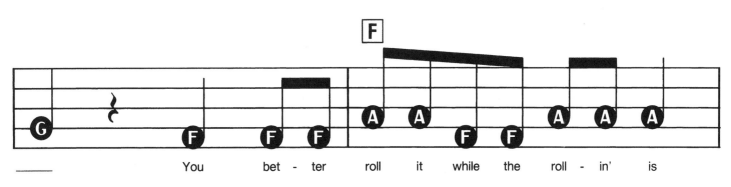

____ You bet - ter roll it while the roll - in' is

D.S. and Fade
(Return to 𝄋 and fade)

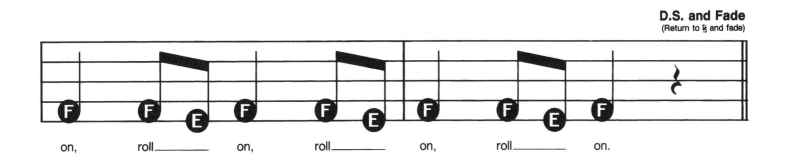

on, roll____ on, roll____ on, roll____ on.

Diana

Registration 7
Rhythm: Rock or 8 Beat

Words and Music by
Paul Anka

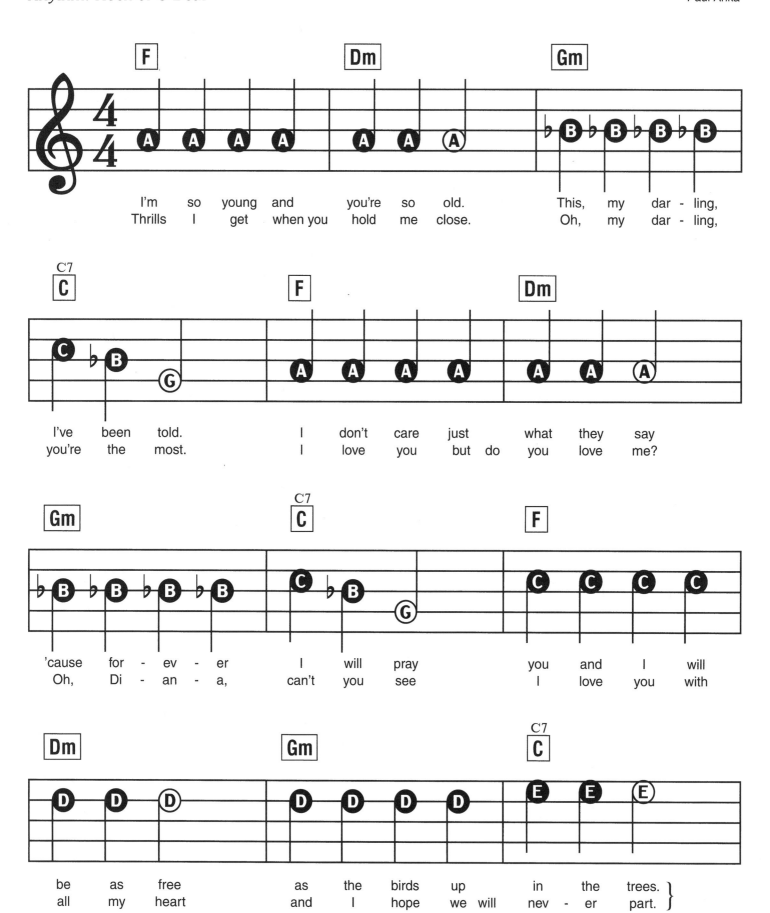

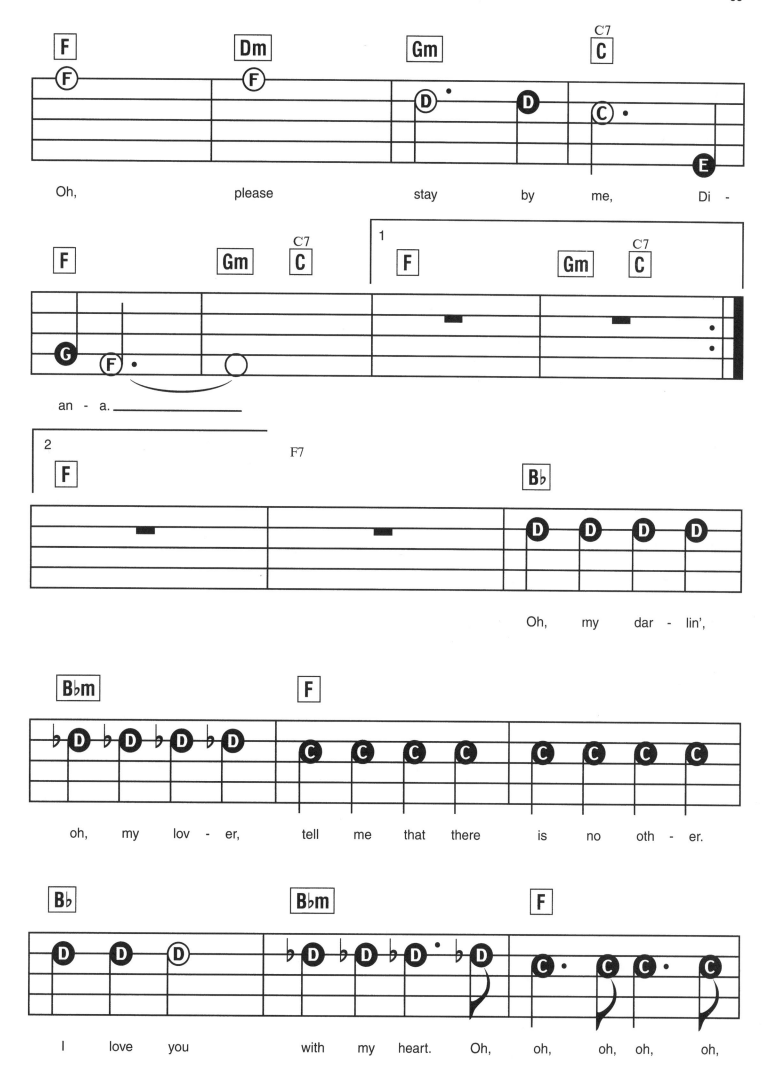

54

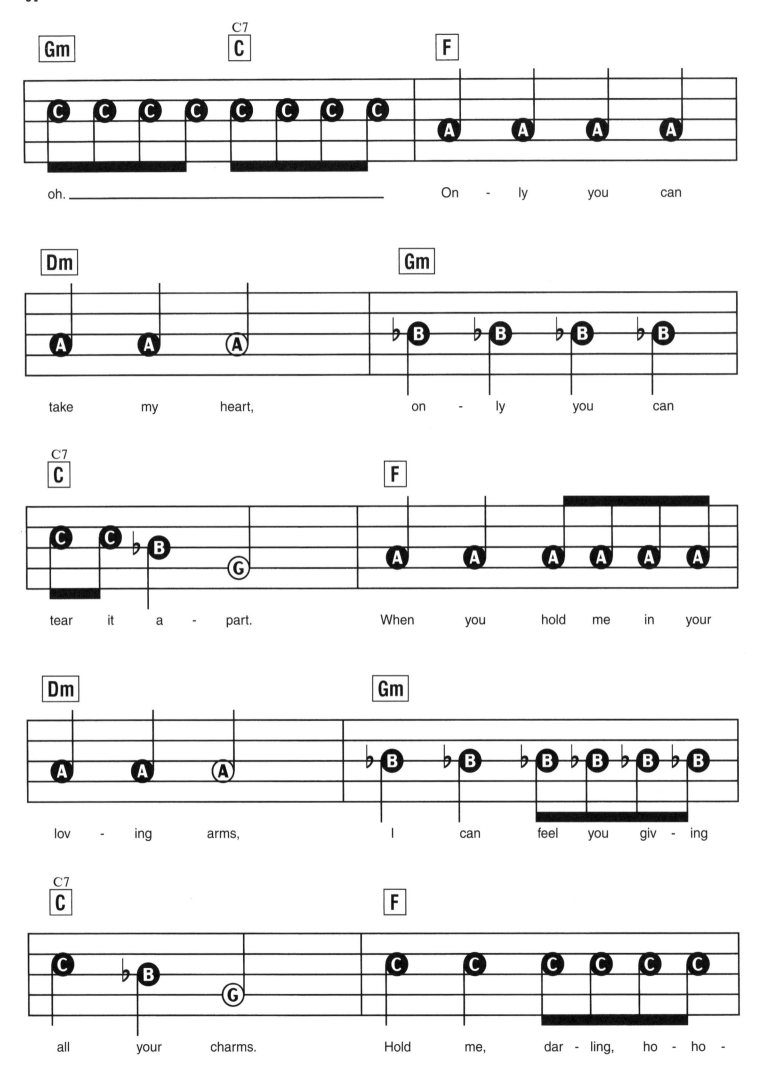

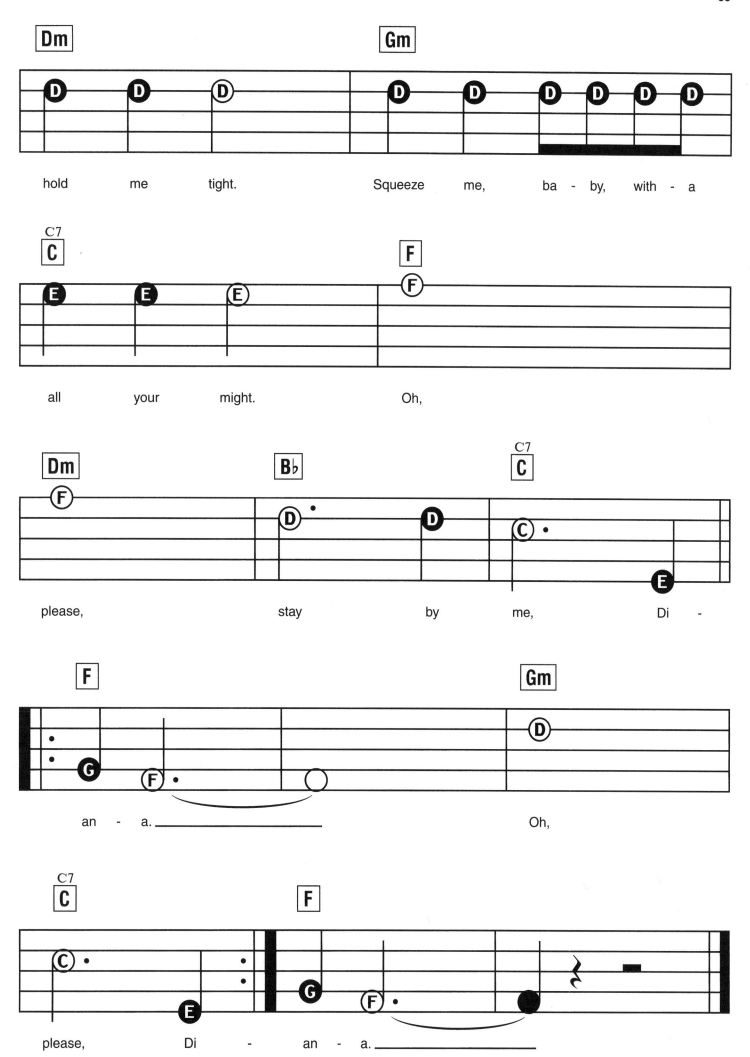

Don't

Registration 1
Rhythm: Slow Rock or Fifties Ballad

Words and Music by Jerry Leiber
and Mike Stoller

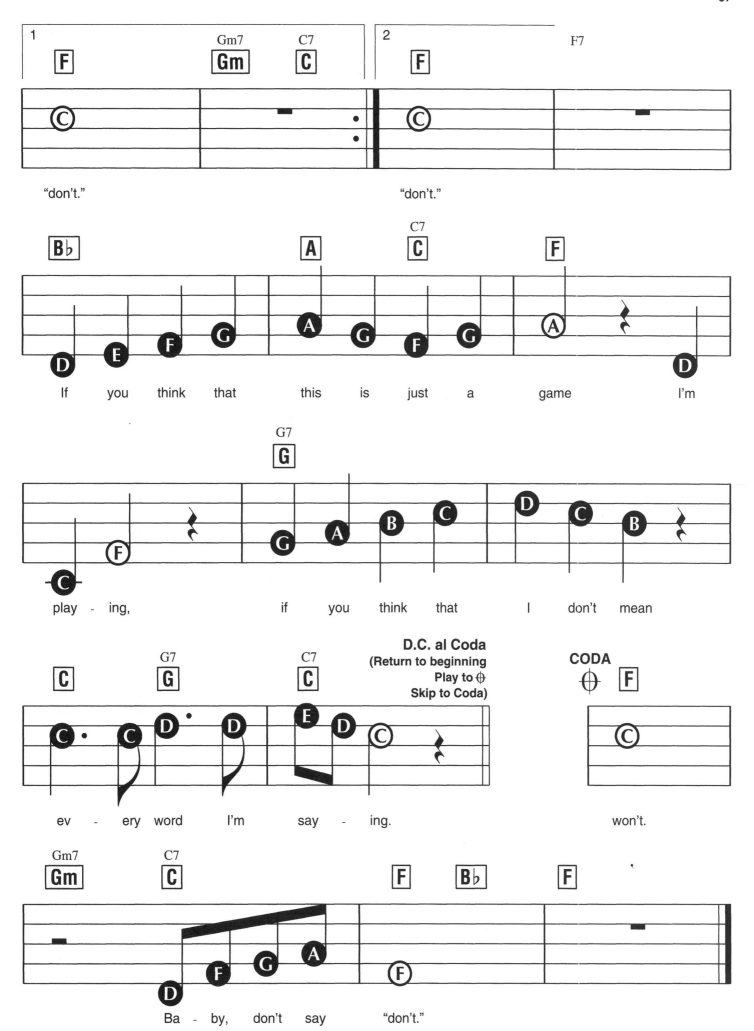

Don't Be Cruel
(To a Heart That's True)

Registration 4
Rhythm: Rock

Words and Music by Otis Blackwell
and Elvis Presley

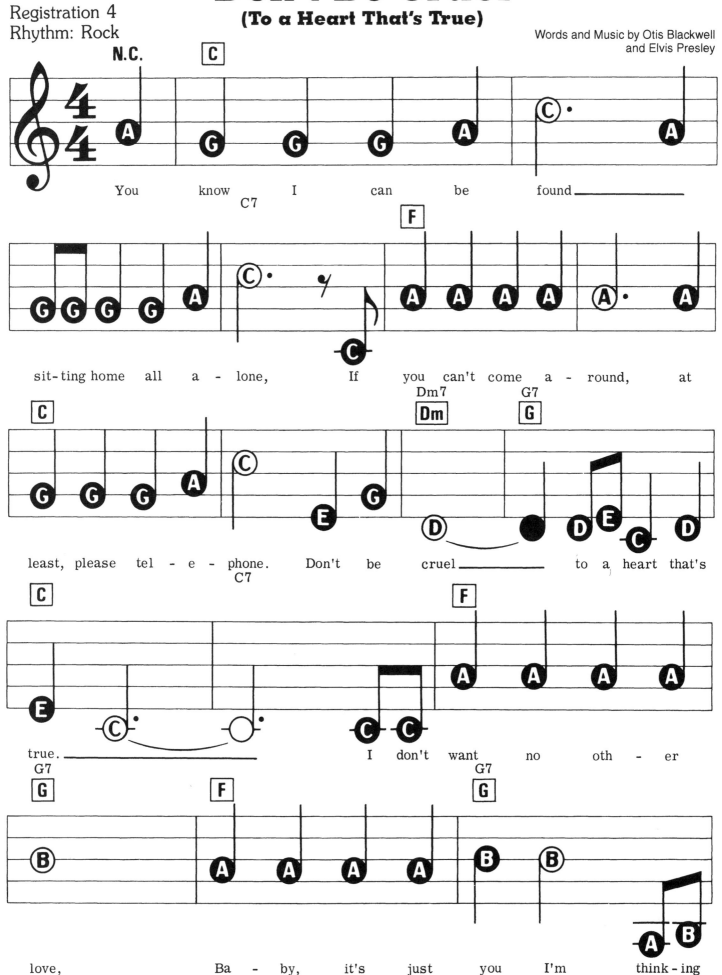

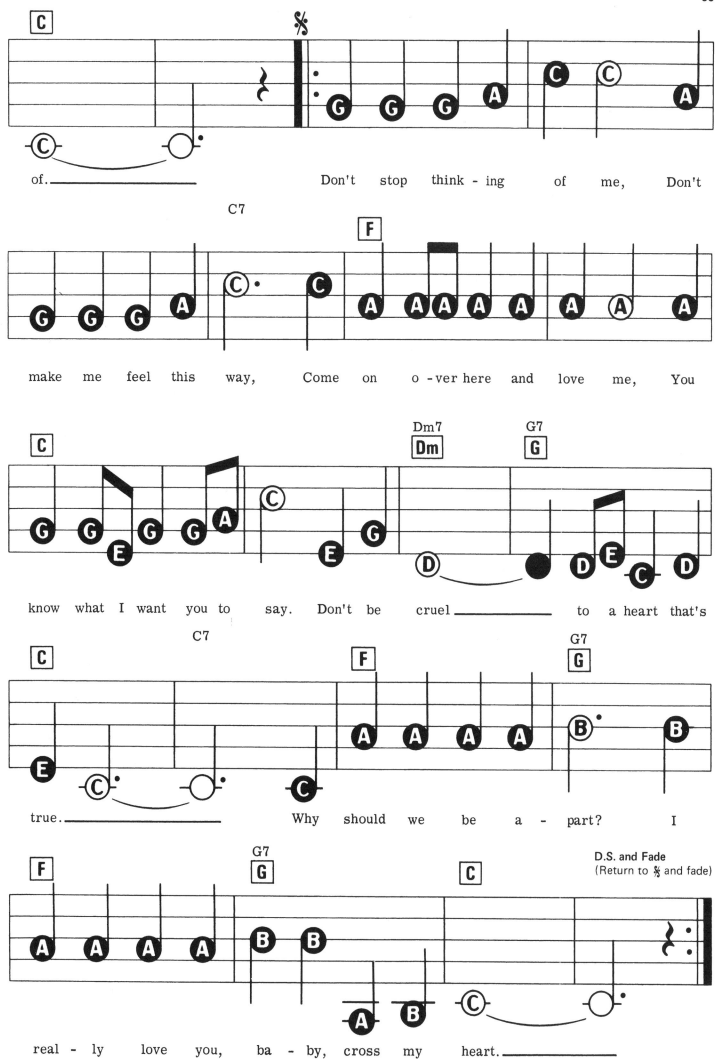

Don't You Know?

Registration 10
Rhythm: Waltz

Words and Music by
Bobby Worth

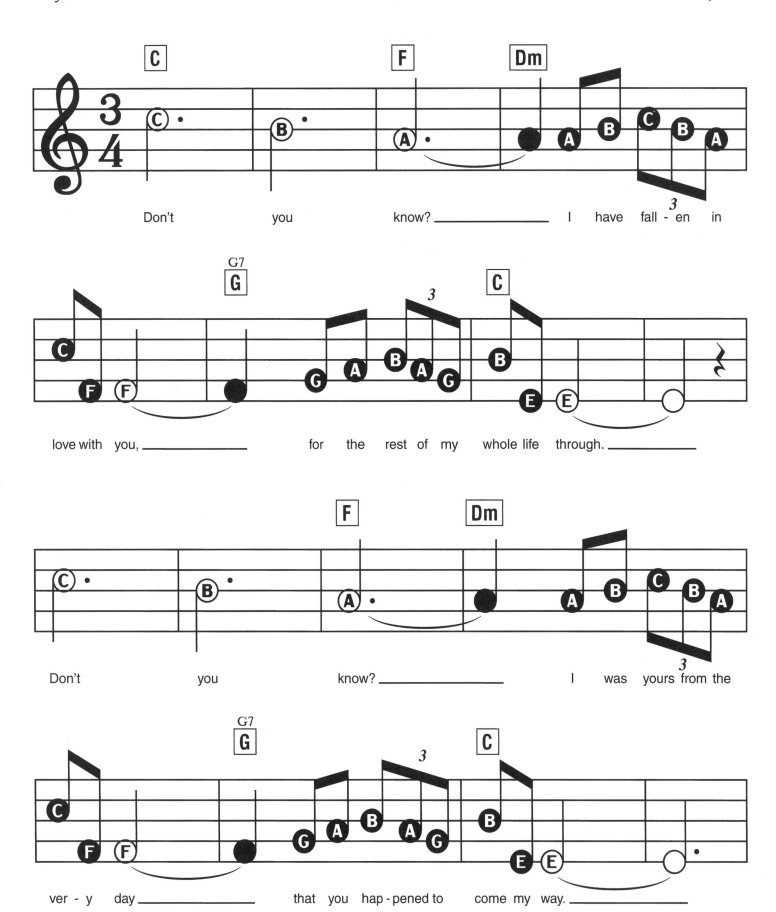

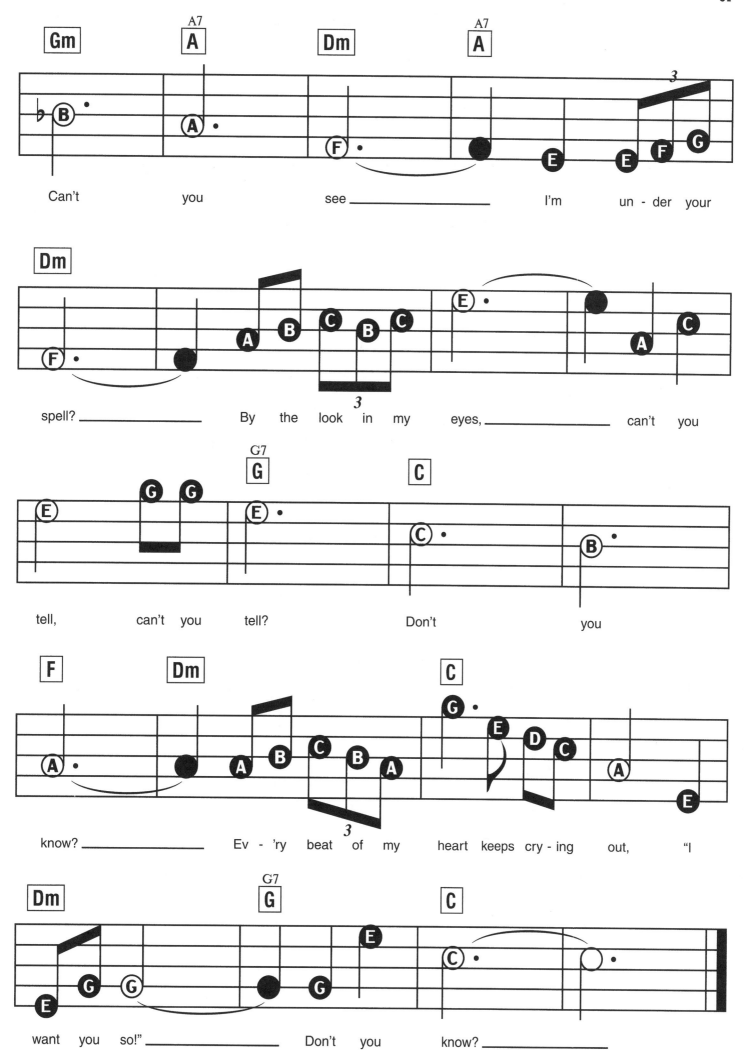

Earth Angel

Registration 5
Rhythm: Slow Rock or 12 Beat

Words and Music by
Jesse Belvin

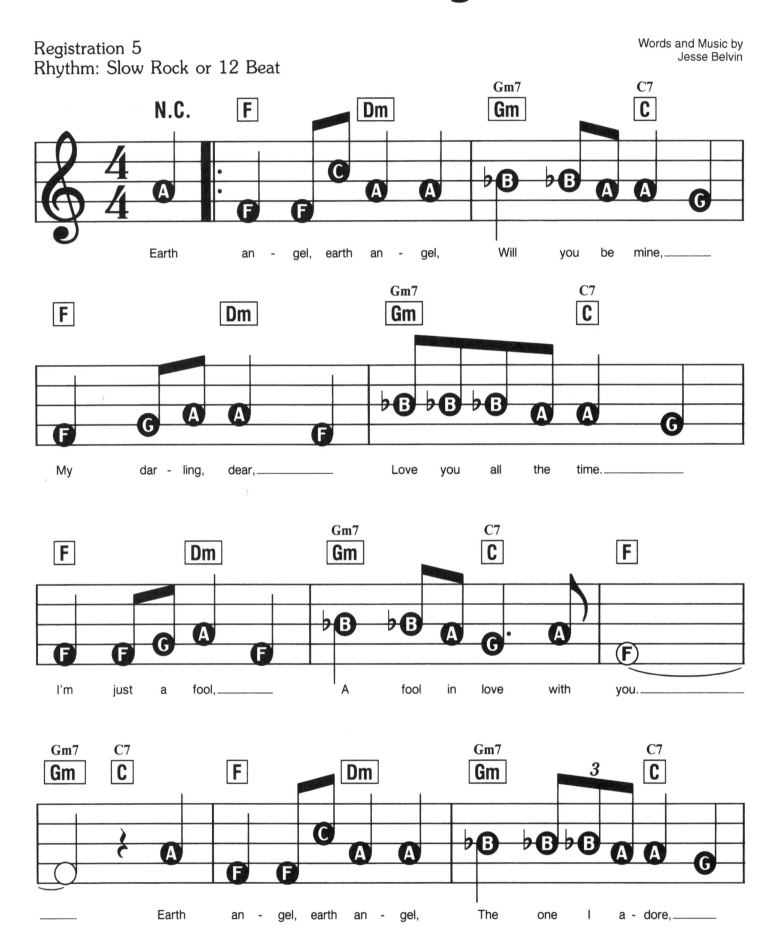

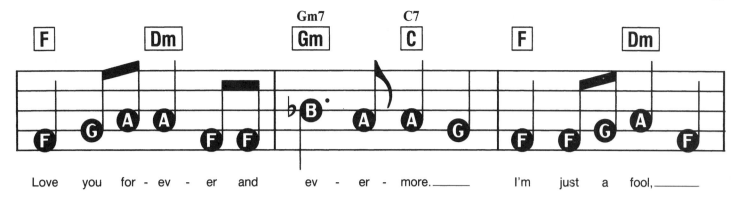

Love you for - ev - er and ev - er - more._____ I'm just a fool,_____

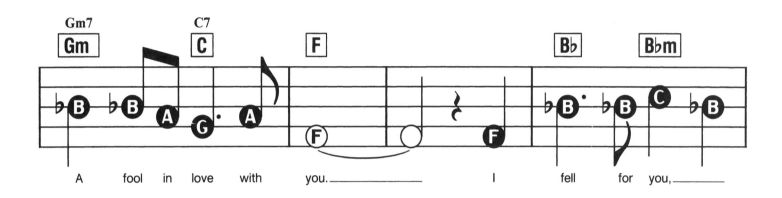

A fool in love with you._____ I fell for you,_____

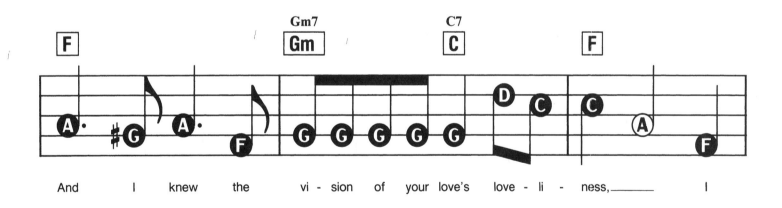

And I knew the vi - sion of your love's love - li - ness,_____ I

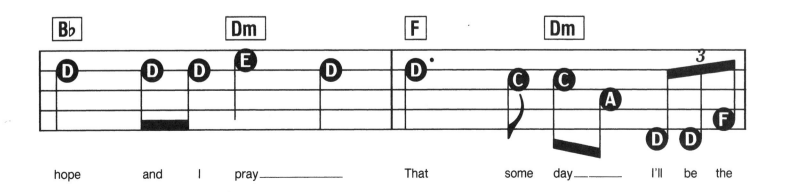

hope and I pray_____ That some day_____ I'll be the

64

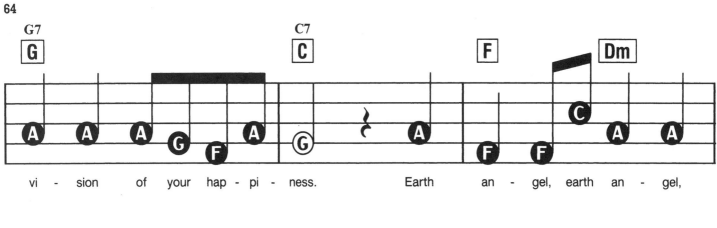

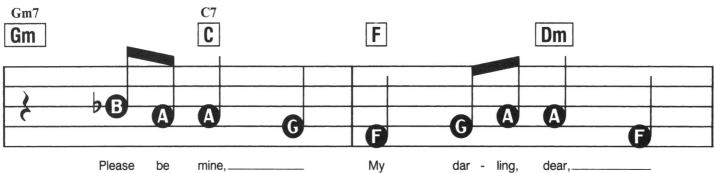

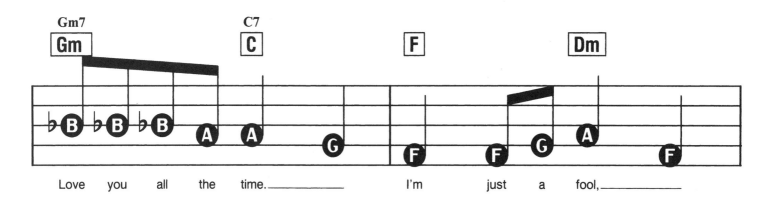

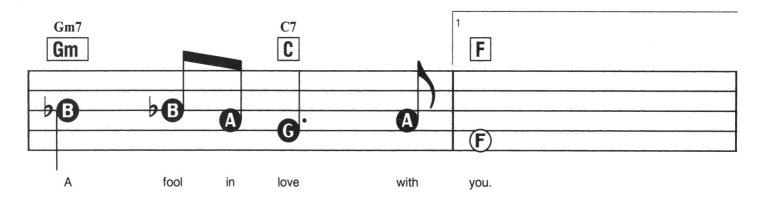

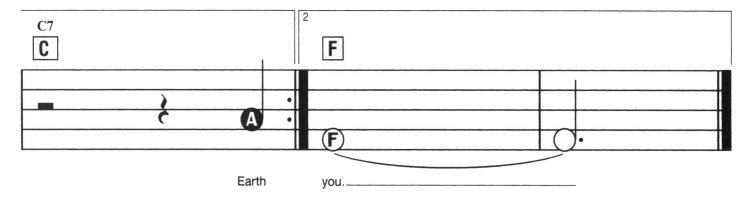

Eddie My Love

Registration 8
Rhythm: Slow Rock or Rock

Words and Music by Aaron Collins,
Maxwell Davis and Saul Sam Ling

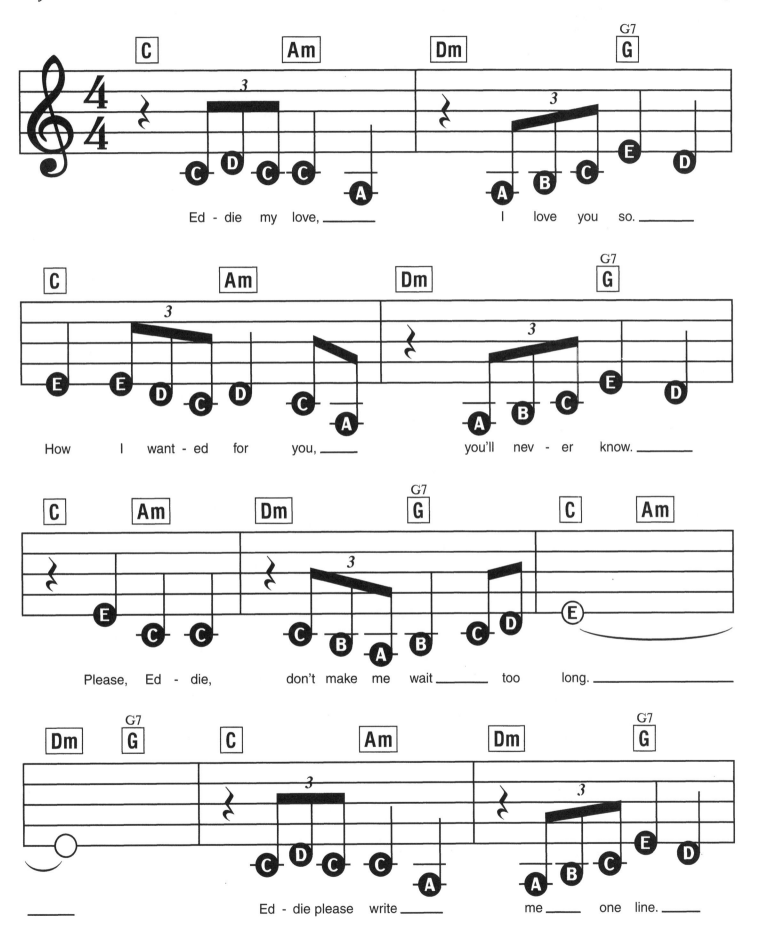

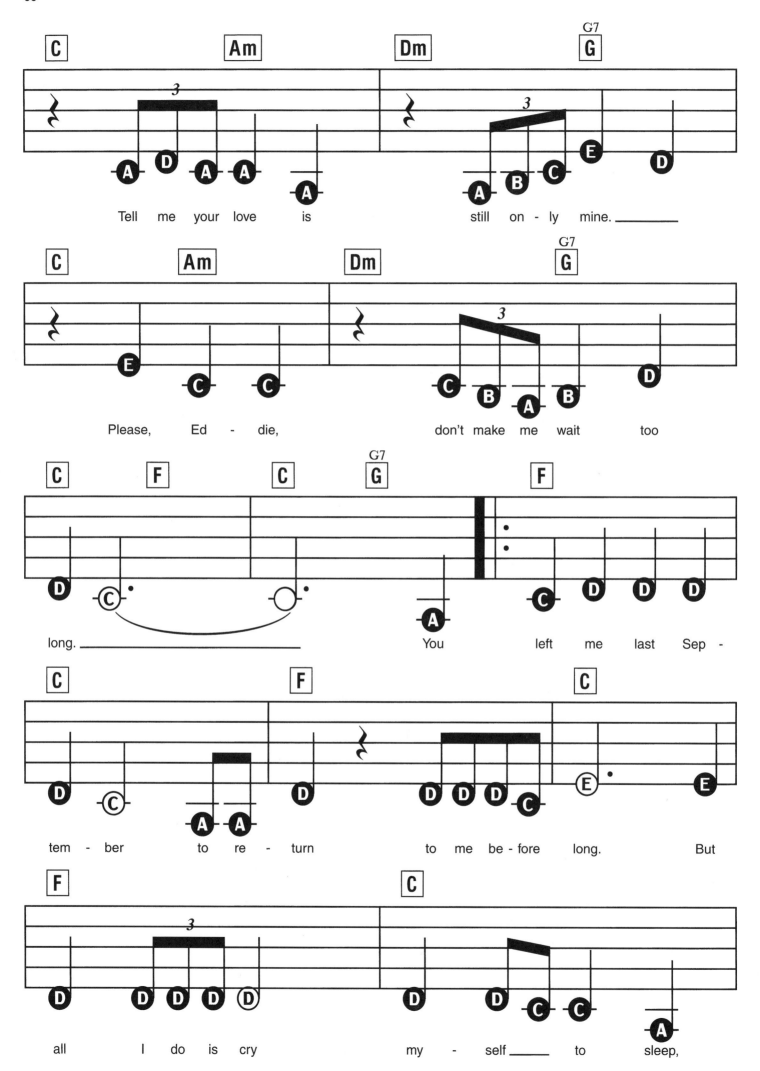

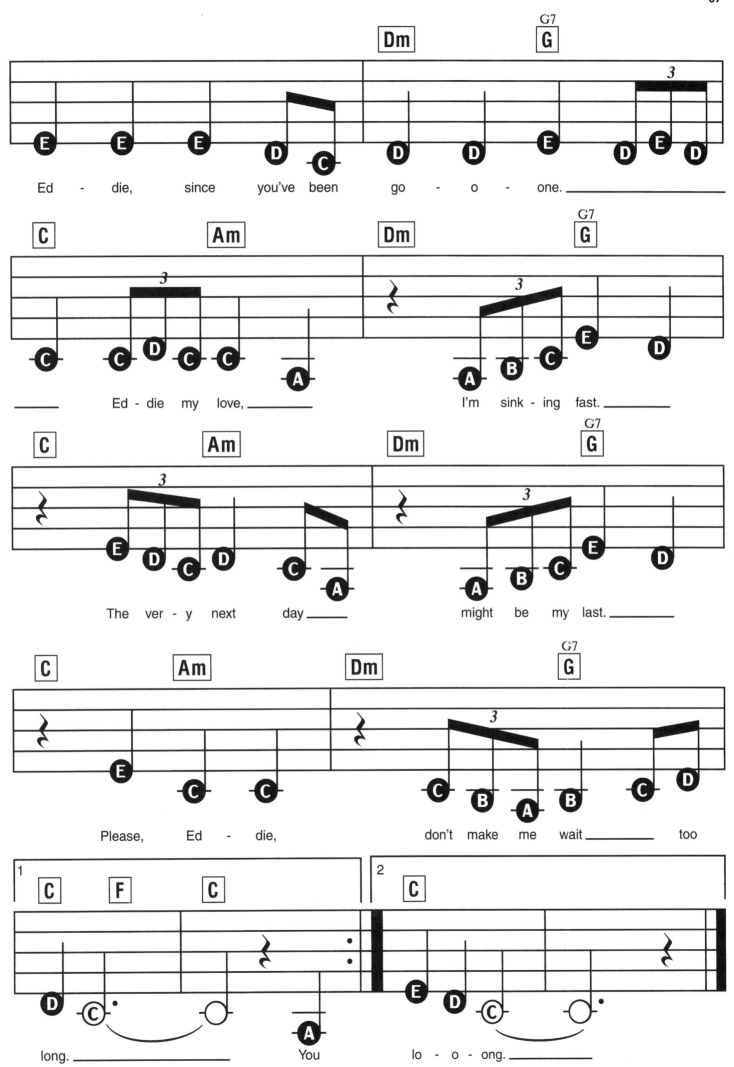

Fever

Registration 9
Rhythm: Ballad

Words and Music by John Davenport
and Eddie Cooley

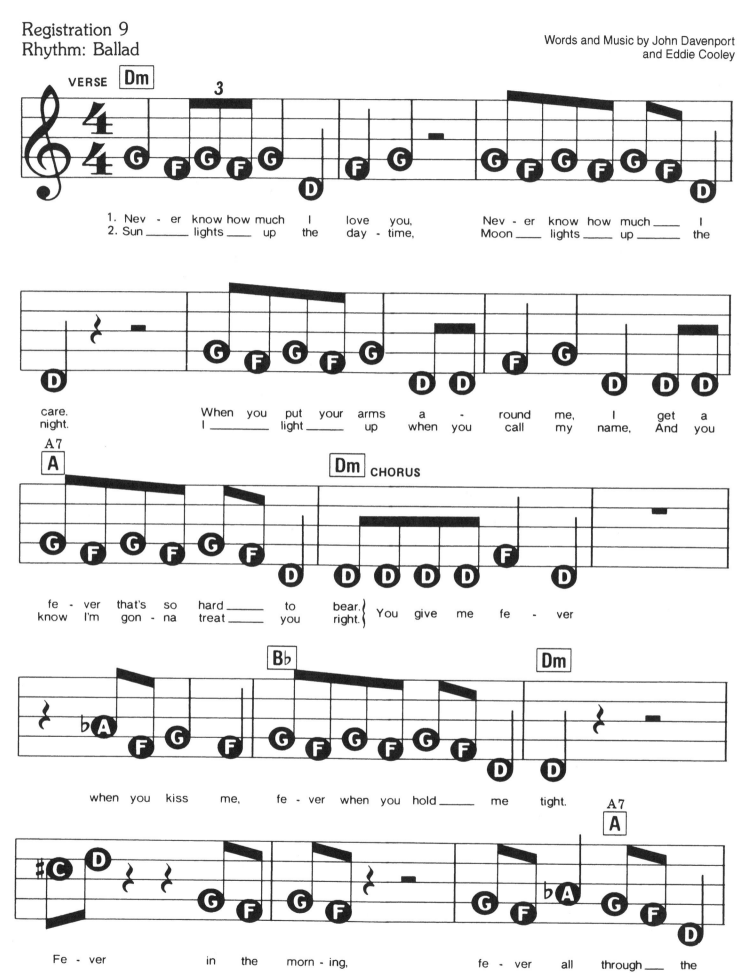

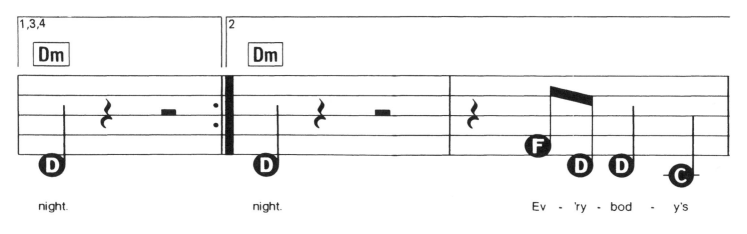

night.　　　　　　　night.　　　　　　　Ev - 'ry - bod - y's

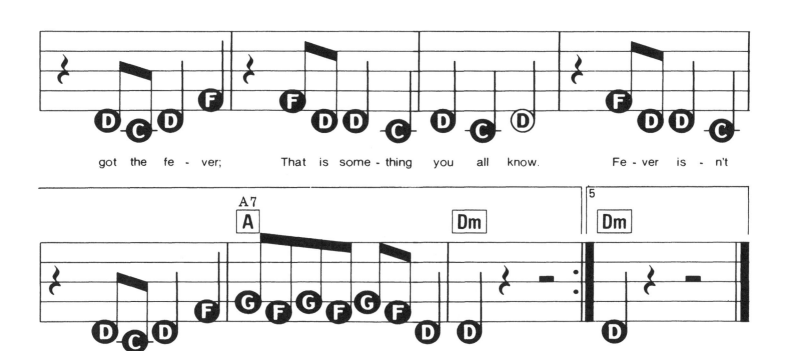

got　the　fe - ver;　　That　is　some - thing　you　all　know.　　Fe - ver　is - n't

such　a　new　thing,　Fe - ver　start - ed　long ____ a - go.　　　　burn.

Additional Verses

Verse 3
Romeo loved Juliet,
Juliet she felt the same.
When he put his arms around her, he said,
"Julie, baby, you're my flame."

Chorus:
Thou givest fever, when we kisseth,
FEVER with thy flaming youth.
FEVER — I'm afire,
FEVER, yea I burn forsooth.

Verse 4
Captain Smith and Pocahantas
Had a very mad affair,
When her Daddy tried to kill him, she said,
"Daddy-o don't you dare."

Chorus:
Give me fever, with his kisses,
FEVER when he holds me tight.
FEVER — I'm his Missus,
Oh Daddy won't you treat him right.

Verse 5
Now you've listened to my story
Here's the point that I have made.
Chicks were born to give you FEVER
Be it fahrenheit or centigrade.

Chorus:
They give you FEVER, when you kiss them,
FEVER if you live and learn.
FEVER — till you sizzle,
What a lovely way to burn.

(Now and Then There's)
A Fool Such As I

Registration 7
Rhythm: Swing

Words and Music by
Bill Trader

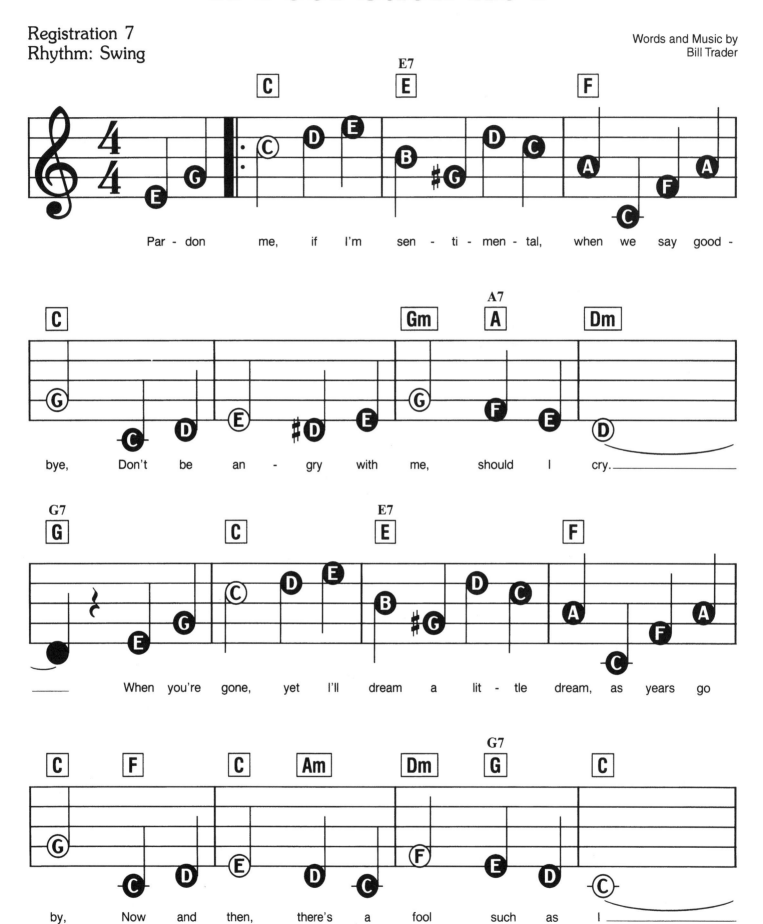

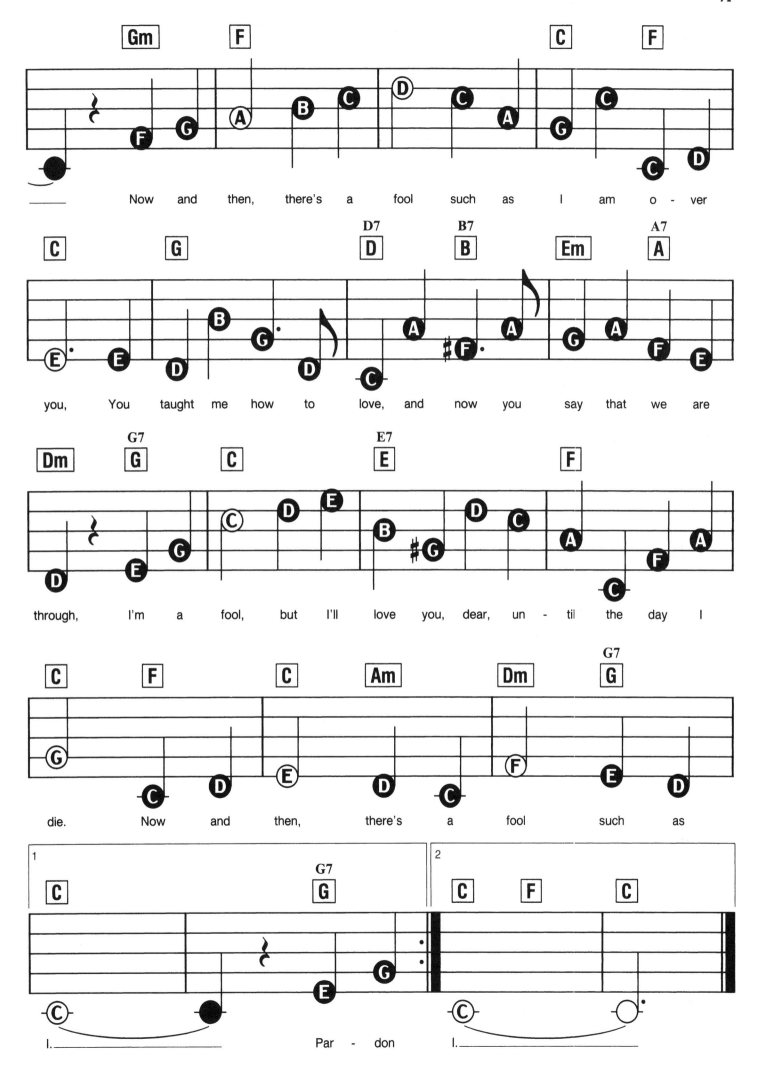

Friendly Persuasion

Registration 10
Rhythm: Ballad or Fox Trot

Words by Paul Francis Webster
Music by Dimitri Tiomkin

Thee I love. More than the mead - ows so green and still,

more than the mul - ber - ries on the hill, more than the buds on the

May ap - ple tree, _____ I love thee. _____

Arms have I, strong as the oak, for this oc - ca - sion.
(D.S.) *Instrumental*

Great Balls of Fire

Registration 5
Rhythm: Rock or Jazz Rock

Words and Music by Otis Blackwell
and Jack Hammer

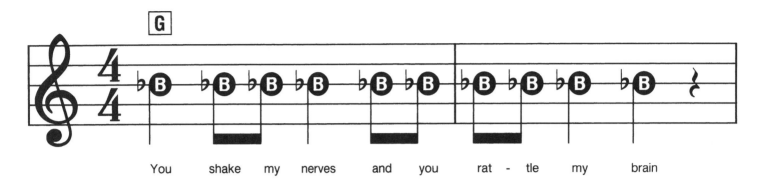

You shake my nerves and you rat - tle my brain

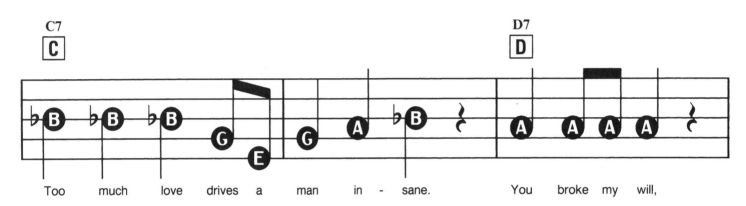

Too much love drives a man in - sane. You broke my will,

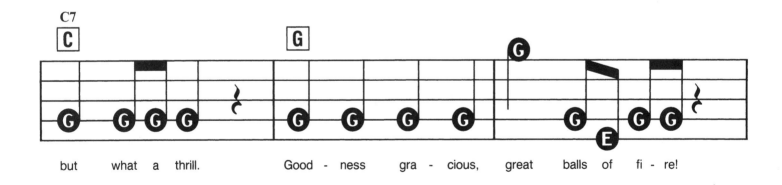

but what a thrill. Good - ness gra - cious, great balls of fi - re!

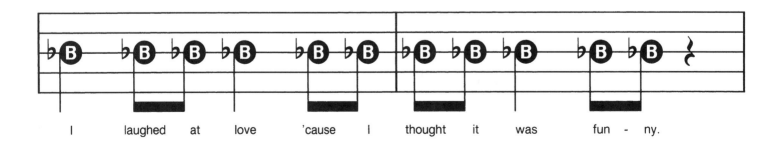

I laughed at love 'cause I thought it was fun - ny.

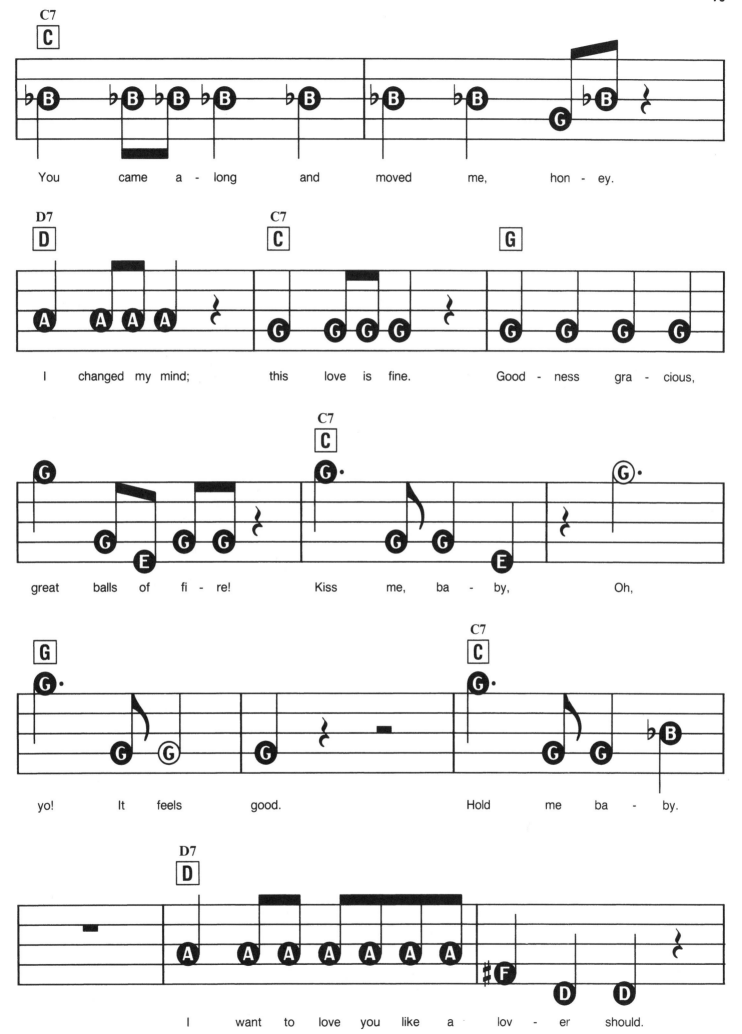

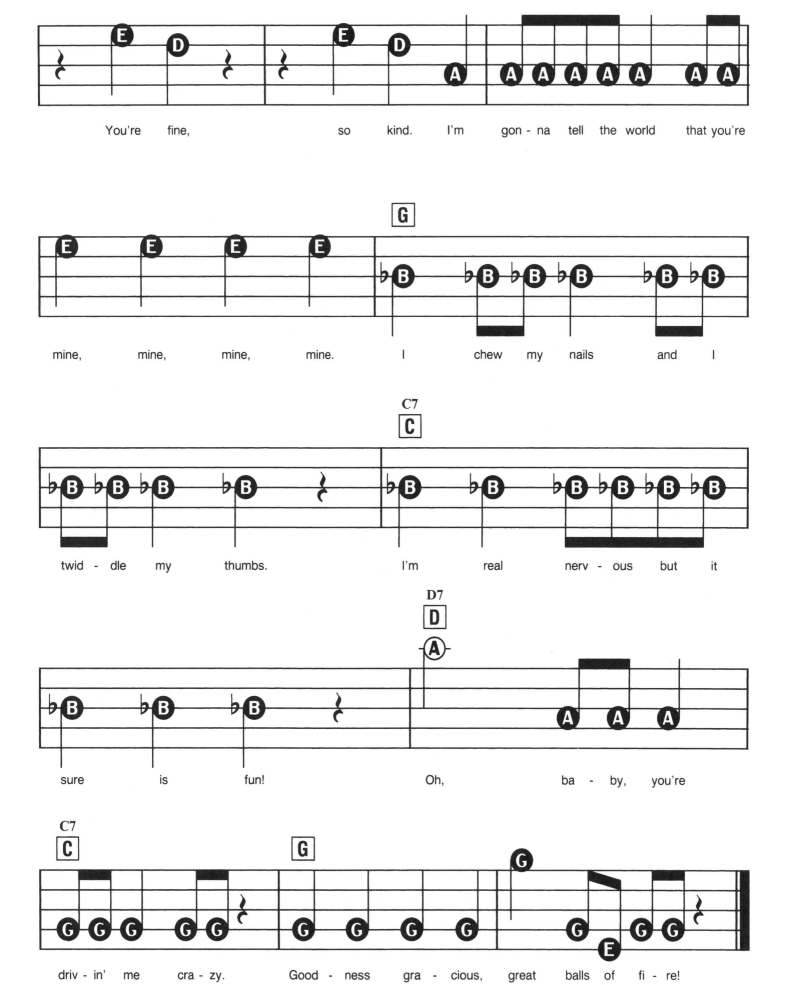

Honeycomb

Registration 2
Rhythm: Swing

Words and Music by
Bob Merrill

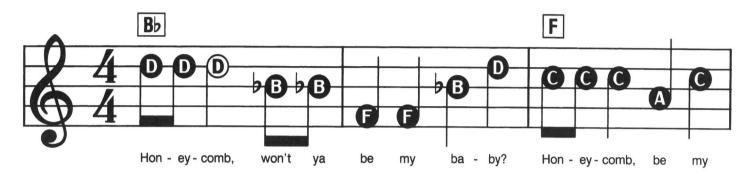

Hon - ey - comb, won't ya be my ba - by? Hon - ey - comb, be my

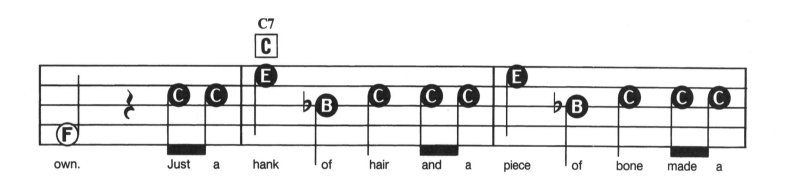

own. Just a hank of hair and a piece of bone made a

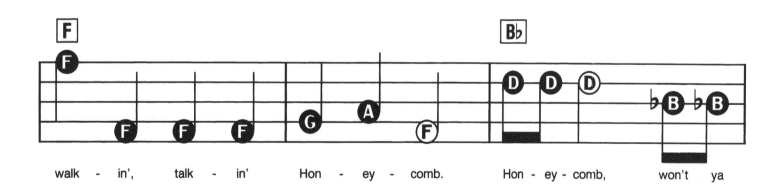

walk - in', talk - in' Hon - ey - comb. Hon - ey - comb, won't ya

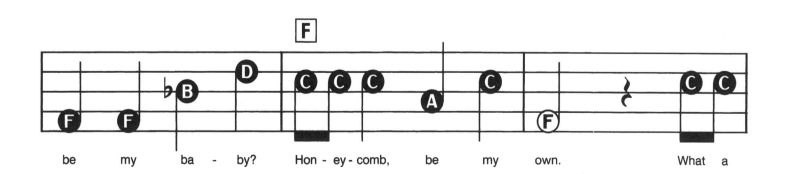

be my ba - by? Hon - ey - comb, be my own. What a

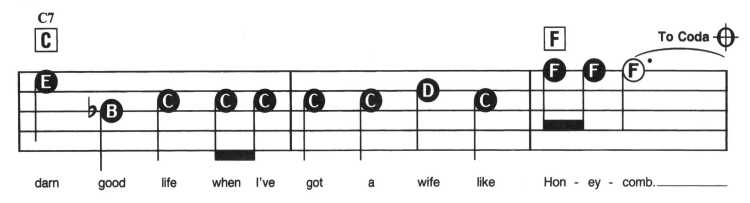

darn good life when I've got a wife like Hon - ey - comb._____

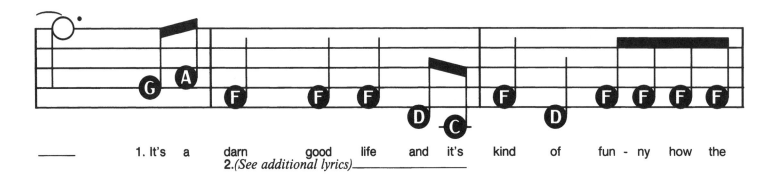

_____ 1. It's a darn good life and it's kind of fun - ny how the
2.*(See additional lyrics)*_____

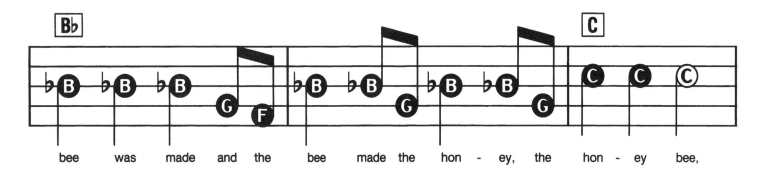

bee was made and the bee made the hon - ey, the hon - ey bee,

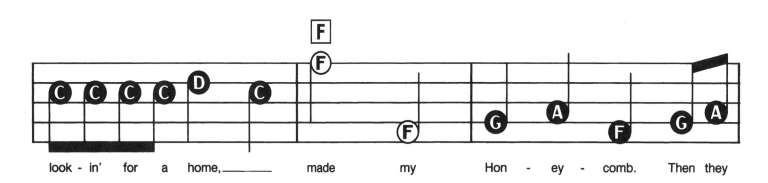

look - in' for a home,_____ made my Hon - ey - comb. Then they

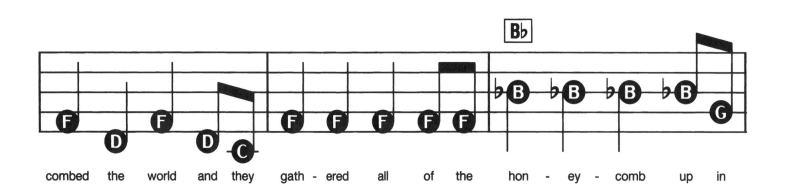

combed the world and they gath - ered all of the hon - ey - comb up in

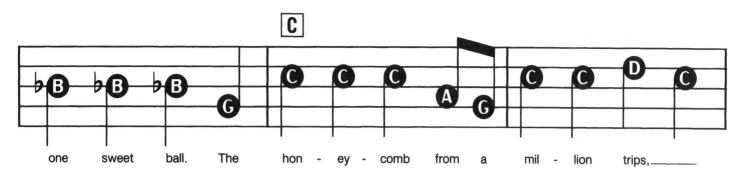

one sweet ball. The hon - ey - comb from a mil - lion trips,

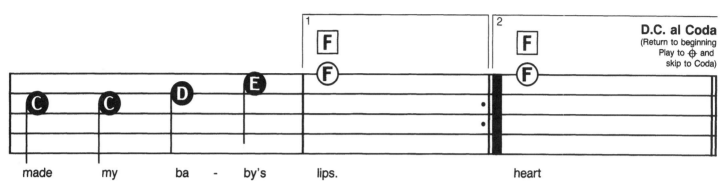

D.C. al Coda
(Return to beginning
Play to ⊕ and
skip to Coda)

made my ba - by's lips. heart

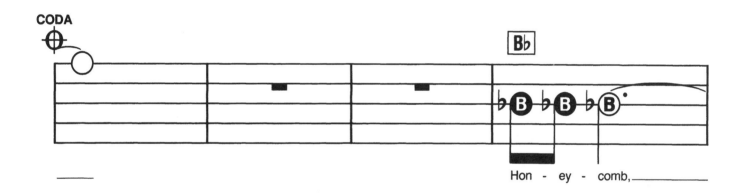

CODA

Hon - ey - comb,

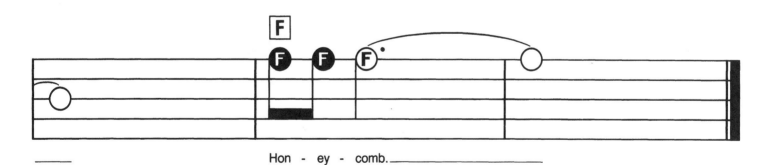

Hon - ey - comb.

Additional Lyrics

2. Now have you heard tell how they made a bee?
   Then tried a hand at a green, green tree.
   So the tree was made and I guess you've heard,
   Next they made a bird.
   Then they went around lookin' everywhere,
   Takin' love from here and from there,
   And they stored it up in a little cart,
   For my honey's heart.

Chorus

The Green Door

Registration 5
Rhythm: Rock

Words and Music by Bob Davie
and Marvin Moore

81

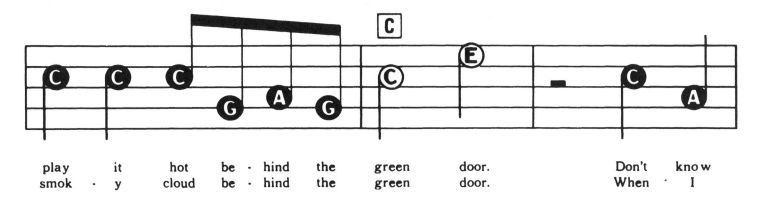

play it hot be · hind the green door. Don't know
smok · y cloud be · hind the green door. When · I

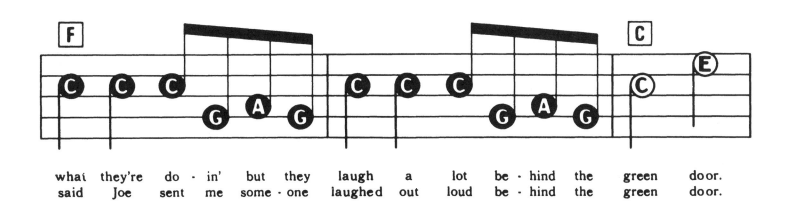

what they're do · in' but they laugh a lot be · hind the green door.
said Joe sent me some · one laughed out loud be · hind the green door.

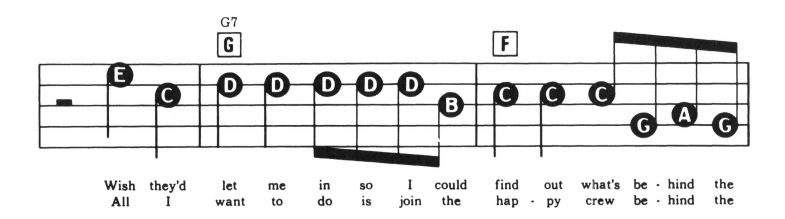

Wish they'd let me in so I could find out what's be · hind the
All I want to do is join the hap · py crew be · hind the

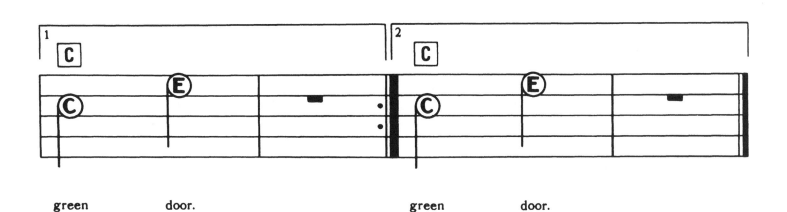

green door. green door.

The Hawaiian Wedding Song
(Ke Kali Nei Au)

Registration 10
Rhythm: Ballad or Slow Rock

English Lyrics by Al Hoffman and Dick Manning
Hawaiian Lyrics and Music by Charles E. King

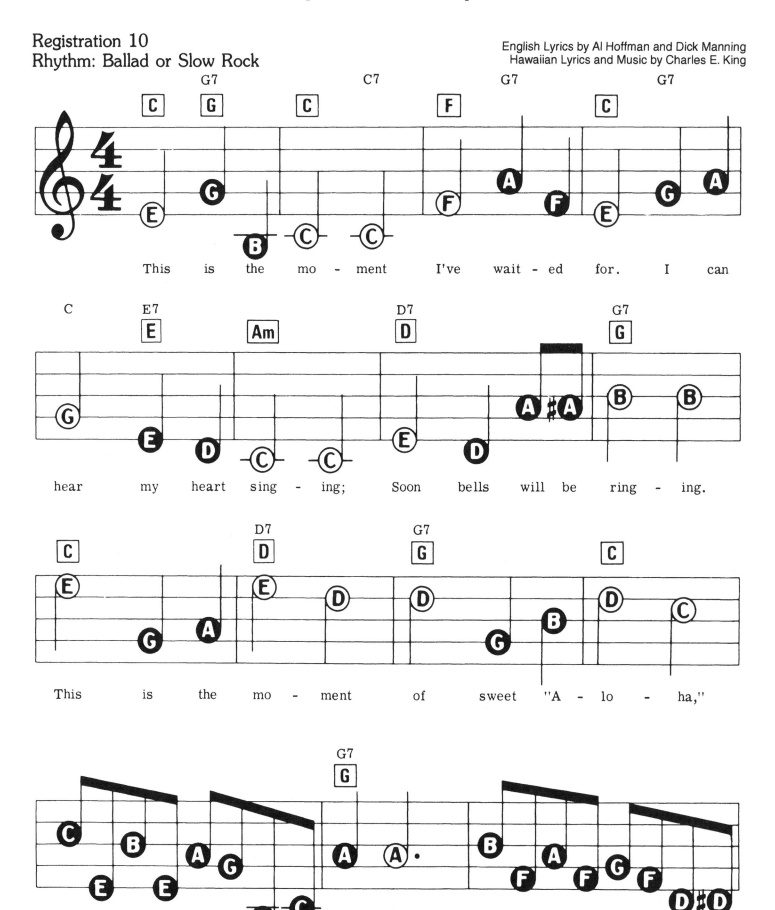

This is the mo - ment I've wait - ed for. I can

hear my heart sing - ing; Soon bells will be ring - ing.

This is the mo - ment of sweet "A - lo - ha,"

I will love you long - er than for - ev - er, Pro - mise me that you will leave me

83

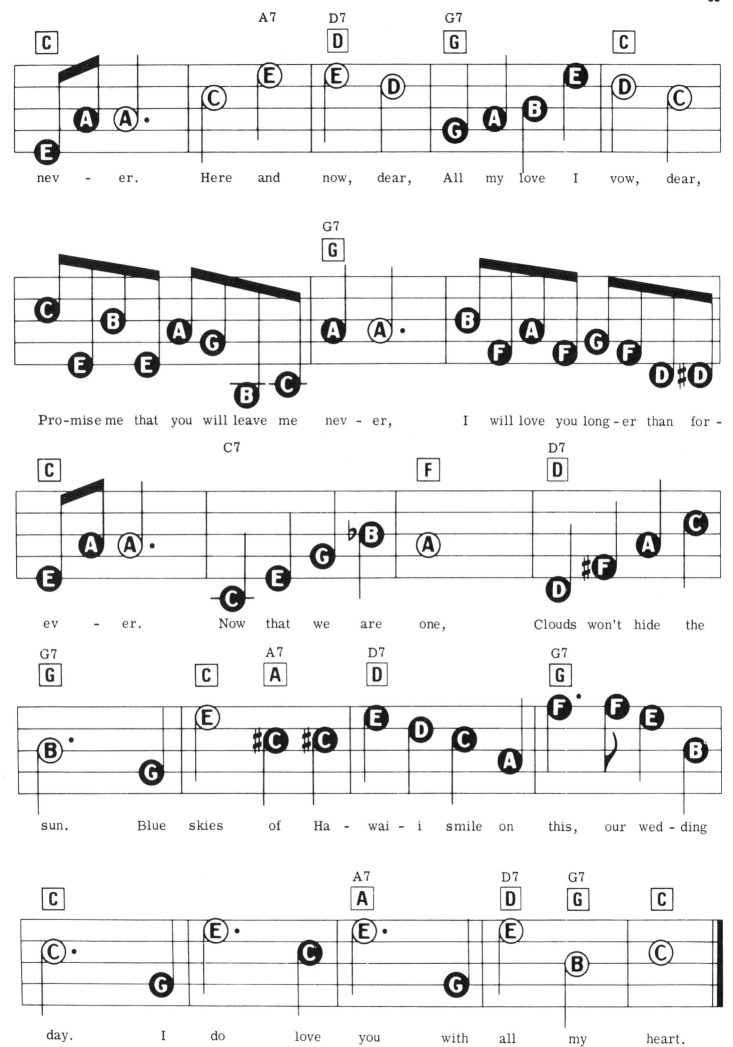

Heartaches by the Number

Registration 4
Rhythm: Country

Words and Music by
Harlan Howard

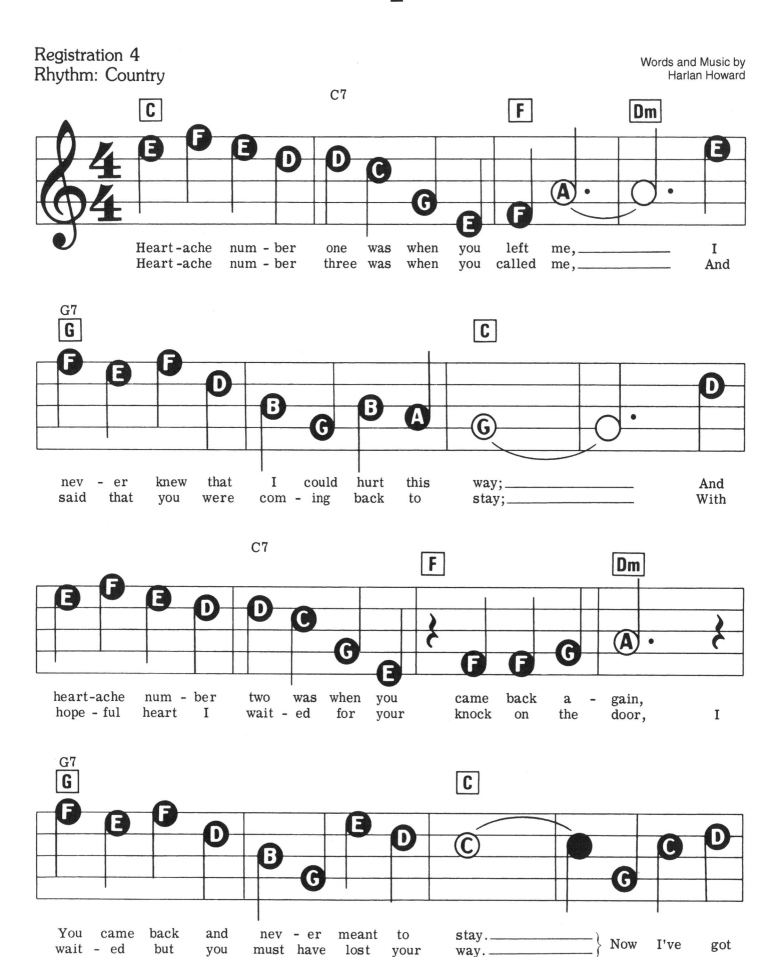

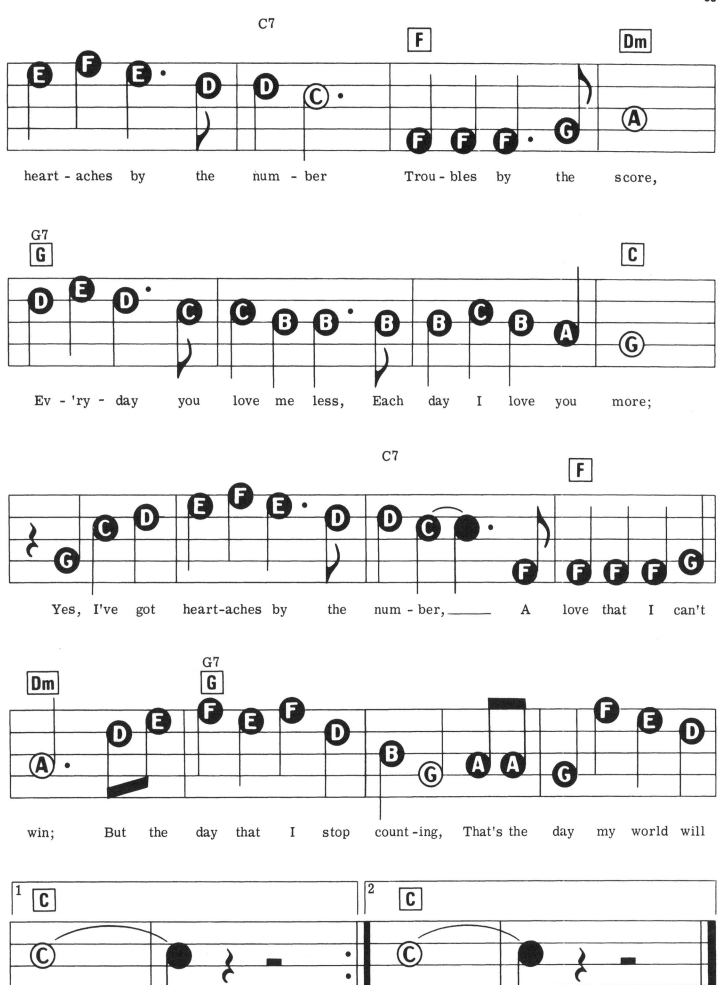

Heartbreak Hotel

Registration 3
Rhythm: Rock

Words and Music by Mae Boren Axton,
Tommy Durden and Elvis Presley

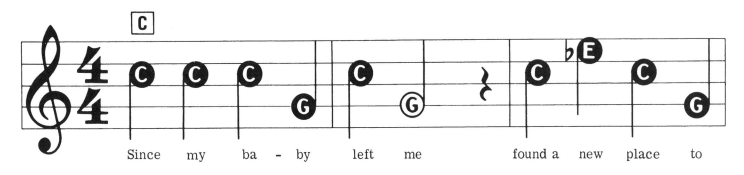

Since my ba - by left me found a new place to

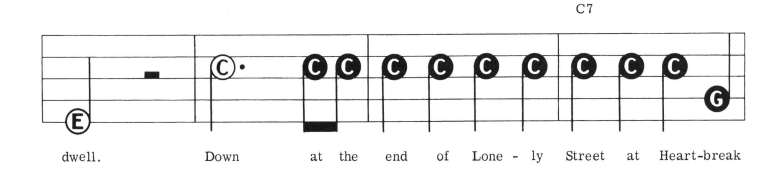

dwell. Down at the end of Lone - ly Street at Heart-break

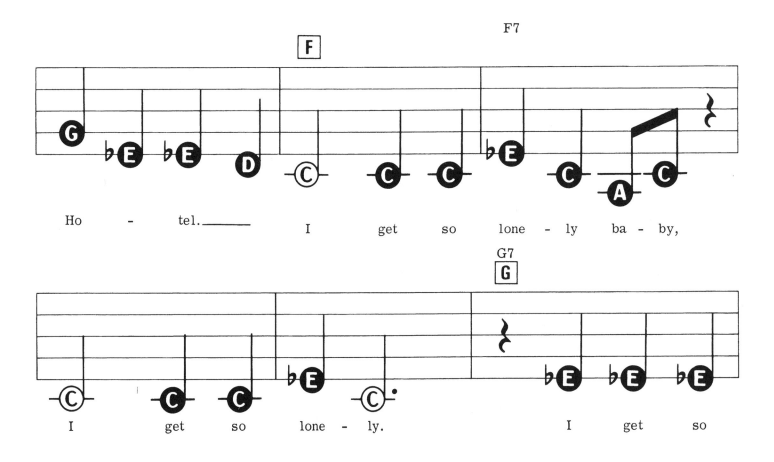

Ho - tel. _____ I get so lone - ly ba - by,

I get so lone - ly. I get so

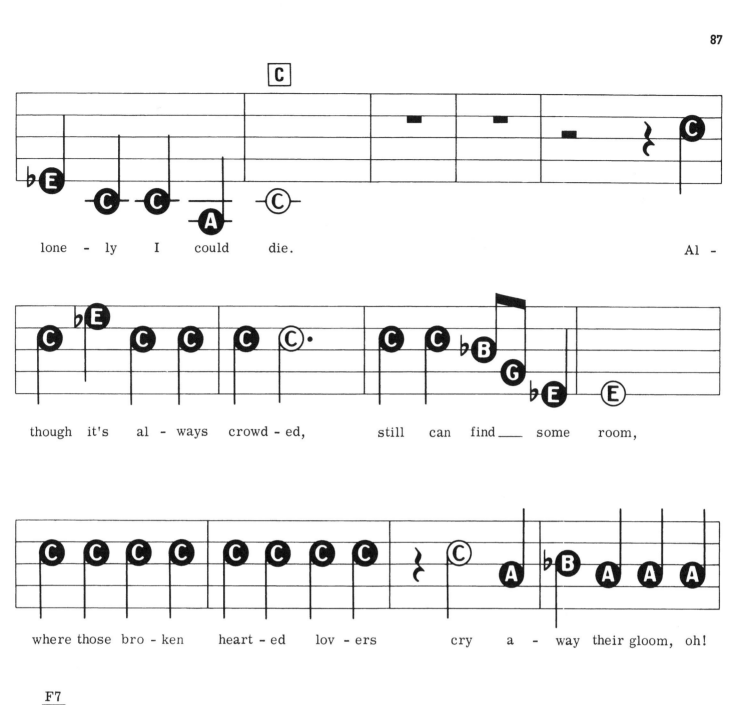

lone - ly I could die. Al -

though it's al - ways crowd - ed, still can find___ some room,

where those bro - ken heart - ed lov - ers cry a - way their gloom, oh!

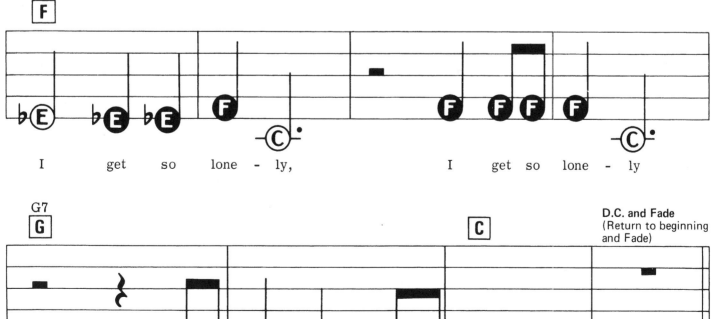

I get so lone - ly, I get so lone - ly

D.C. and Fade
(Return to beginning
and Fade)

get so lone - ly I could die.

Hot Diggity
(Dog Ziggity Boom)

Registration 9
Rhythm: Waltz

Words and Music by Al Hoffman
and Dick Manning

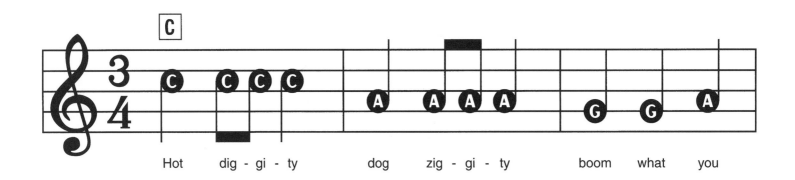

Hot dig-gi-ty dog zig-gi-ty boom what you

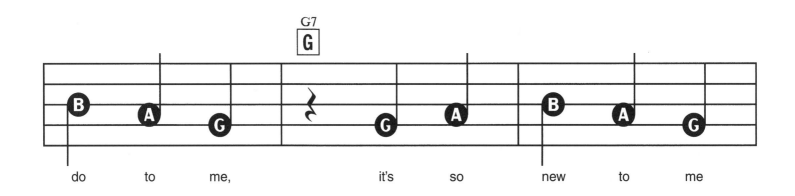

do to me, it's so new to me

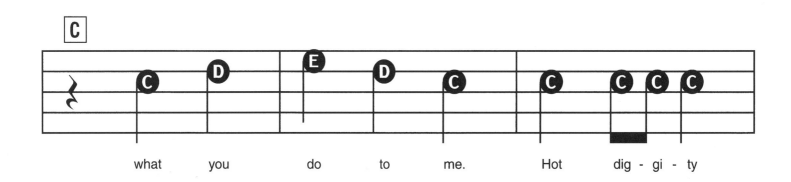

what you do to me. Hot dig-gi-ty

To Coda ⊕

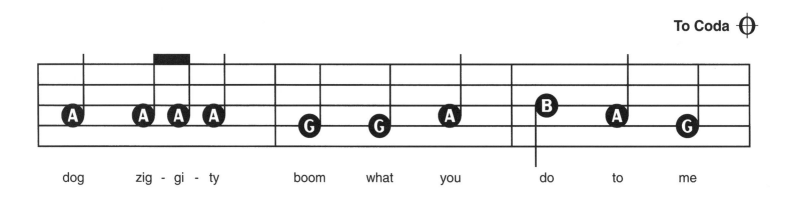

dog zig-gi-ty boom what you do to me

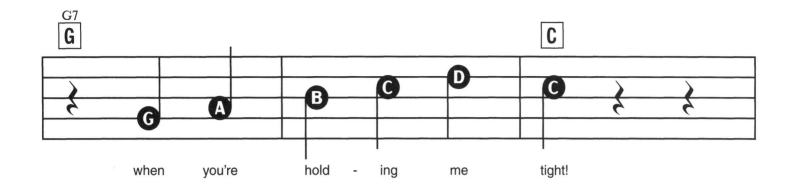

when you're hold - ing me tight!

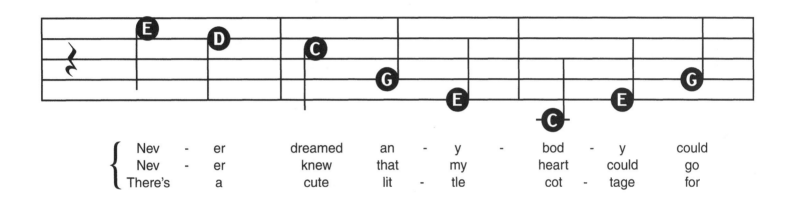

Nev - er dreamed an - y - bod - y could
Nev - er knew that my heart could go
There's a cute lit - tle cot - tage for

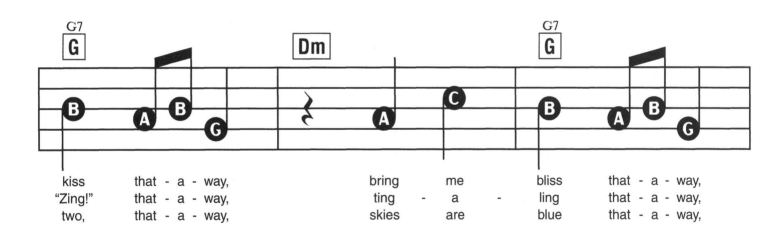

kiss that - a - way, bring me bliss that - a - way,
"Zing!" that - a - way, ting - a - ling that - a - way,
two, that - a - way, skies are blue that - a - way,

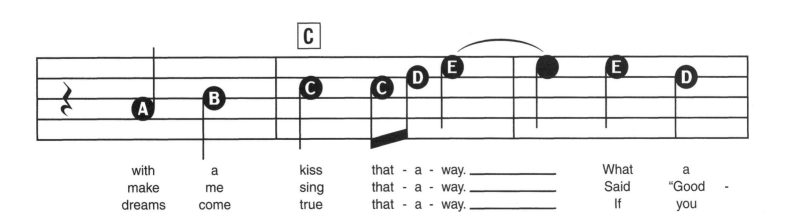

with a kiss that - a - way. _____ What a
make me sing that - a - way. _____ Said "Good -
dreams come true that - a - way. _____ If you

90

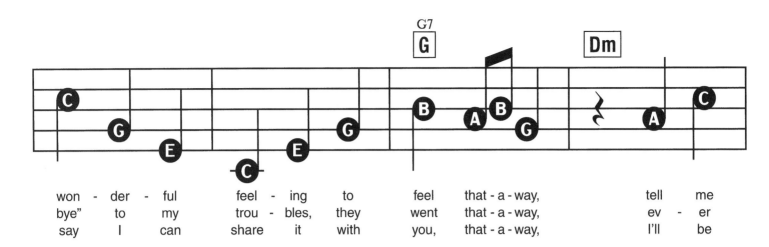

won - der - ful   feel - ing   to   feel   that - a - way,   tell   me
bye"   to   my   trou - bles,   they   went   that - a - way,   ev - er
say   I   can   share   it   with   you,   that - a - way,   I'll   be

D.C. al Coda
(3rd time)
(Return to beginning
Play to ⊕ and
Skip to Coda)

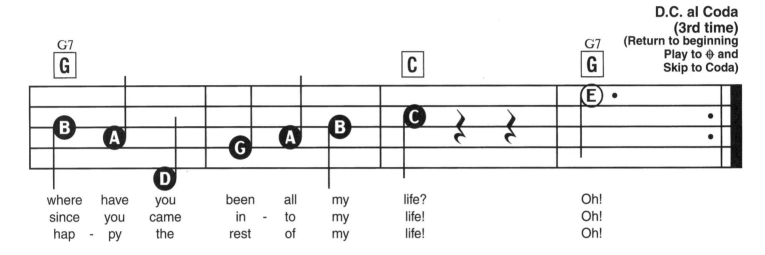

where   have   you   been   all   my   life?   Oh!
since   you   came   in - to   my   life!   Oh!
hap - py   the   rest   of   my   life!   Oh!

CODA

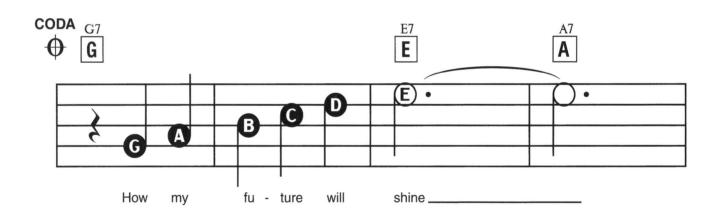

How   my   fu - ture   will   shine _____

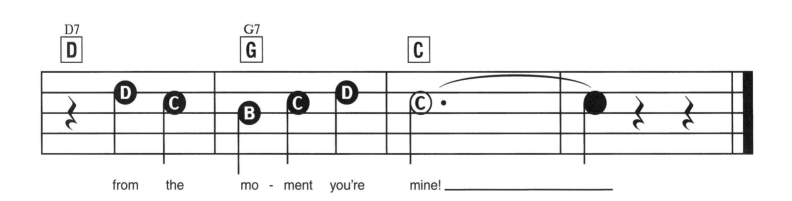

from   the   mo - ment   you're   mine! _____

Hushabye

Registration 1
Rhythm: Ballad

Words and Music by Doc Pomus
and Mort Shuman

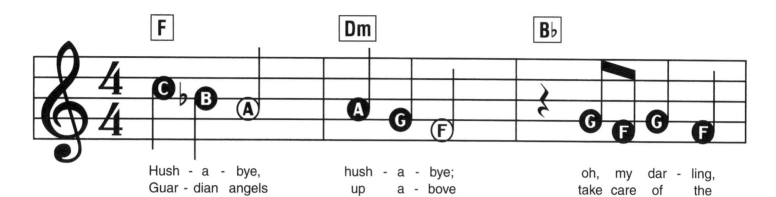

Hush - a - bye,   hush - a - bye;   oh, my dar - ling,
Guar - dian angels   up a - bove   take care of the

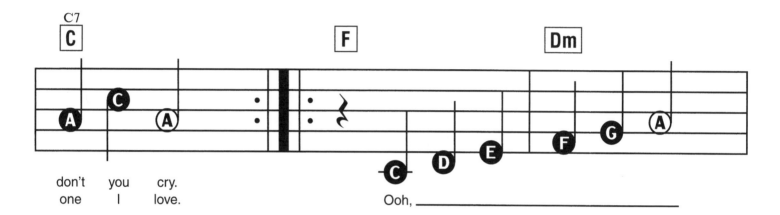

don't you cry.   Ooh, _____
one I love.

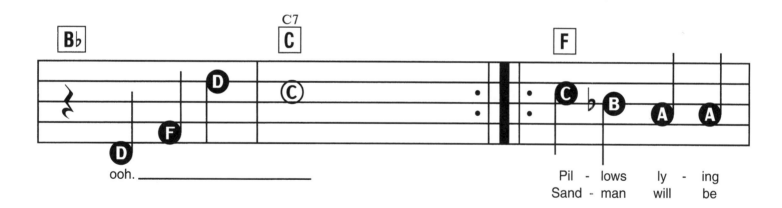

ooh. _____   Pil - lows ly - ing
                                Sand - man will be

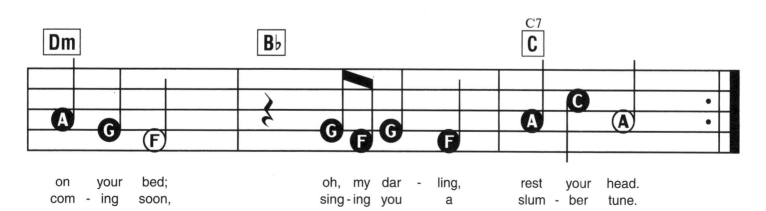

on your bed;   oh, my dar - ling,   rest your head.
com - ing soon,   sing - ing you a   slum - ber tune.

92

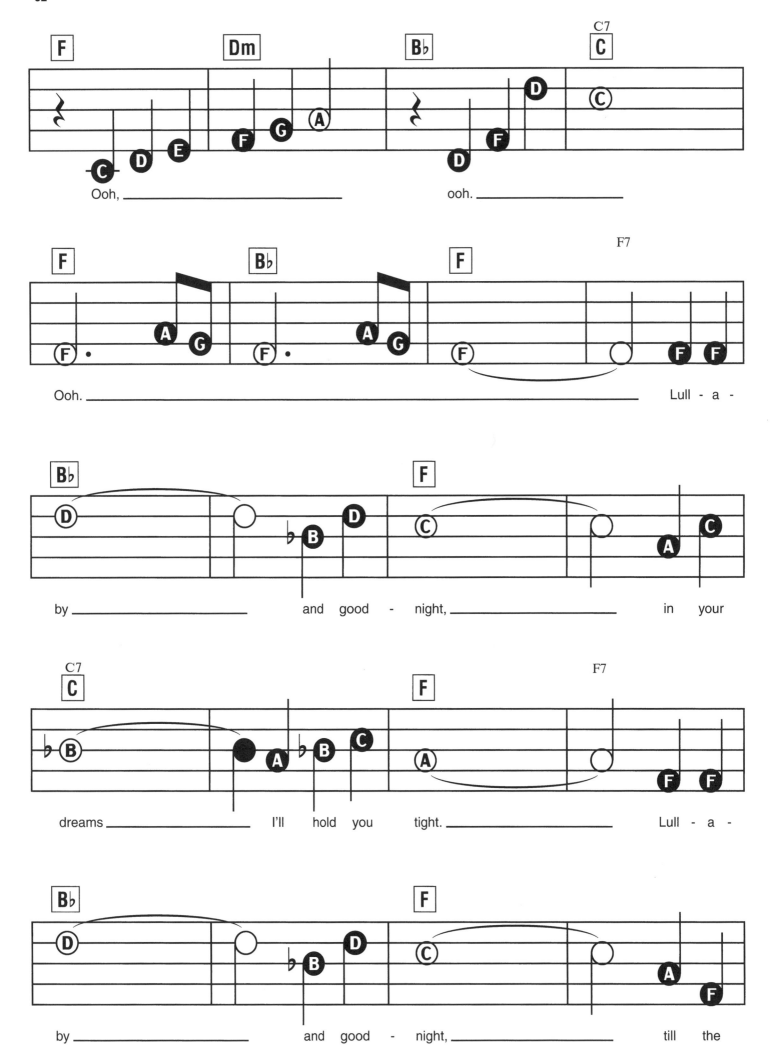

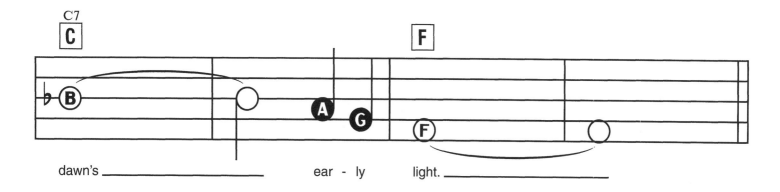

dawn's _____ ear - ly light. _____

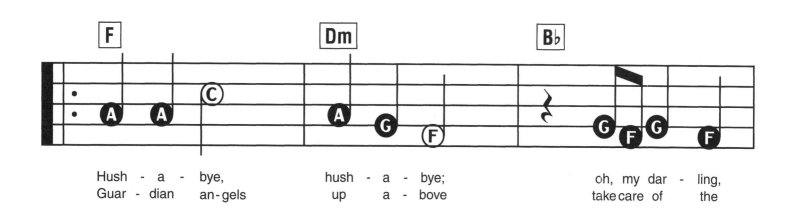

Hush - a - bye,   hush - a - bye;   oh, my dar - ling,
Guar - dian an - gels   up a - bove   take care of the

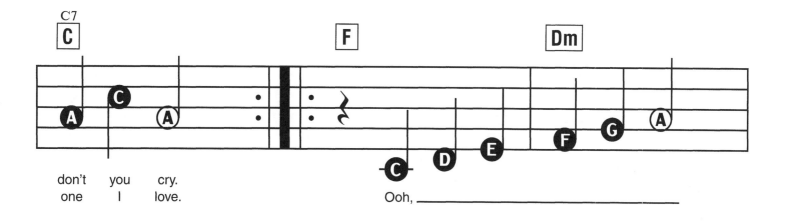

don't you cry.   Ooh, _____
one I love.

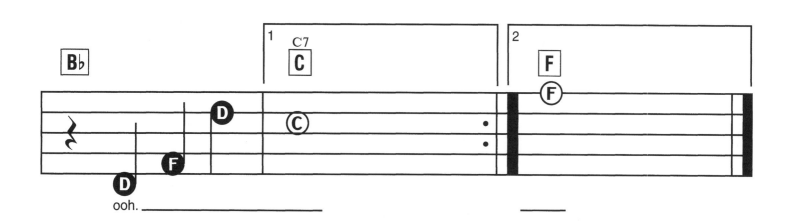

ooh. _____ _____

I Beg of You

Registration 2
Rhythm: Rock

Words and Music by Rose Marie McCoy
and Kelly Owens

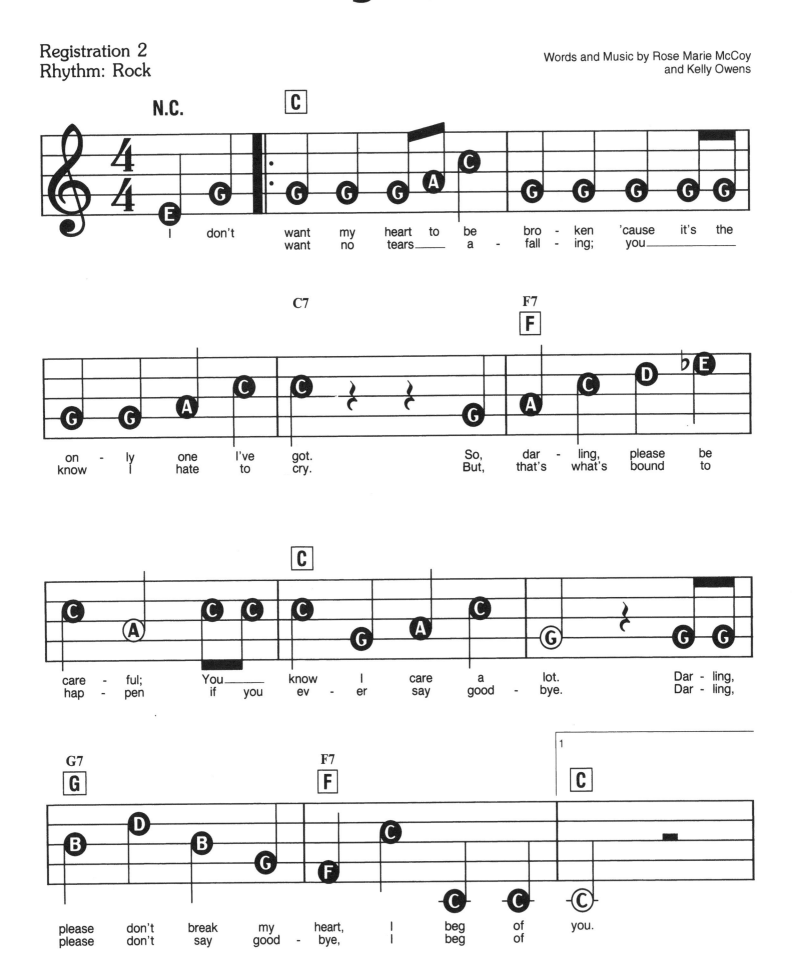

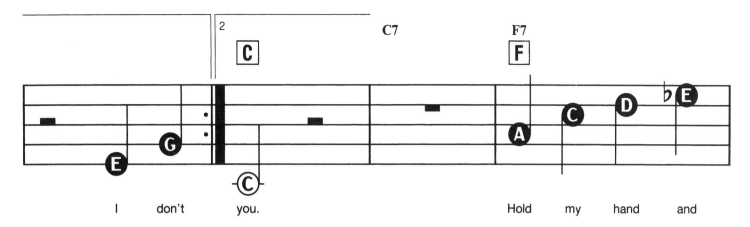

I don't you. Hold my hand and

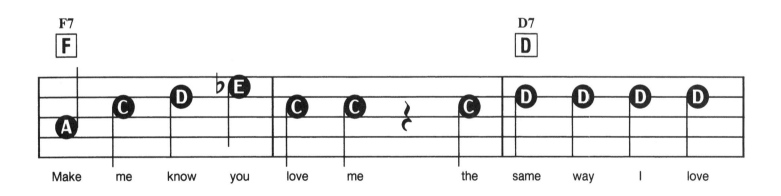

prom - ise that you'll al - ways love me true.

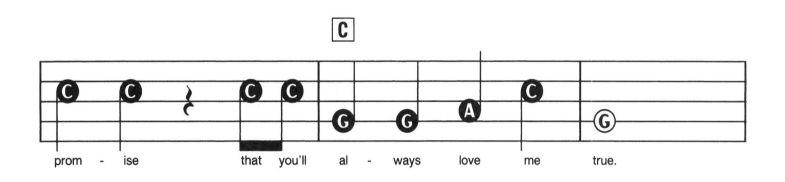

Make me know you love me the same way I love

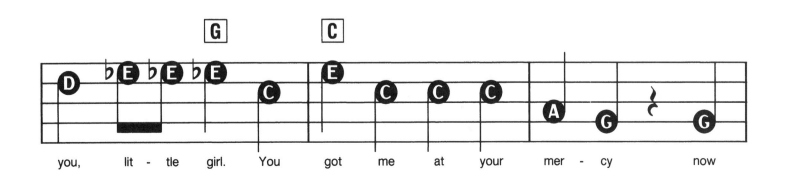

you, lit - tle girl. You got me at your mer - cy now

96

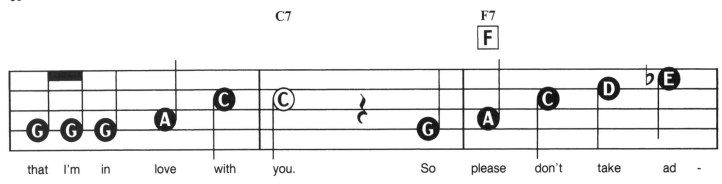

that I'm in love with you. So please don't take ad -

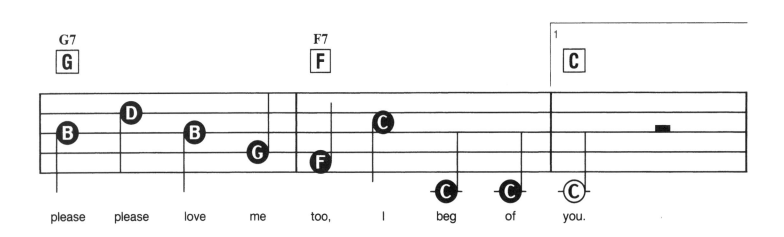

van - tage 'cause you know my love is true My dar - ling,

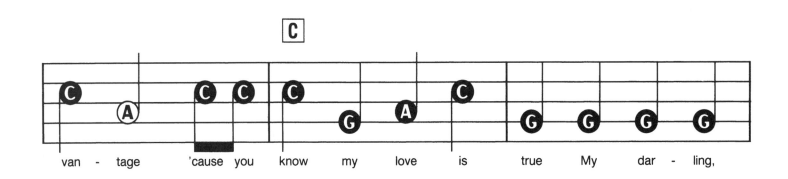

please please love me too, I beg of you.

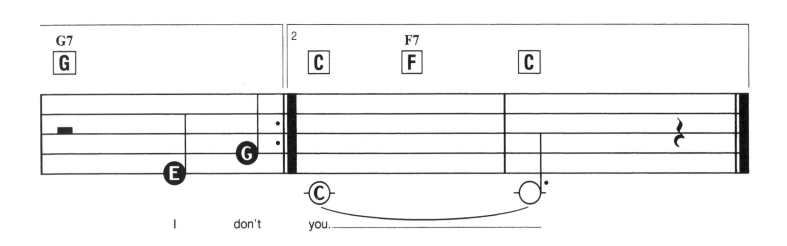

I don't you.

I Don't Care If the Sun Don't Shine

Registration 1
Rhythm: Fox Trot or Swing

Words and Music by
Mack David

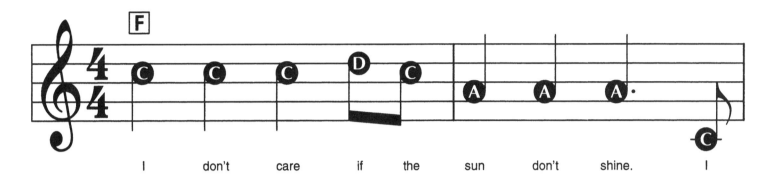

I don't care if the sun don't shine. I

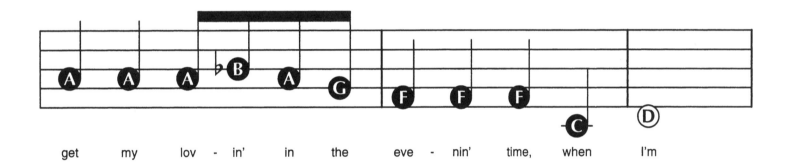

get my lov - in' in the eve - nin' time, when I'm

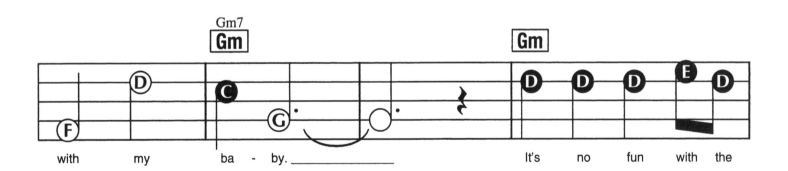

with my ba - by. _____ It's no fun with the

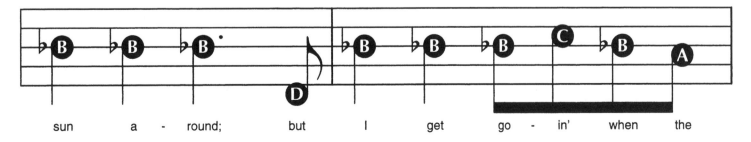

sun a - round; but I get go - in' when the

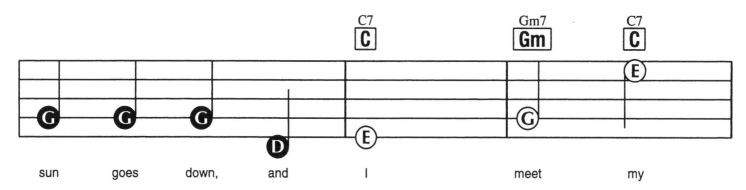

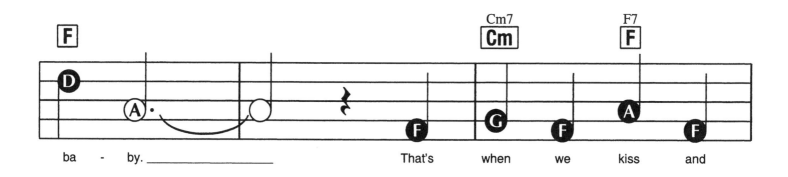

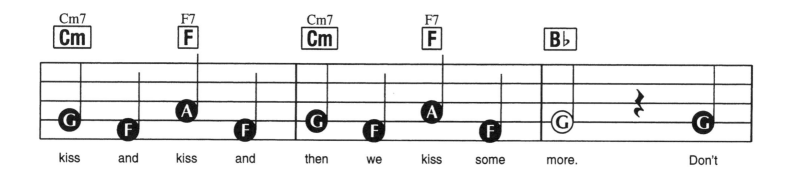

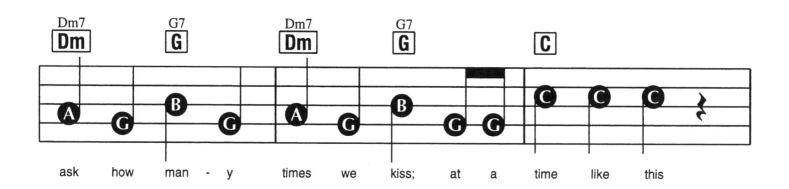

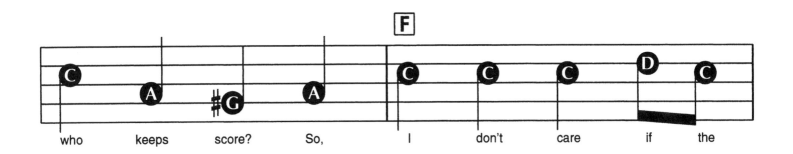

who keeps score? So, I don't care if the

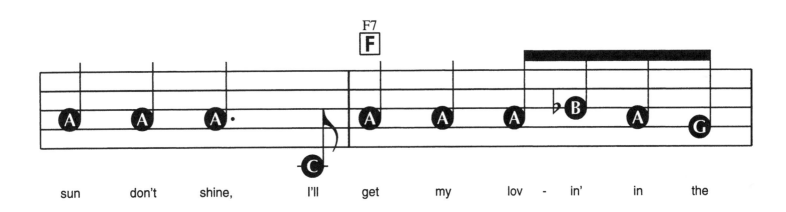

sun don't shine, I'll get my lov - in' in the

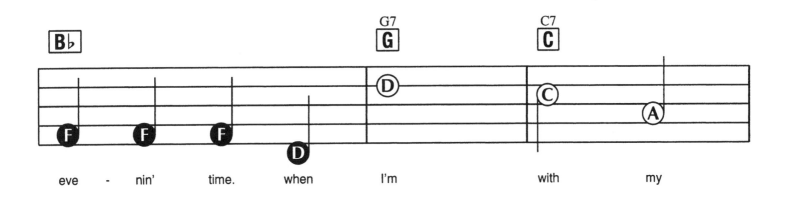

eve - nin' time. when I'm with my

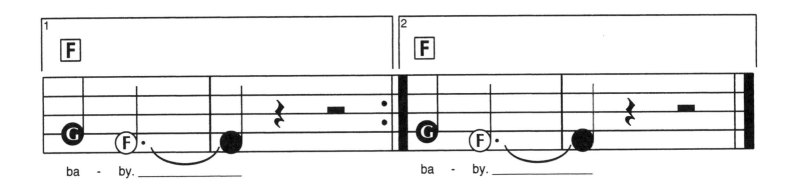

ba - by. _____ ba - by. _____

I'm Walking Behind You
(Look Over Your Shoulder)

Registration 7
Rhythm: Ballad or Fox Trot

Words and Music by
Billy Reid

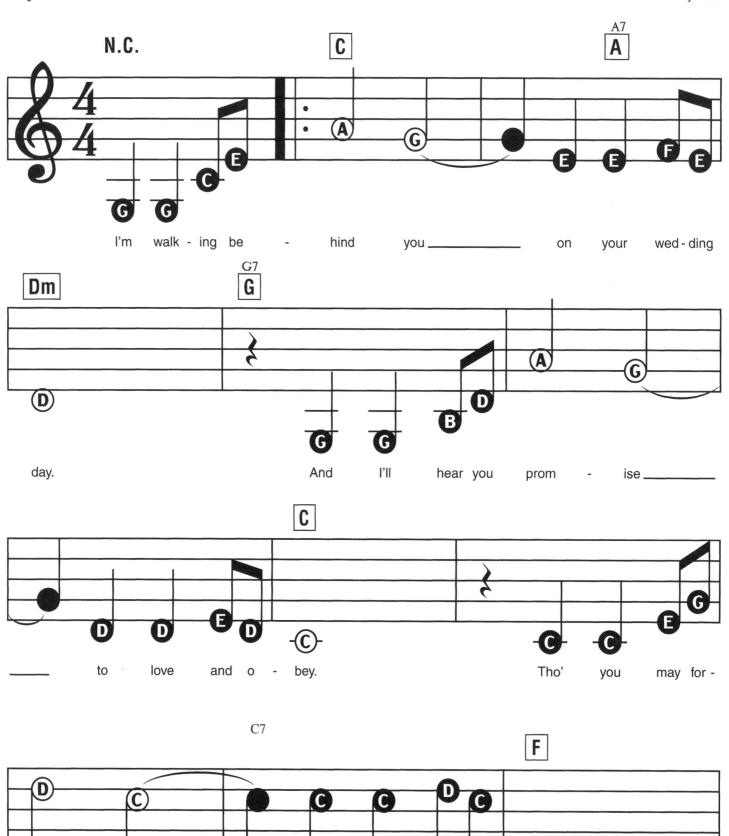

101

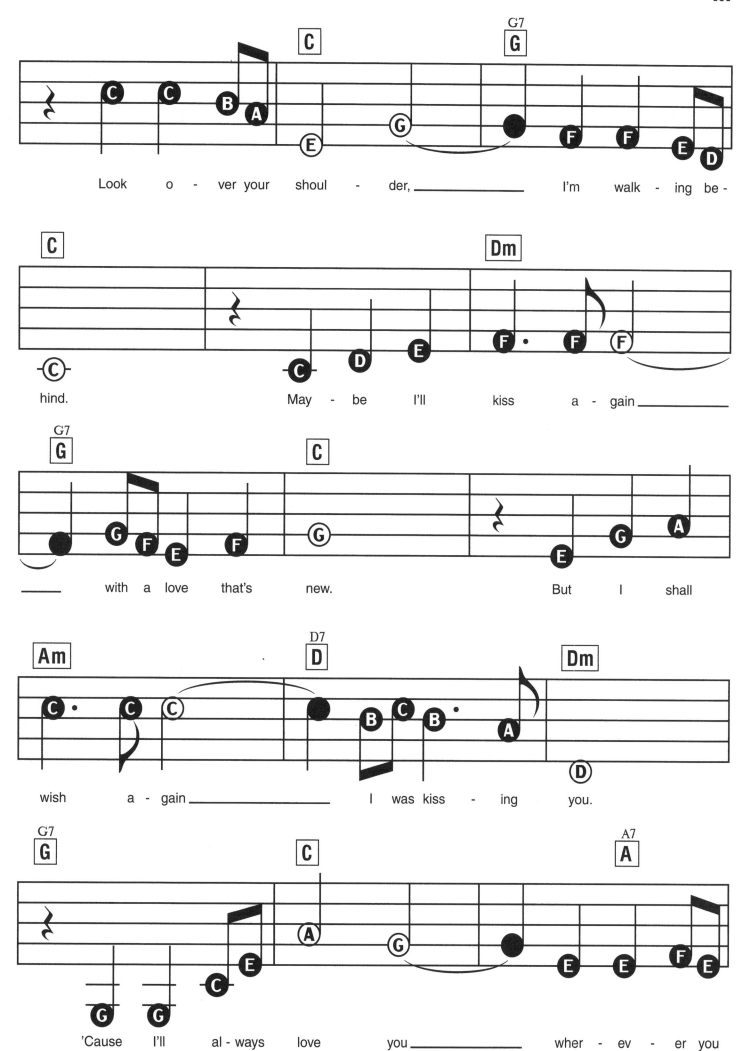

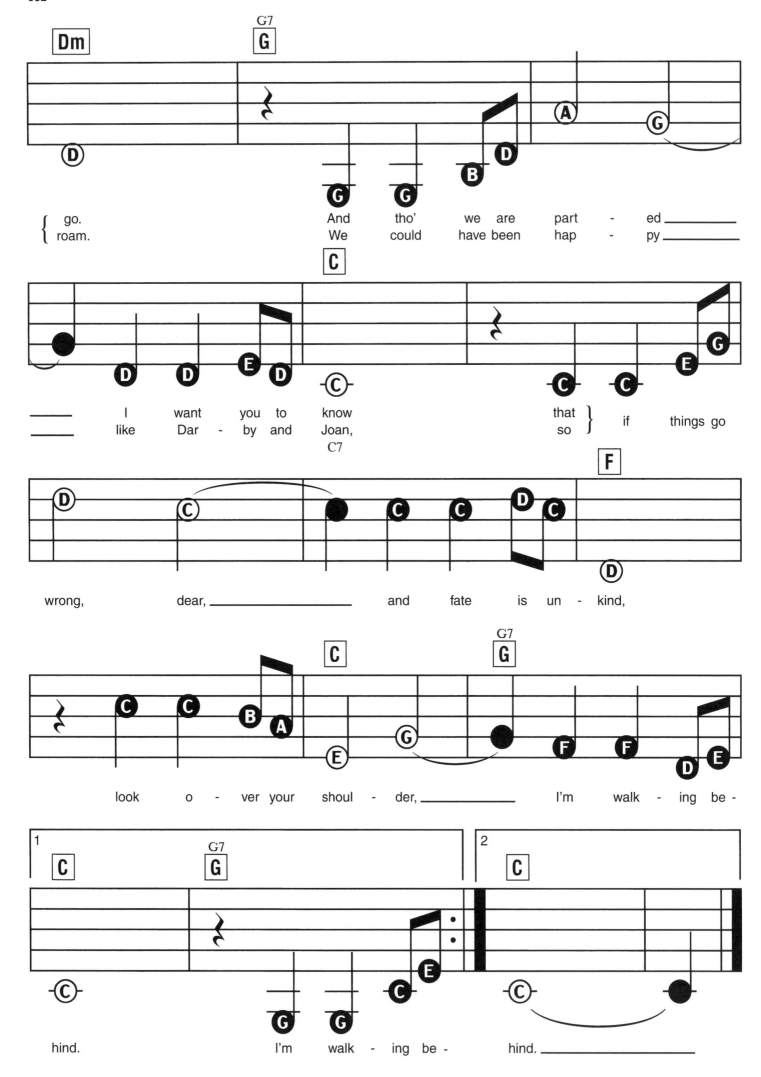

It's Almost Tomorrow

Registration 8
Rhythm: Waltz

Words and Music by Wade Buff
and Gene Adkinson

It's al - most to - mor - row, but what do I

do? Your kiss - es all tell me that your

love is un - true. I'll love you for -

ev - er till stars cease to shine, and hope some - day,

dar - ling, that you'll al - ways be mine. It's mine.

It's Only Make Believe

Registration 1
Rhythm: Slow Rock or Rock

Words and Music by Conway Twitty
and Jack Nance

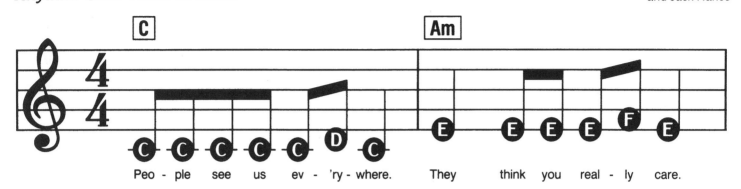

Peo - ple see us ev - 'ry - where. They think you real - ly care.

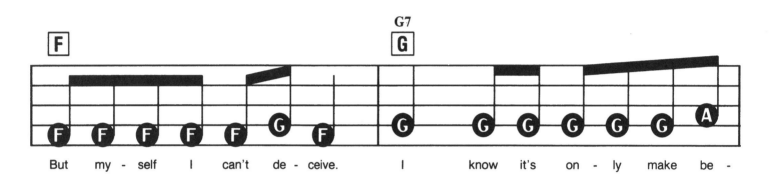

But my - self I can't de - ceive. I know it's on - ly make be -

Rhythm: Slow Rock or 12 Beat

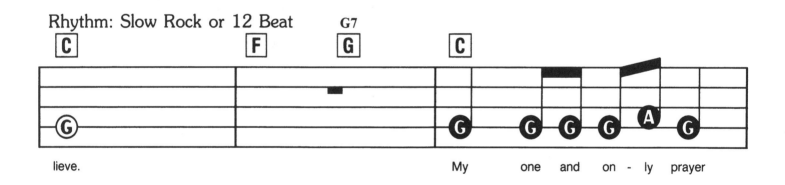

lieve. My one and on - ly prayer

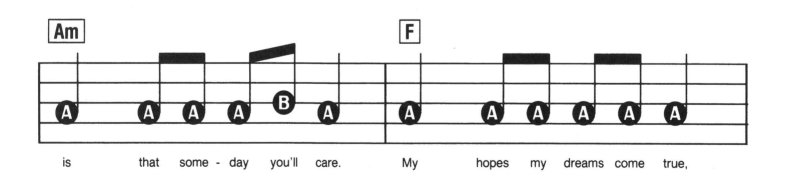

is that some - day you'll care. My hopes my dreams come true,

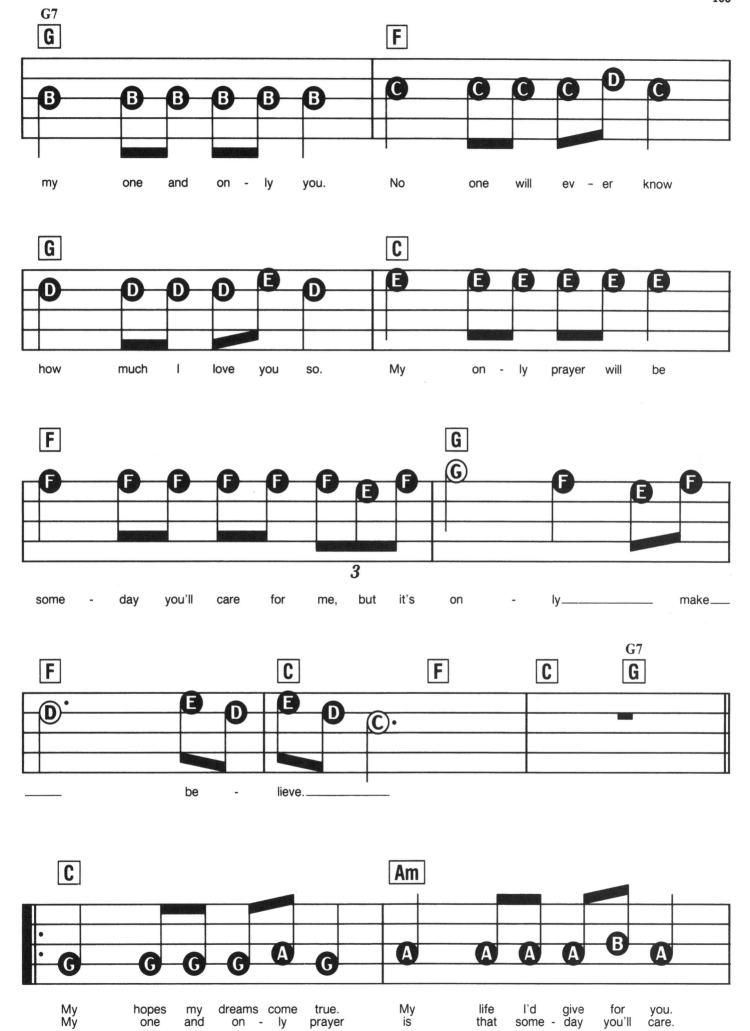

Lollipop

Registration 5
Rhythm: Rock or 8 Beat

Words and Music by Beverly Ross
and Julius Dixon

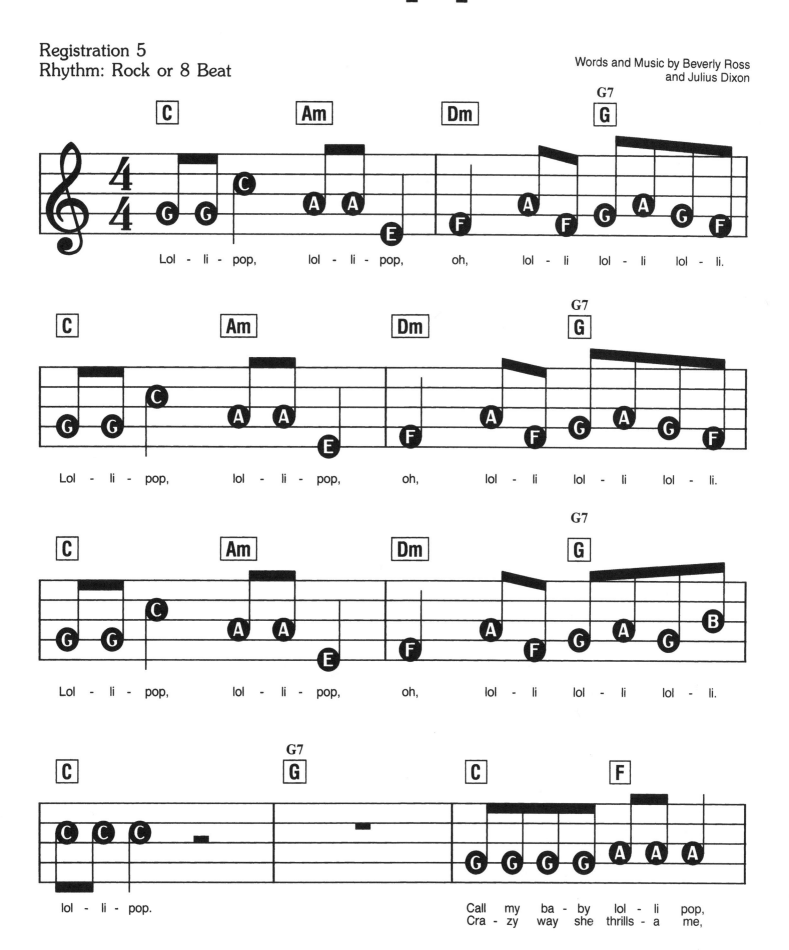

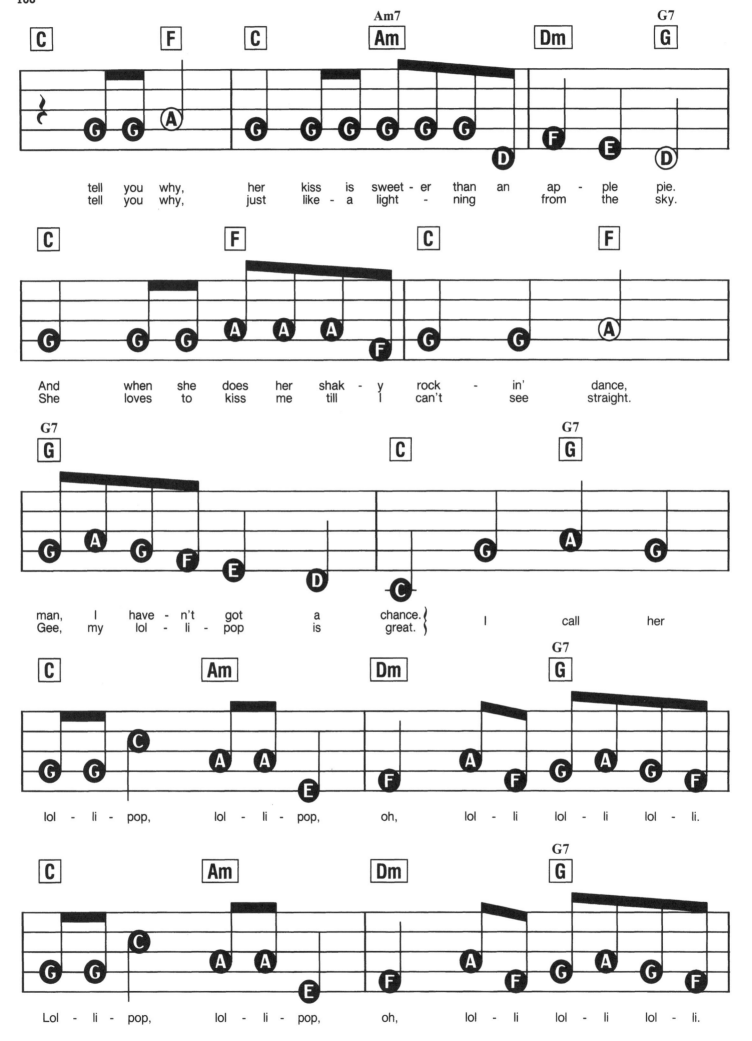

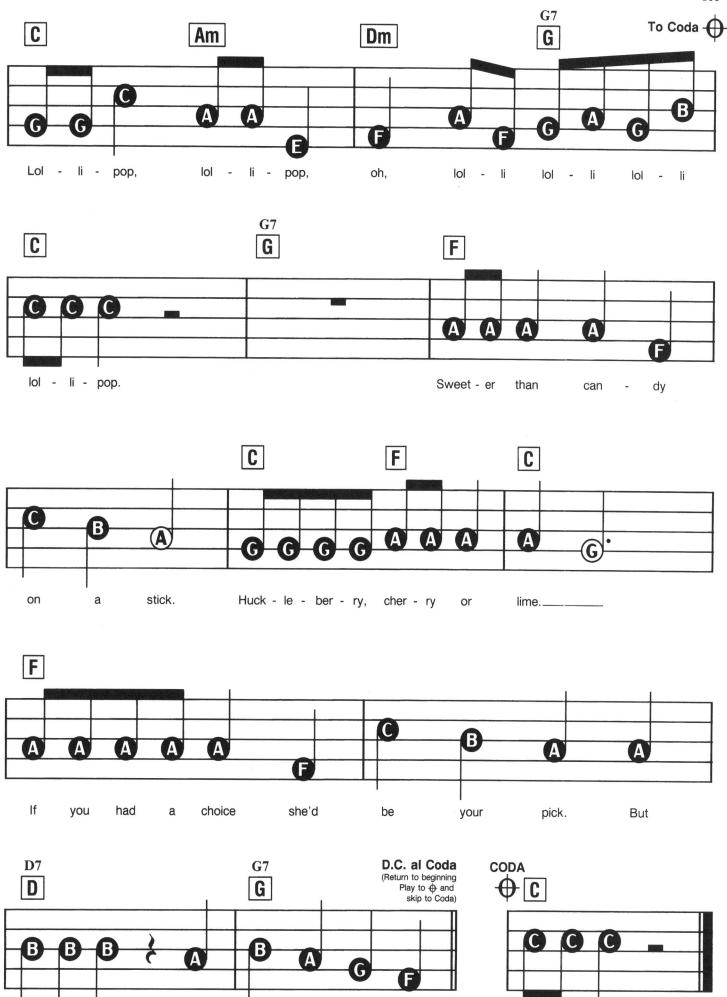

Ivory Tower

Registration 1
Rhythm: Waltz

Words and Music by Jack Fulton
and Lois Steele

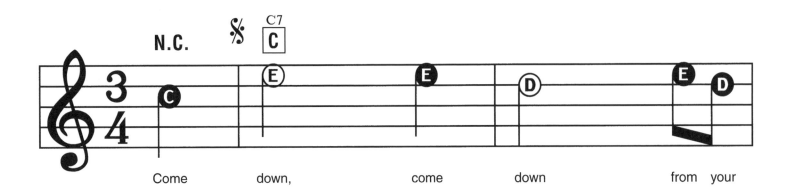

Come   down,   come   down   from your

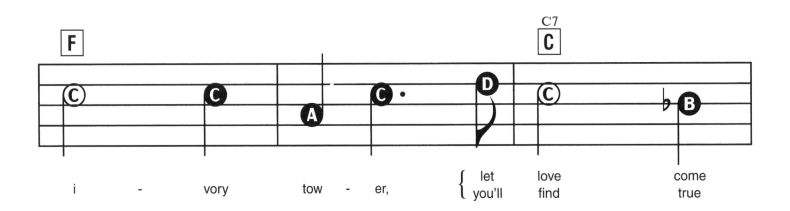

i - vory   tow - er,   { let   love   come
                   you'll   find   true

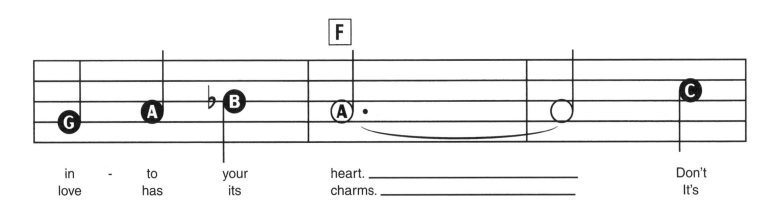

in - to   your   heart. _____   Don't
love   has   its   charms. _____   It's

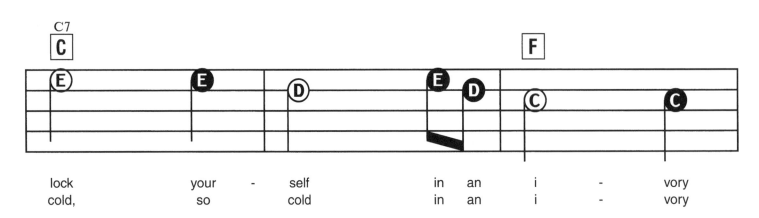

lock   your - self   in an   i - vory
cold,   so   cold   in an   i - vory

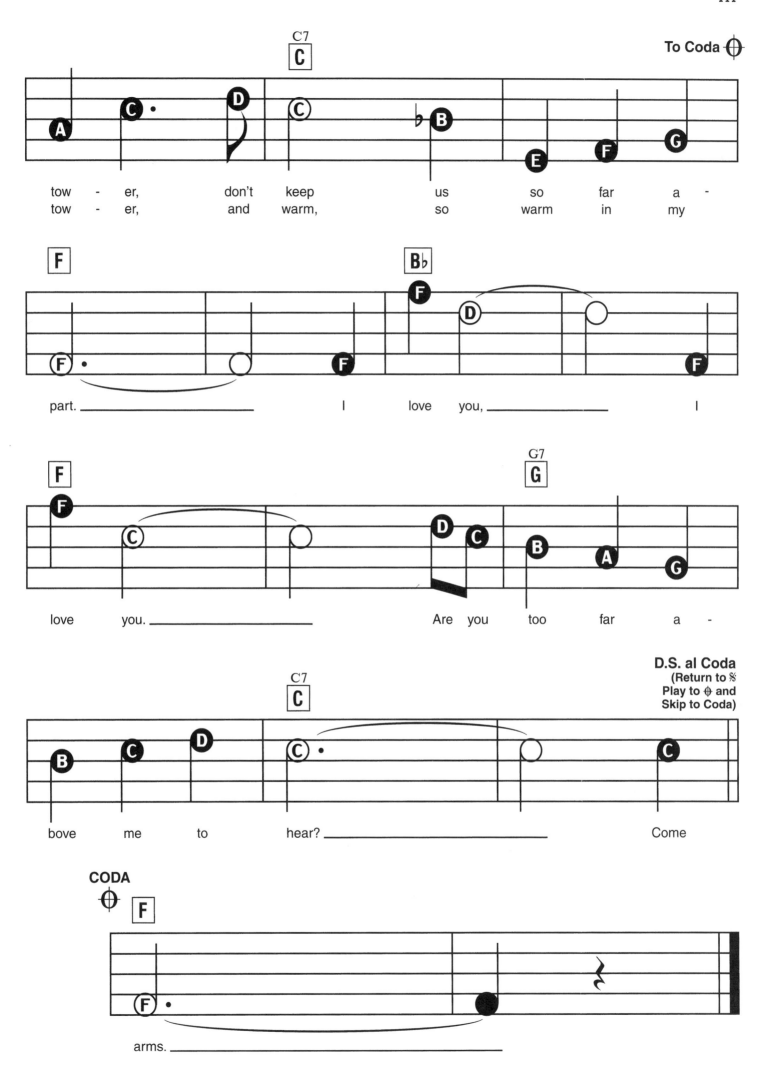

Just Walking in the Rain

Registration 7
Rhythm: Fox Trot

Words and Music by Johnny Bragg
and Robert S. Riley

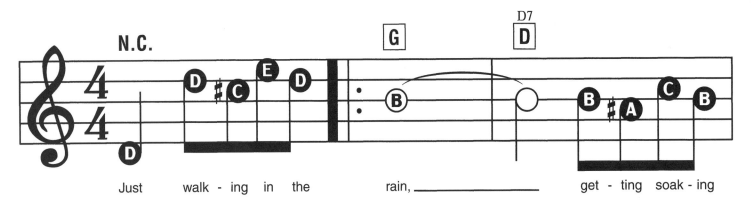

Just walk - ing in the rain, _____ get - ting soak - ing

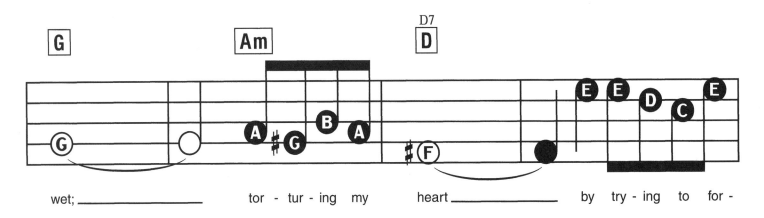

wet; _____ tor - tur - ing my heart _____ by try - ing to for -

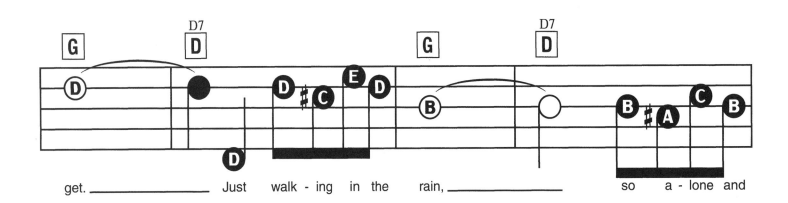

get. _____ Just walk - ing in the rain, _____ so a - lone and

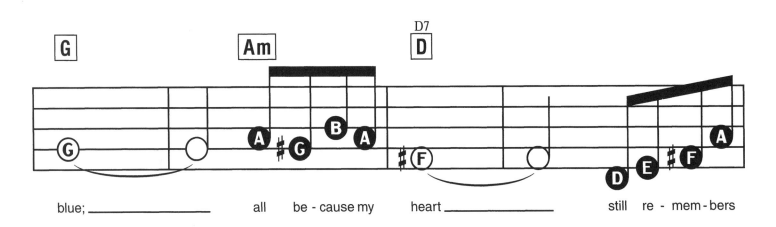

blue; _____ all be - cause my heart _____ still re - mem - bers

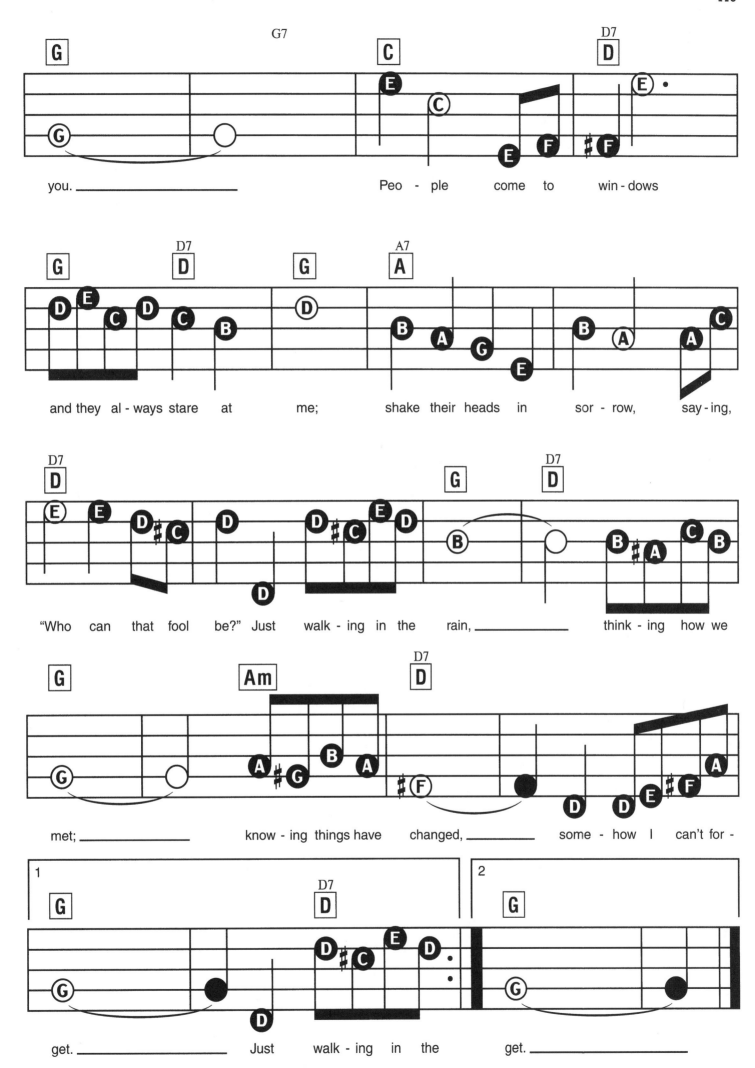

Kansas City

Registration 4
Rhythm: Shuffle or Swing

Words and Music by Jerry Leiber
and Mike Stoller

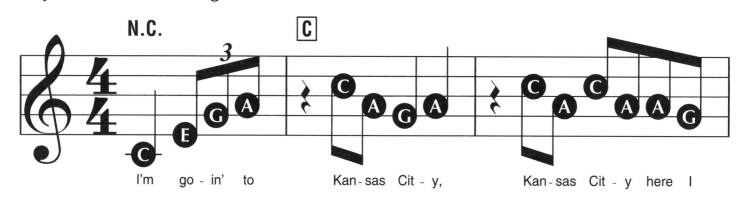

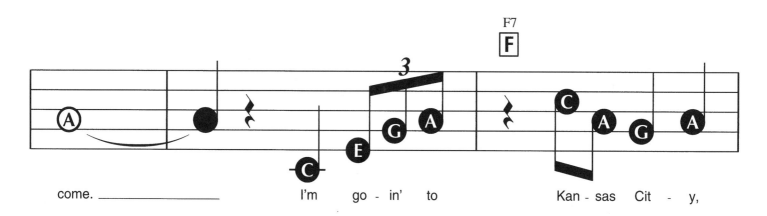

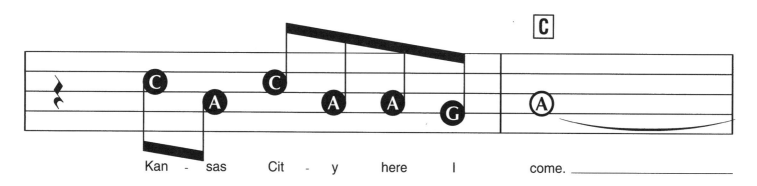

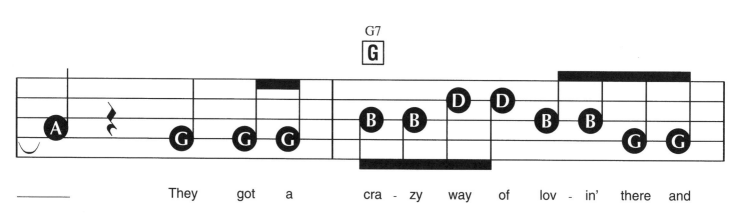

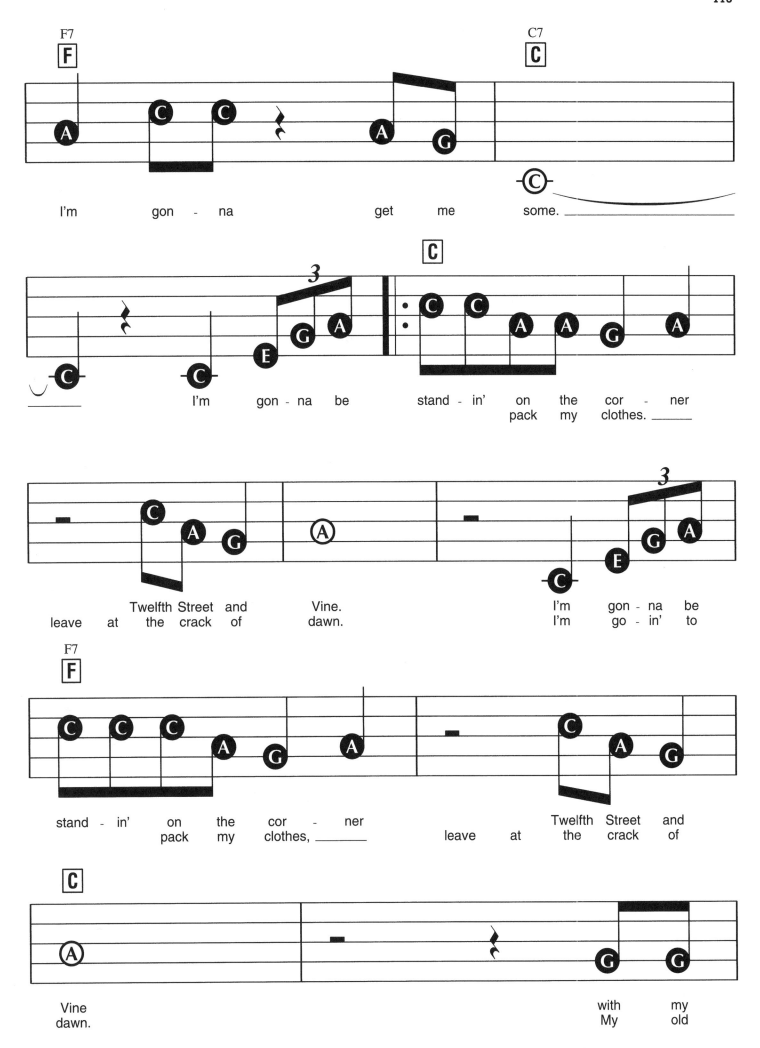

116

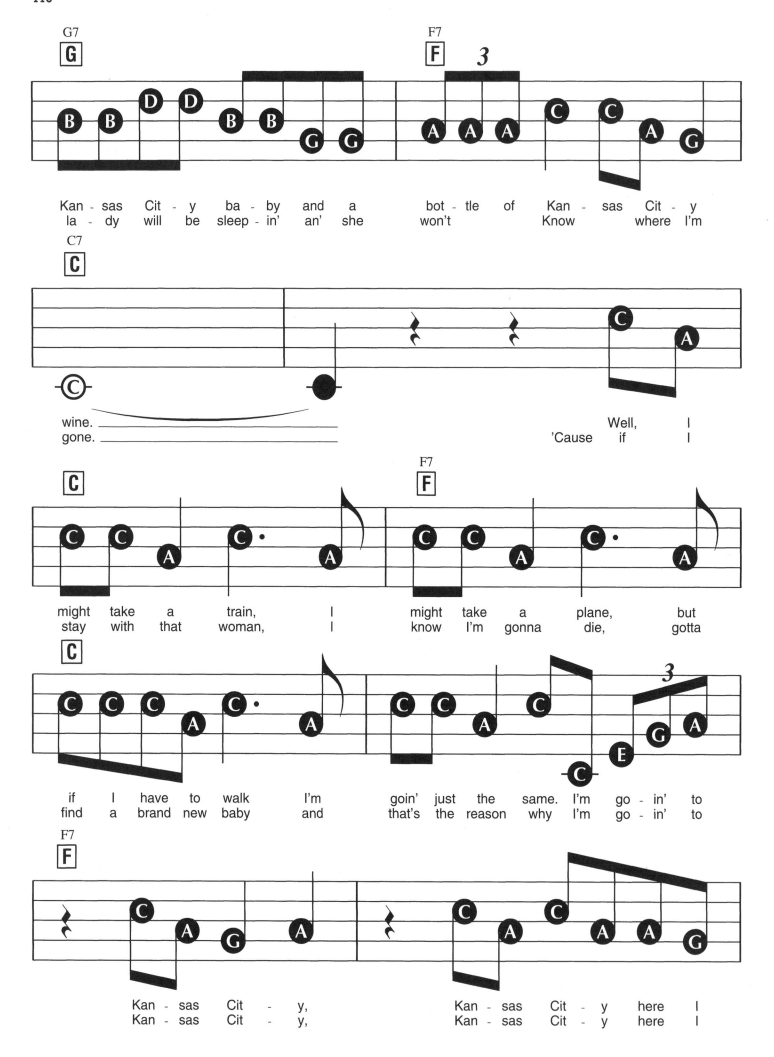

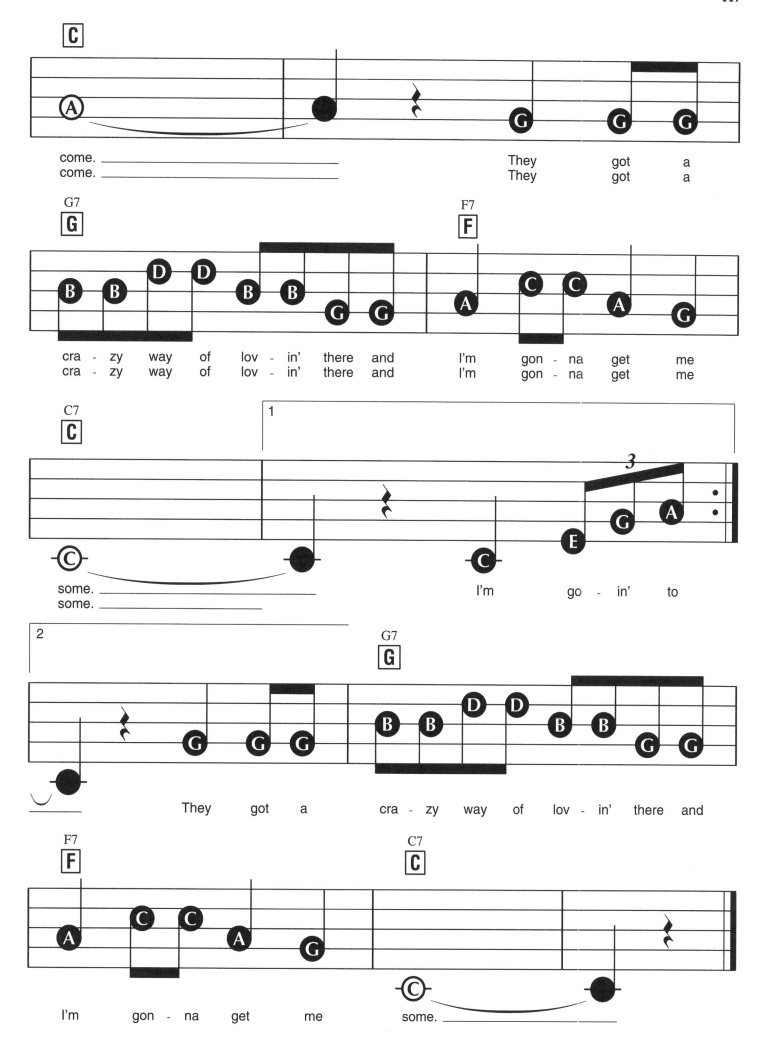

Ko Ko Mo
(I Love You So)

Registration 8
Rhythm: Shuffle or Rock

Words and Music by Eunice Levy,
Jake Porter and Forest Wilson

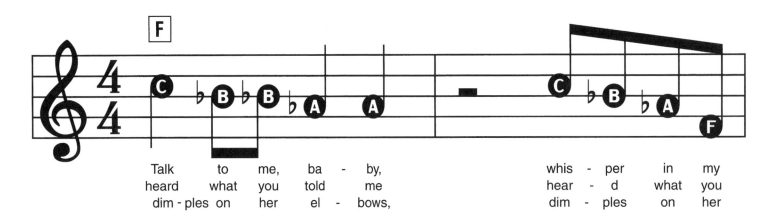

Talk to me, ba - by, whis - per in my
heard what you told me hear - d what you
dim - ples on her el - bows, dim - ples on her

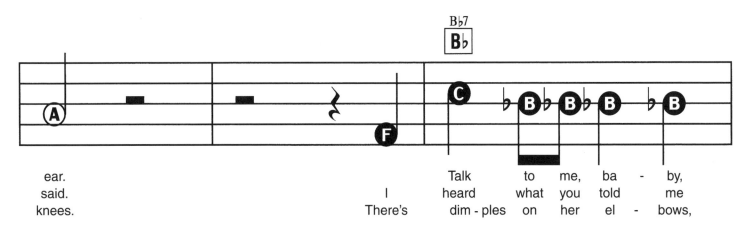

ear. Talk to me, ba - by,
said. I heard what you told me
knees. There's dim - ples on her el - bows,

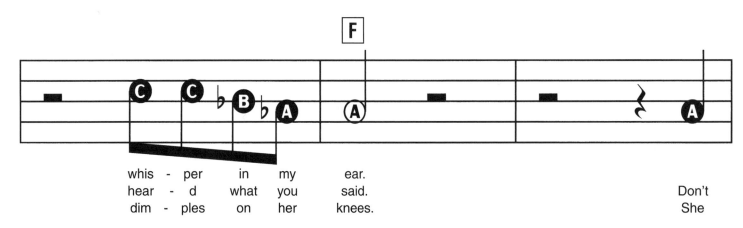

whis - per in my ear. Don't
hear - d what you said. She
dim - ples on her knees.

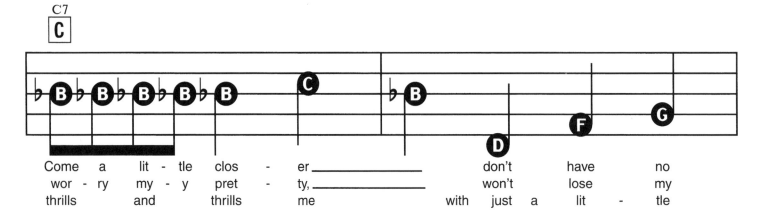

Come a lit - tle clos - er _____ don't have no
wor - ry my - y pret - ty, _____ won't lose my
thrills and thrills me with just a lit - tle

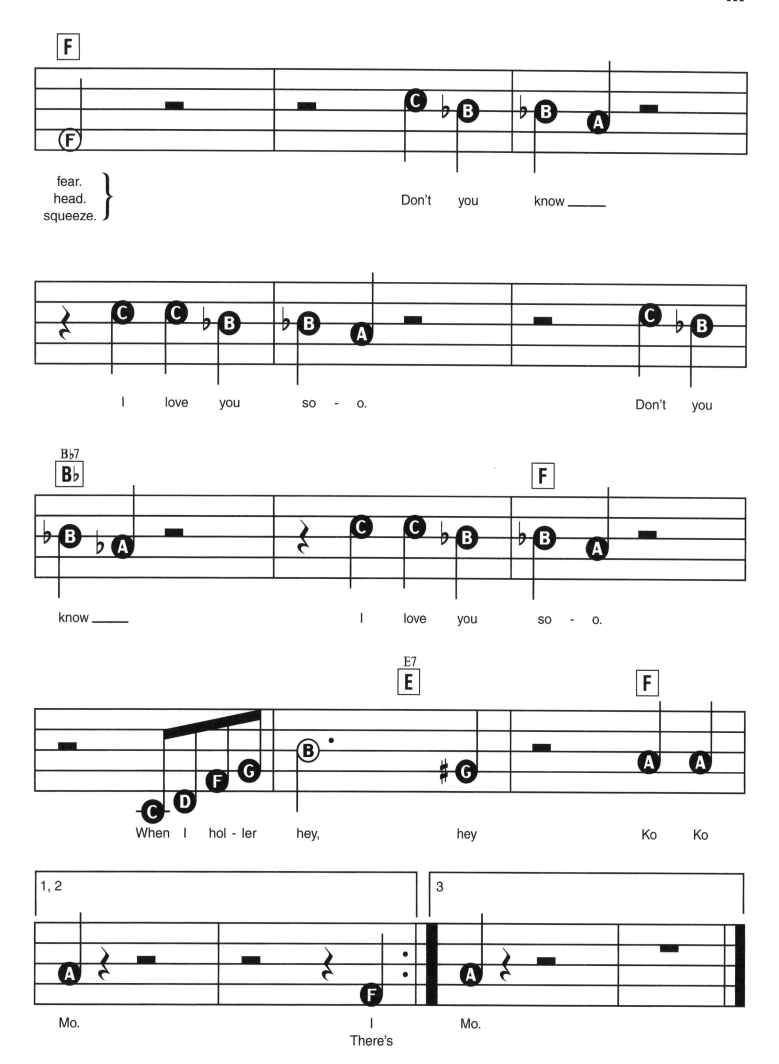

Lipstick on Your Collar

Registration 4
Rhythm: Rock

Words by Edna Lewis
Music by George Goehring

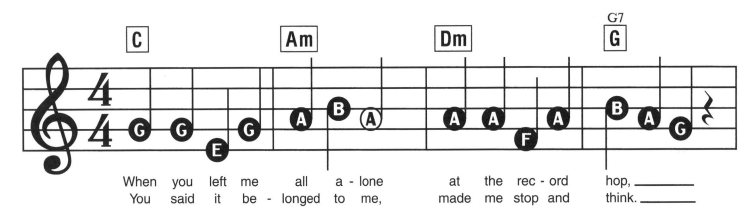

When you left me all a - lone at the rec - ord hop, _____
You said it be - longed to me, made me stop and think. _____

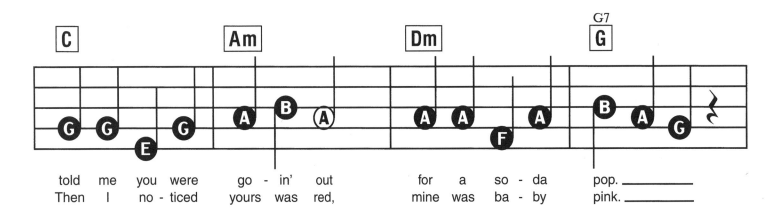

told me you were go - in' out for a so - da pop. _____
Then I no - ticed yours was red, mine was ba - by pink. _____

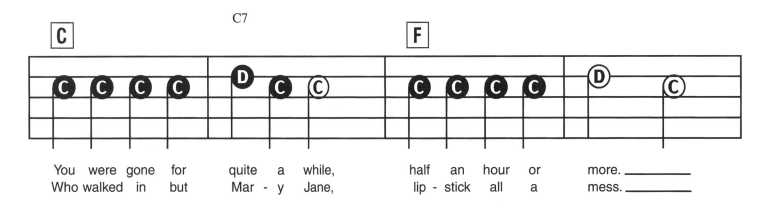

You were gone for quite a while, half an hour or more. _____
Who walked in but Mar - y Jane, lip - stick all a mess. _____

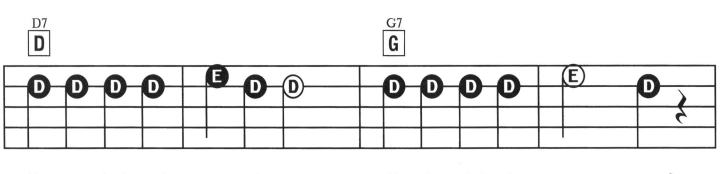

You came back and man, oh man, this is what I saw: _____ }
Were you smooch - in' my best friend? Guess the an - swer's yes. _____ }

121

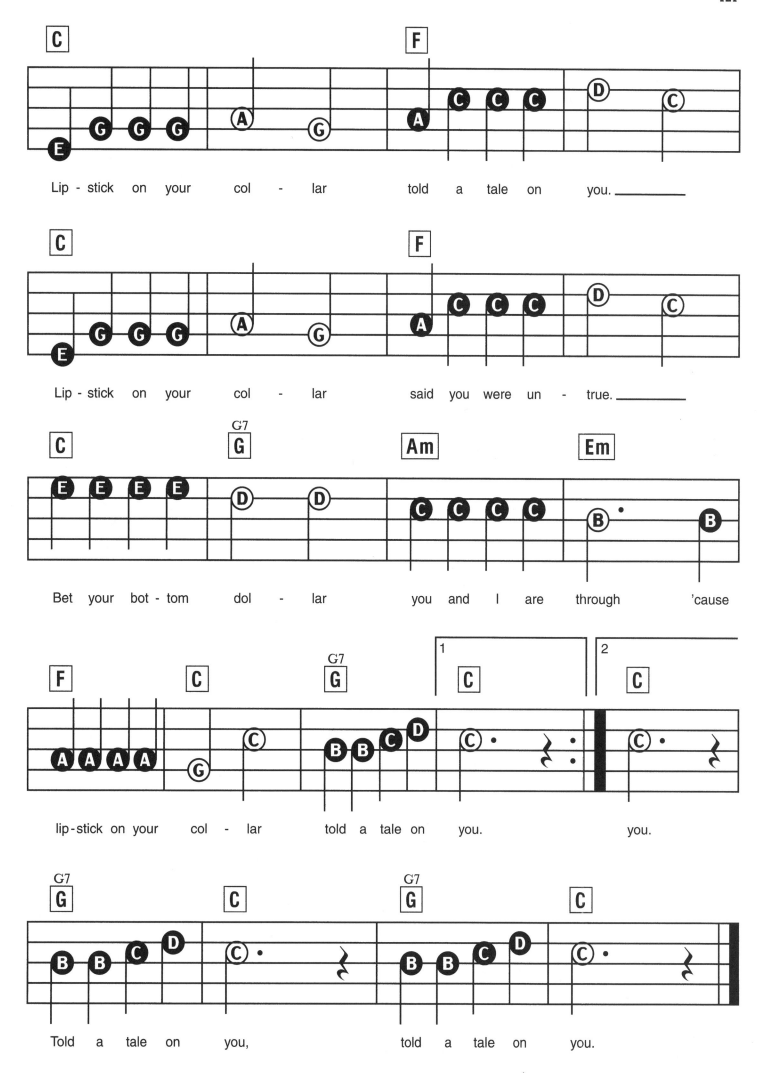

Lonely Boy

Registration 8
Rhythm: Slow Rock or 12 Beat

Words and Music by
Paul Anka

I'm just a lone - ly boy, lone - ly and blue. _____ I'm all a - lone with noth - in' to do. I've got ev - 'ry -

thing you could think of, _____ but all I want is some - one to love. Some - one, yes, some - one to love, _____ some - one to kiss, _____ some - one to

hold at a mo - ment like this. I'd like to hear some - bod - y

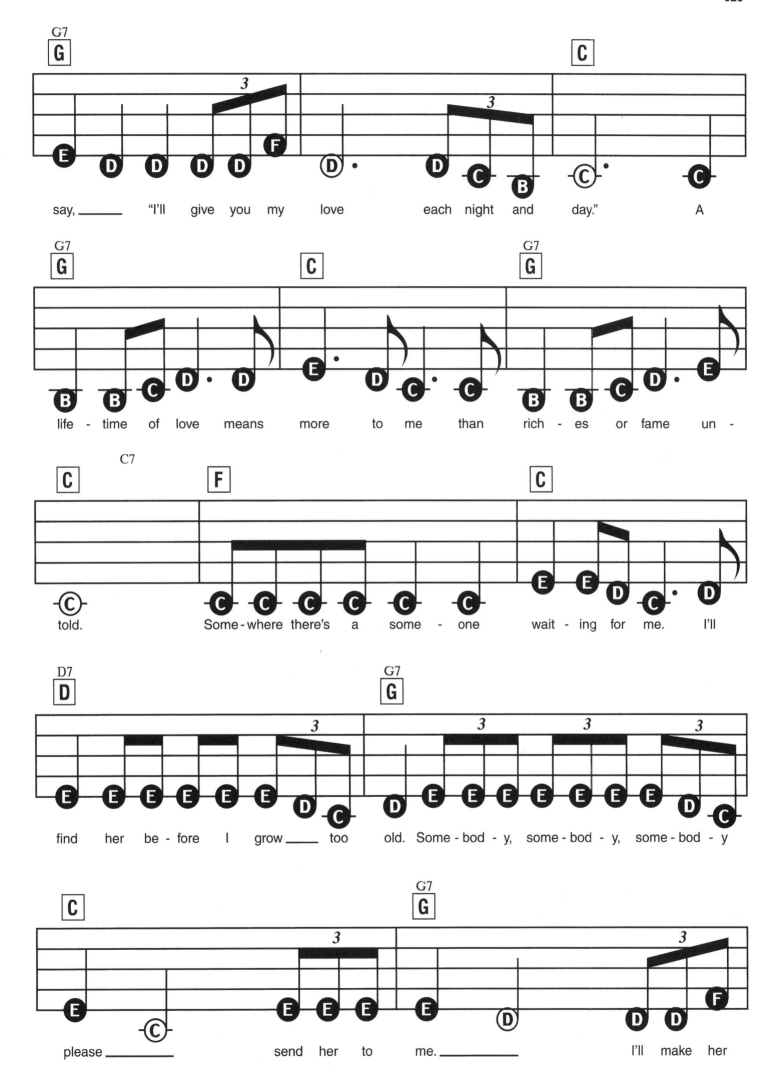

Love and Marriage

Registration 1
Rhythm: Swing or Big Band

Words by Sammy Cahn
Music by James Van Heusen

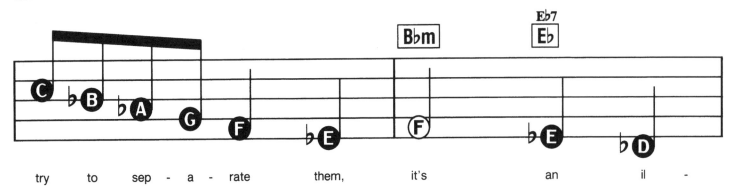

try to sep - a - rate them, it's an il -

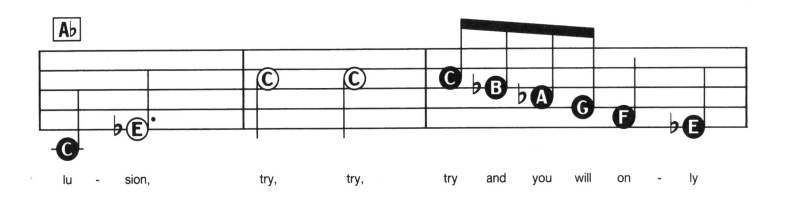

lu - sion, try, try, try and you will on - ly

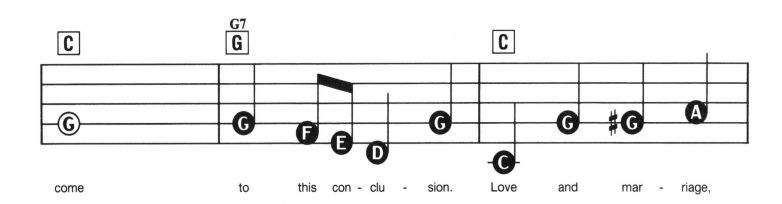

come to this con - clu - sion. Love and mar - riage,

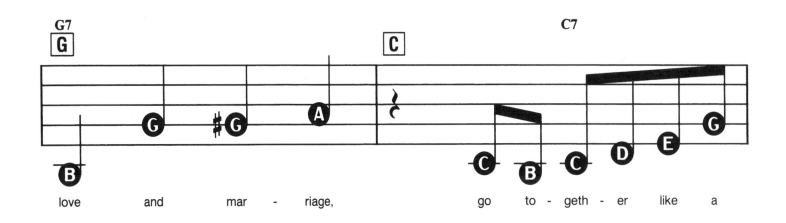

love and mar - riage, go to - geth - er like a

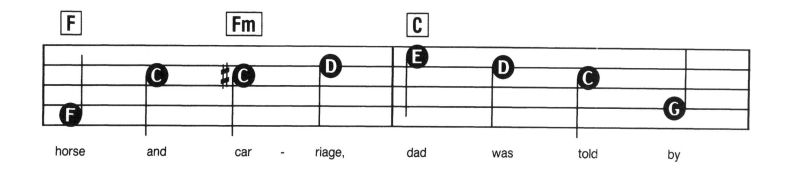

horse and car - riage, dad was told by

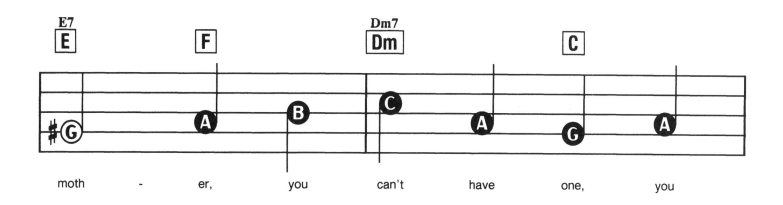

moth - er, you can't have one, you

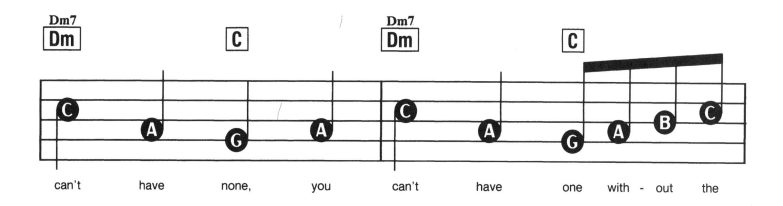

can't have none, you can't have one with - out the

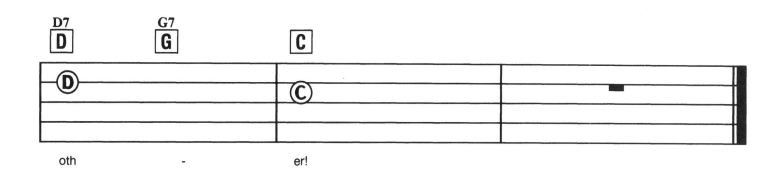

oth - er!

Love Me Tender
from LOVE ME TENDER

Registration 9
Rhythm: Slow Rock or Rock

Words and Music by Elvis Presley
and Vera Matson

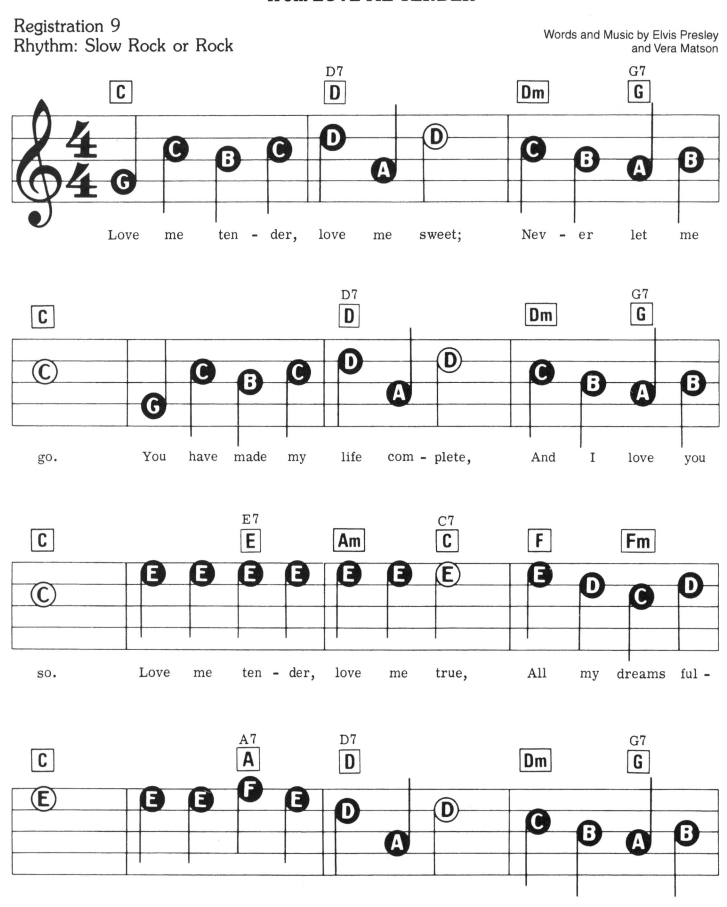

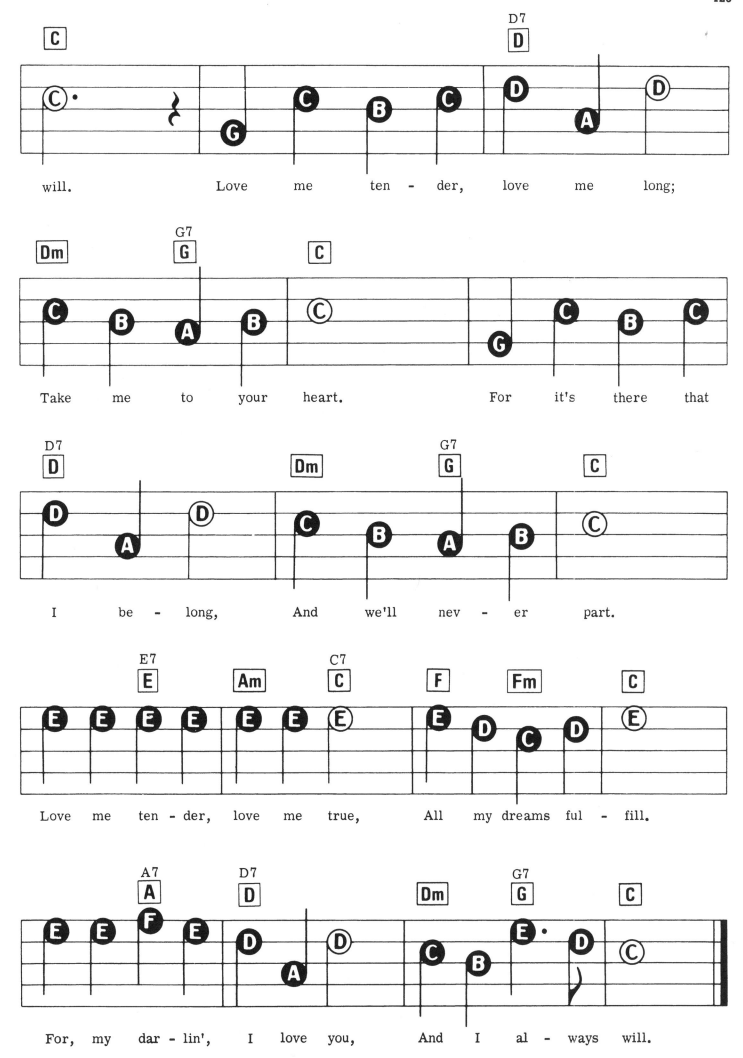

A Lover's Question

Registration 7
Rhythm: Country

Words and Music by Brook Benton
and Jimmy Williams

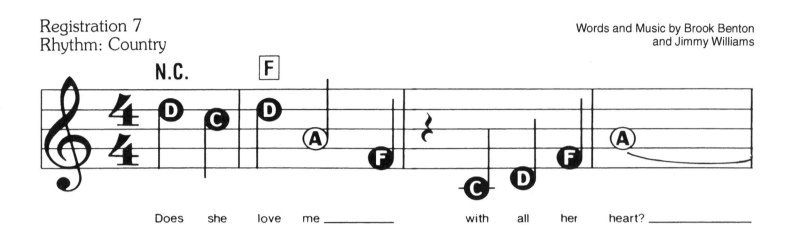

Does she love me _____ with all her heart? _____

_____ Should I wor - ry when we're a - part? _____

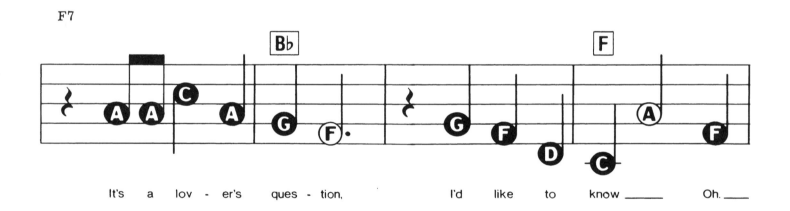

It's a lov - er's ques - tion, I'd like to know _____ Oh. _____

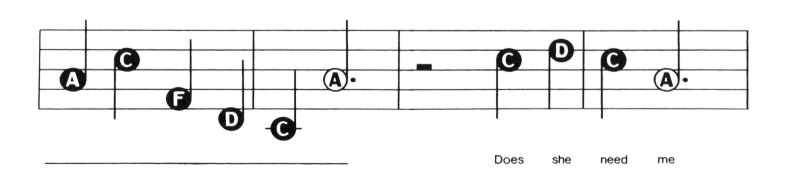

_____ Does she need me

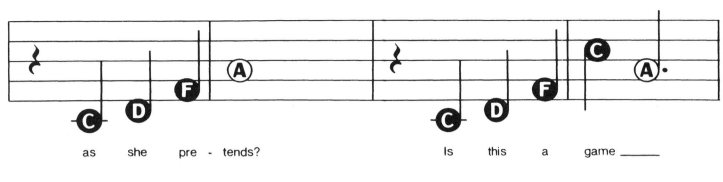

as she pre - tends?   Is   this   a   game _____

F7

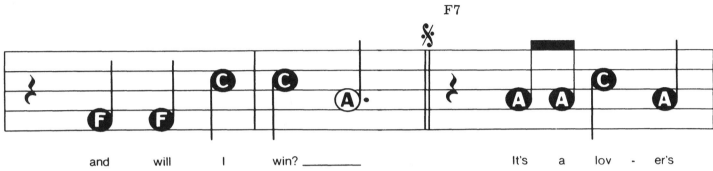

and   will   I   win? _____   It's   a   lov - er's

Bb   F

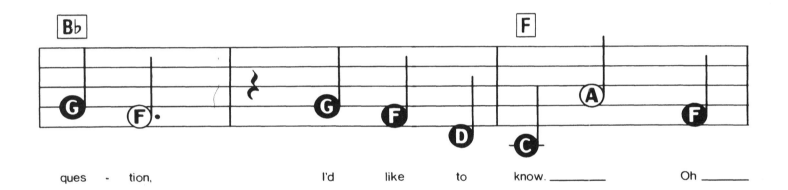

ques - tion,   I'd   like   to   know. _____   Oh _____

                                                    Bb

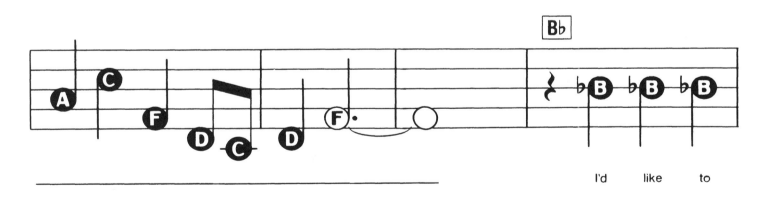

_____   I'd   like   to

F   Bb

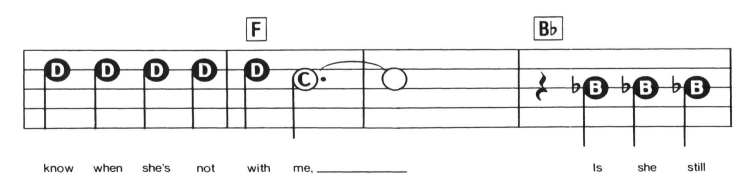

know when she's not with me, _____   Is   she   still

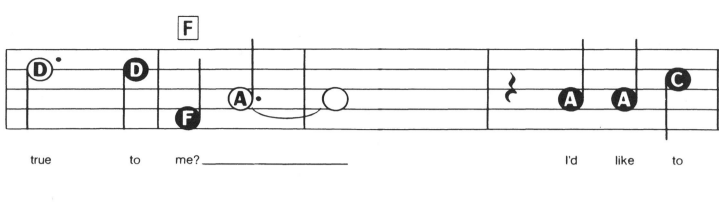

true   to   me?_____   I'd   like   to

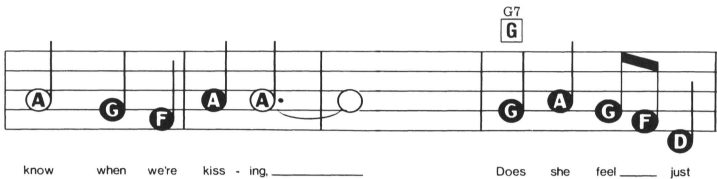

know   when   we're   kiss - ing,_____   Does   she   feel____   just

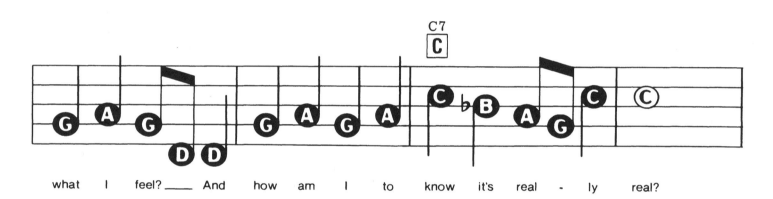

what   I   feel?____ And   how   am   I   to   know   it's   real - ly   real?

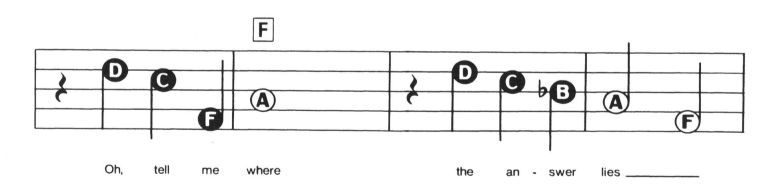

Oh,   tell   me   where   the   an - swer   lies_____

D.S. and Fade
(Return to 𝄋 and Fade)

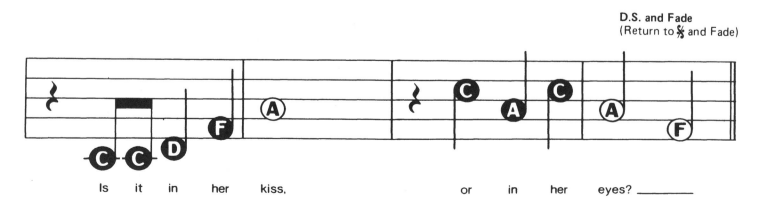

Is   it   in   her   kiss,   or   in   her   eyes?_____

Memories Are Made of This

Registration 1
Rhythm: Swing

Words and Music by Richard Dehr,
Frank Miller and Terry Gilkyson

134

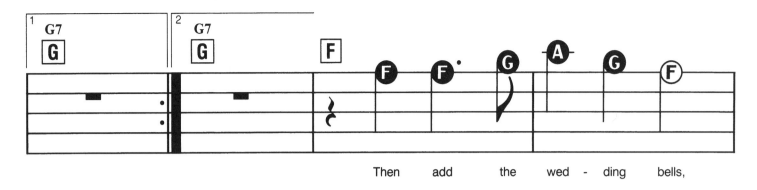

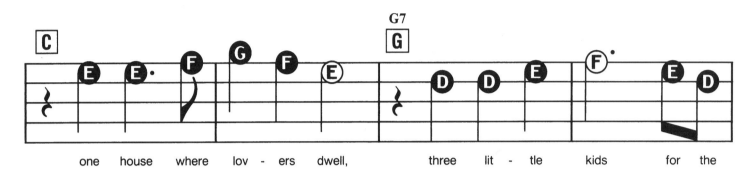

Then add the wed - ding bells,

one house where lov - ers dwell, three lit - tle kids for the

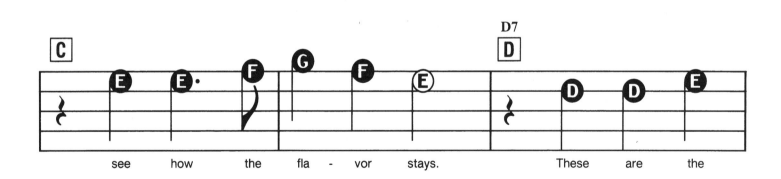

fla - vor._____ Stir care - f'lly through the days,

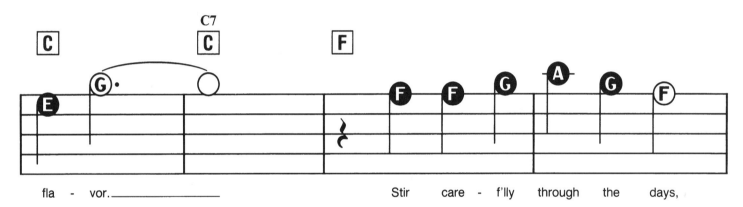

see how the fla - vor stays. These are the

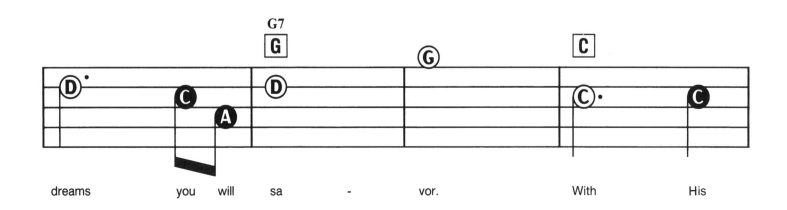

dreams you will sa - vor. With His

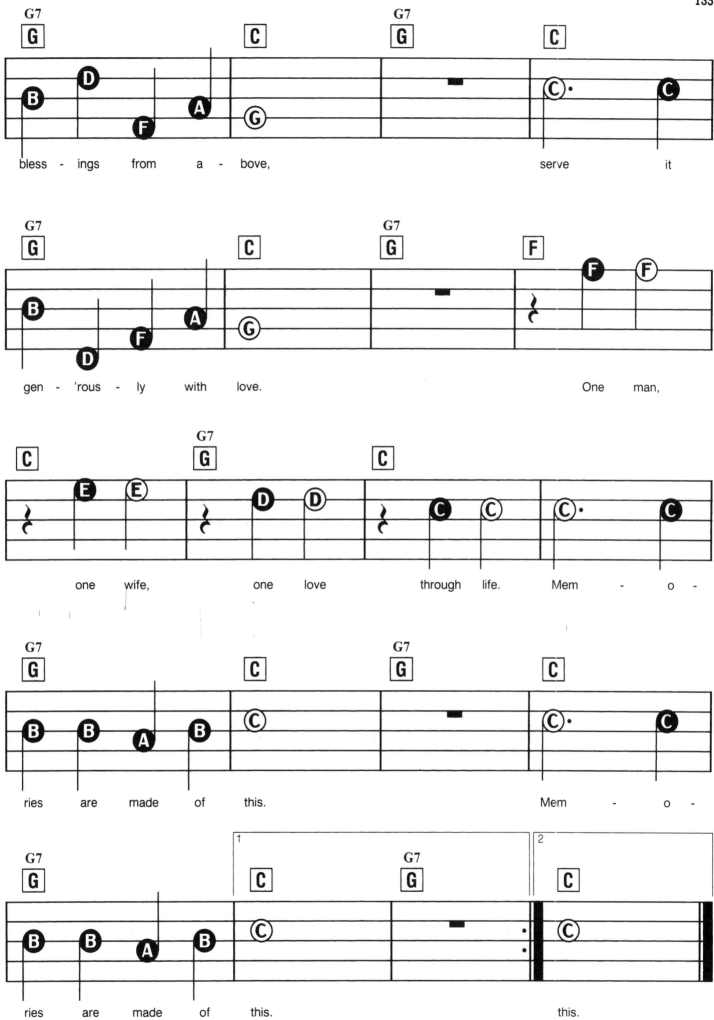

Loving You

Registration 4
Rhythm: Ballad or Fox Trot

Words and Music by Jerry Leiber
and Mike Stoller

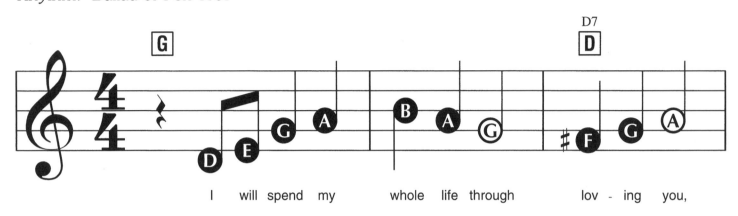

I will spend my whole life through lov - ing you,

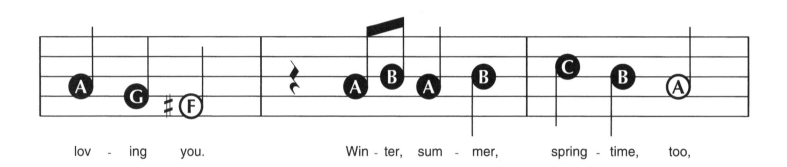

lov - ing you. Win - ter, sum - mer, spring - time, too,

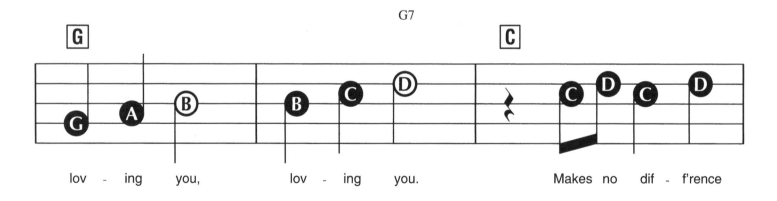

lov - ing you, lov - ing you. Makes no dif - f'rence

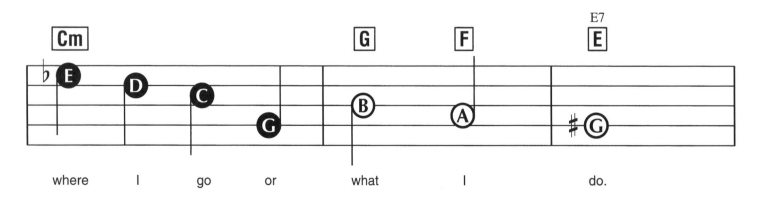

where I go or what I do.

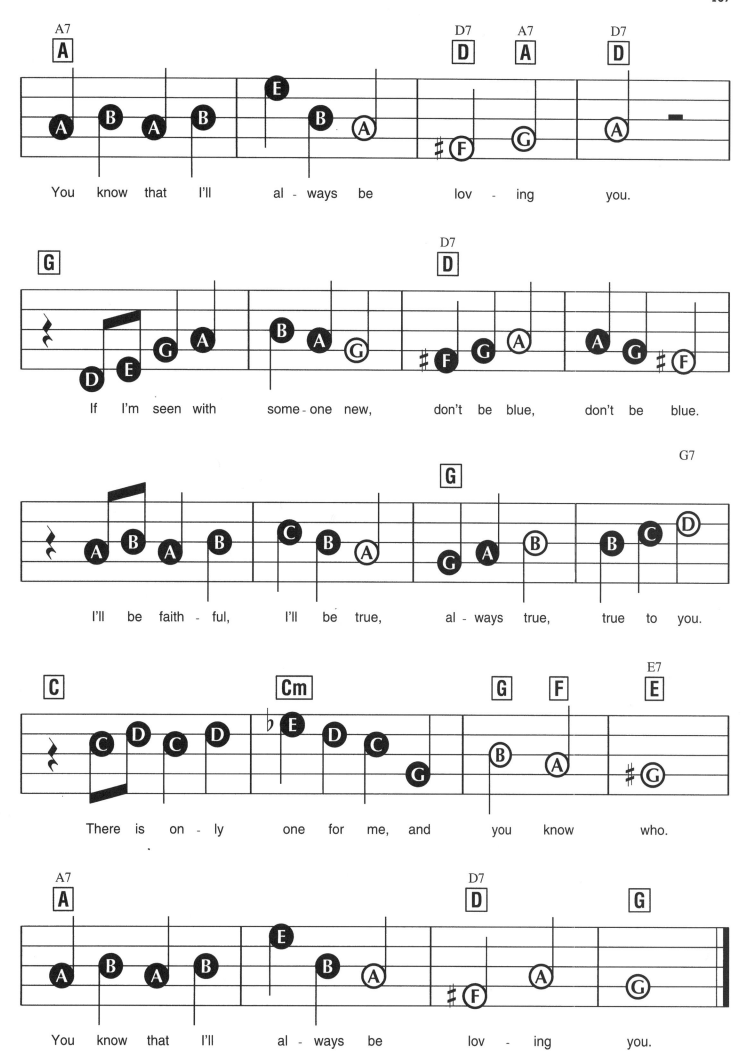

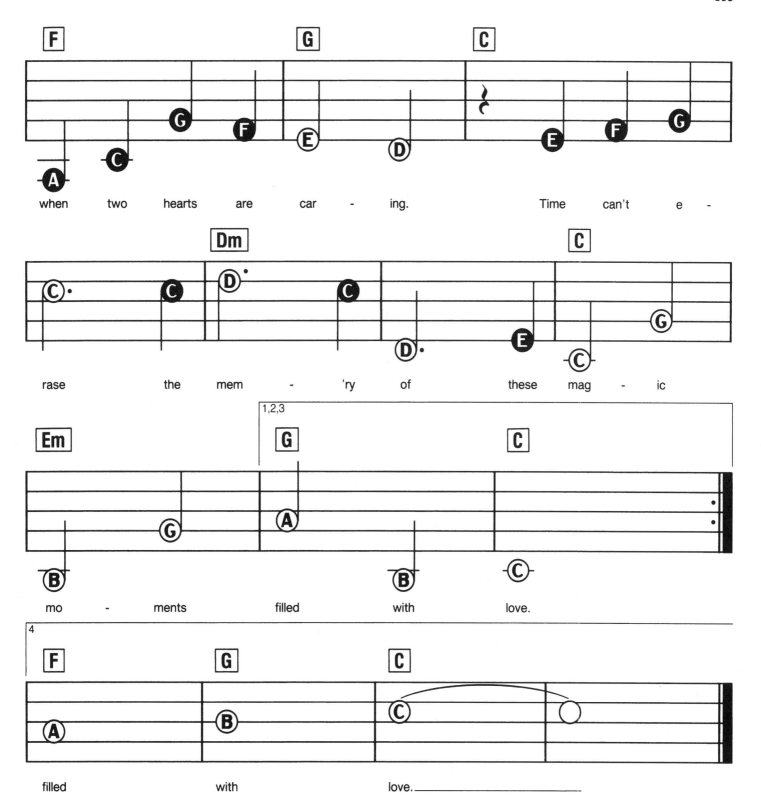

when   two   hearts   are   car - ing.   Time   can't   e -

rase   the   mem - 'ry   of   these   mag - ic

mo - ments   filled   with   love.

filled   with   love._____

Additional Lyrics

3. The way that we cheered whenever our team was scoring a touchdown,
    The time that the floor fell out of {my / your} car when {I / you} put the clutch down;
    (To Chorus)

4. The penny arcade, the games that we played, the fun and the prizes,
    The Halloween hop when ev'ryone came in funny disguises;
    (To Chorus)

(You've Got)
The Magic Touch

Registration 3
Rhythm: Slow Rock, $\frac{12}{8}$, or Swing

Words and Music by
Buck Ram

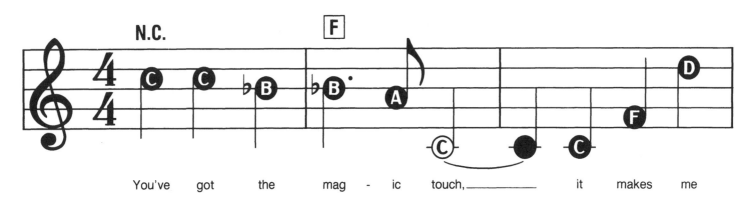

You've got the mag - ic touch,_____ it makes me

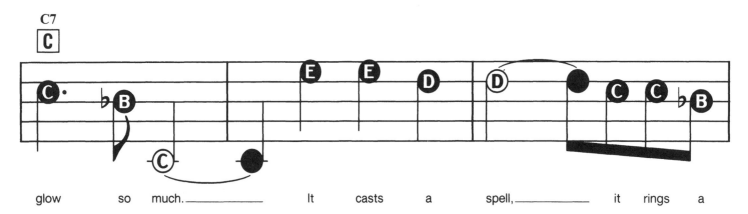

glow so much._____ It casts a spell,_____ it rings a

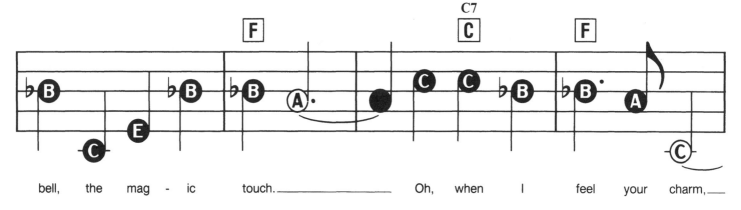

bell, the mag - ic touch._____ Oh, when I feel your charm,_____

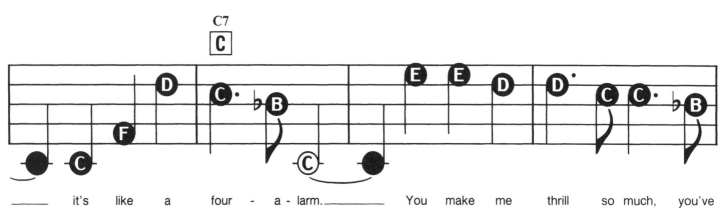

_____ it's like a four - a - larm._____ You make me thrill so much, you've

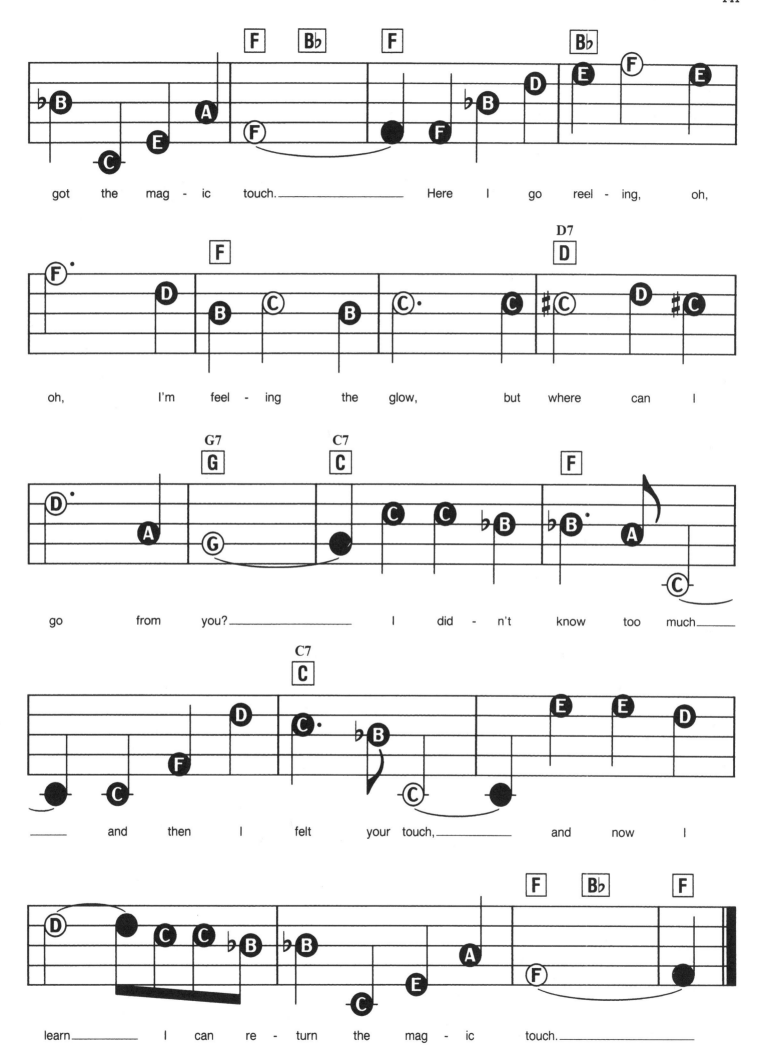

Mister Sandman

Registration 4
Rhythm: Fox Trot or Swing

Lyric and Music by
Pat Ballard

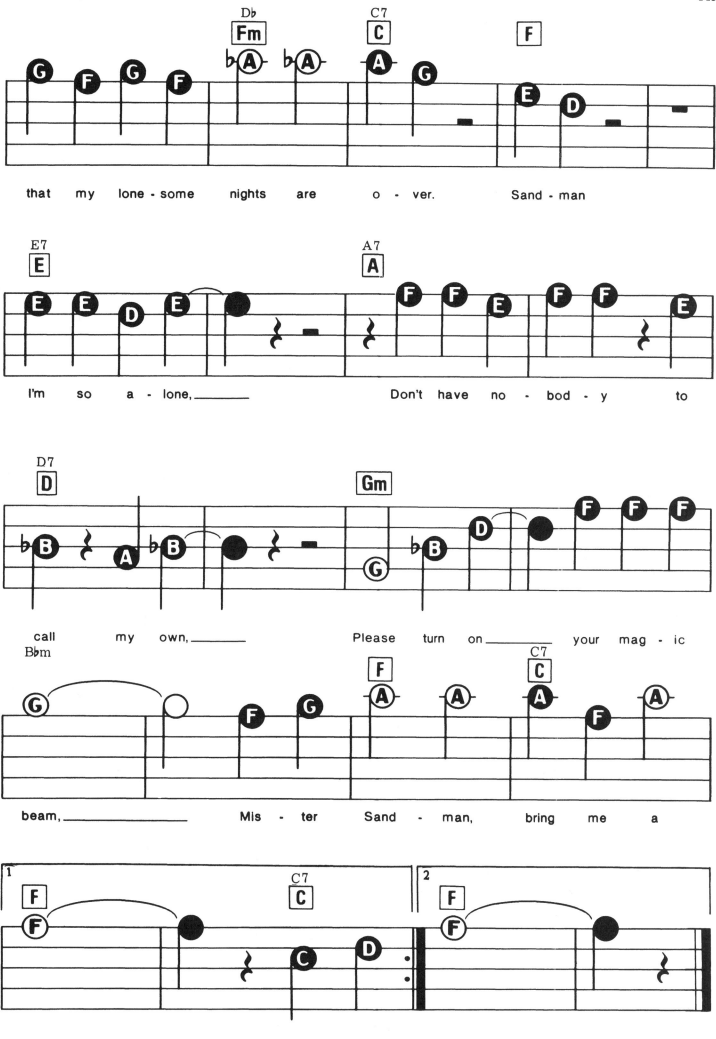

Moments to Remember

Registration 8
Rhythm: Ballad

Words by Al Stillman
Music by Robert Allen

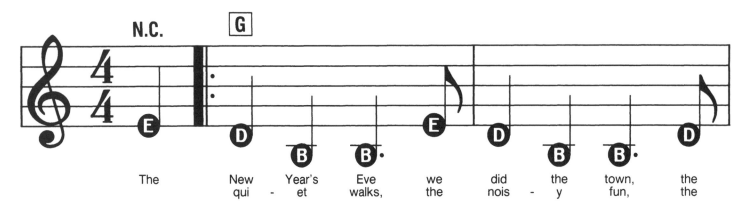

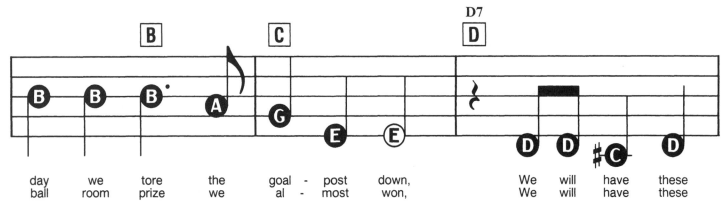

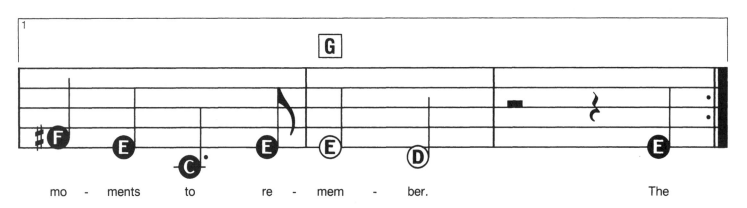

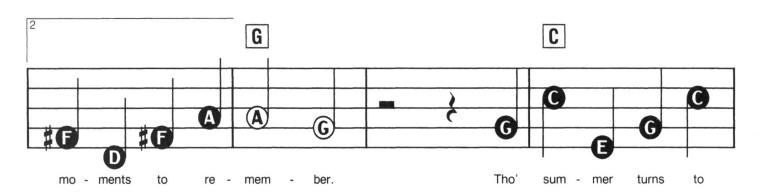

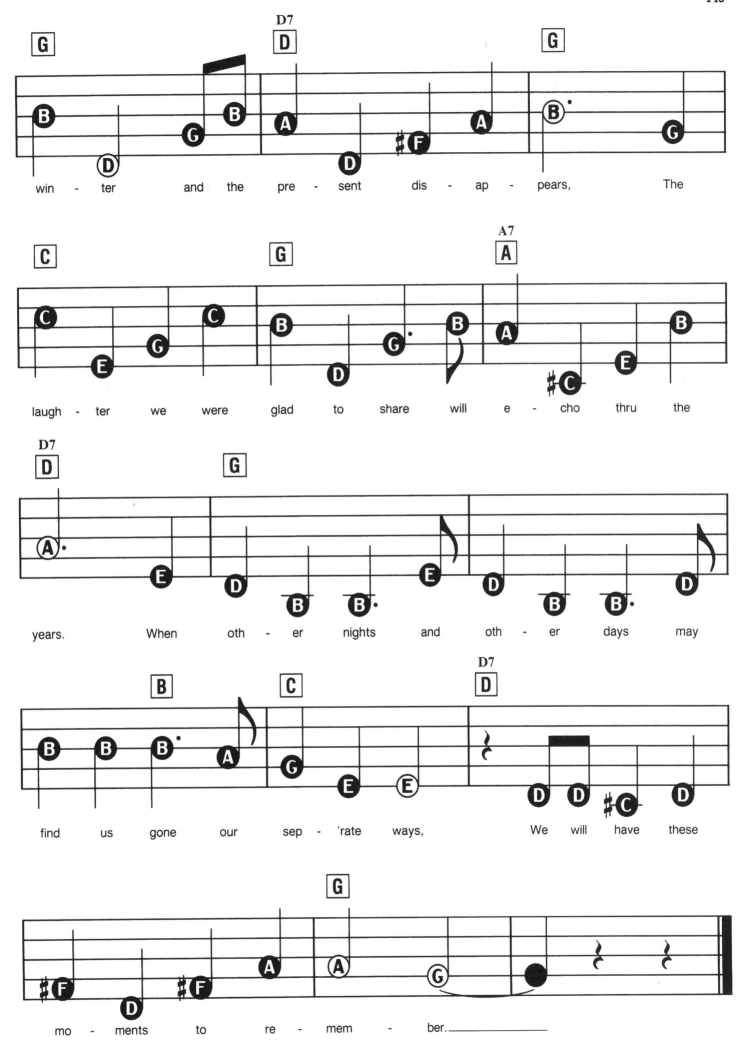

Mona Lisa
from the Paramount Picture CAPTAIN CAREY, U.S.A.

Registration 9
Rhythm: Swing

Words and Music by Jay Livingston
and Ray Evans

(Put Another Nickel In)

Music! Music! Music!

Registration 4
Rhythm: Fox Trot

Words and Music by Stephan Weiss
and Bernie Baum

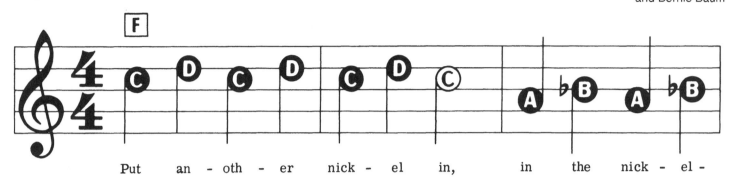

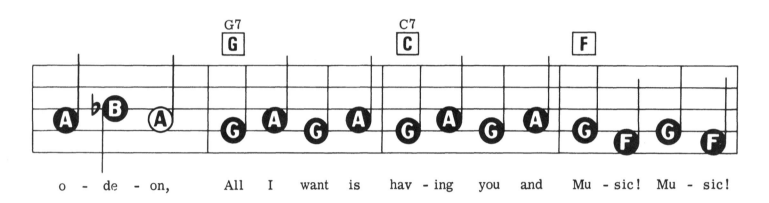

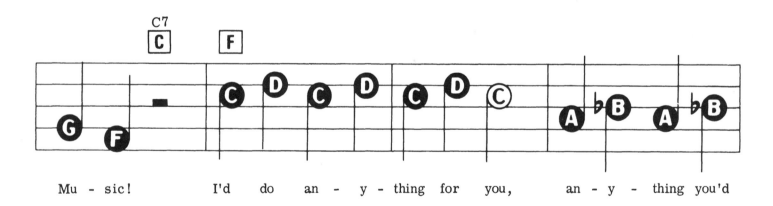

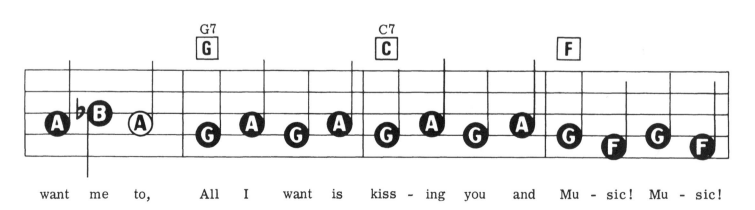

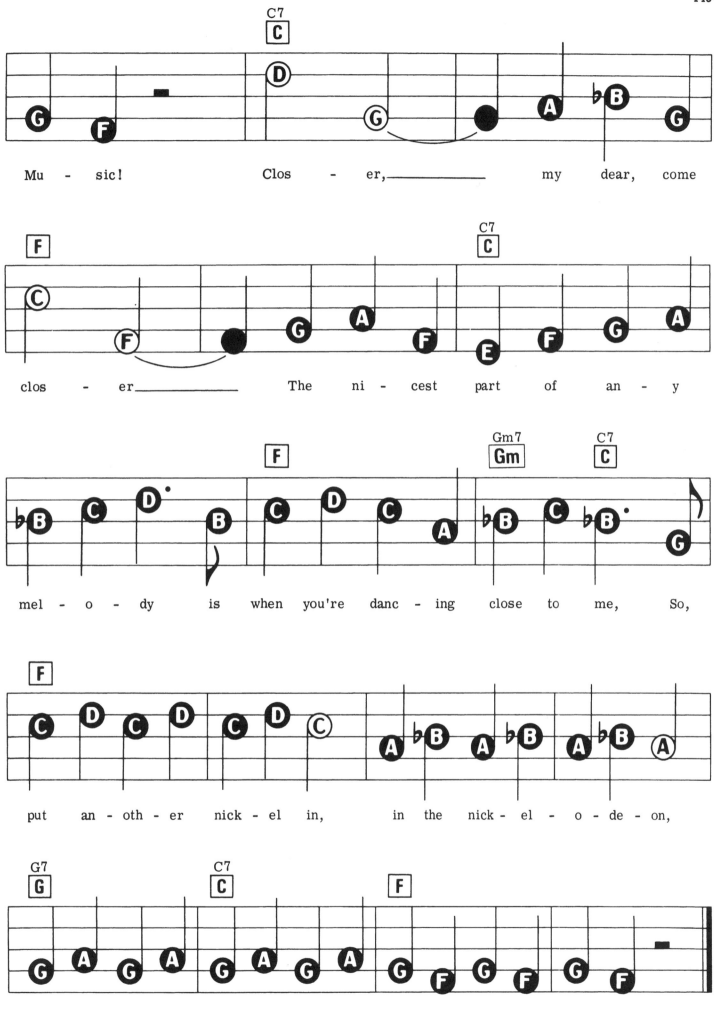

My Heart Cries for You

Registration 3
Rhythm: Waltz

Music by Percy Faith
Lyrics by Carl Sigman

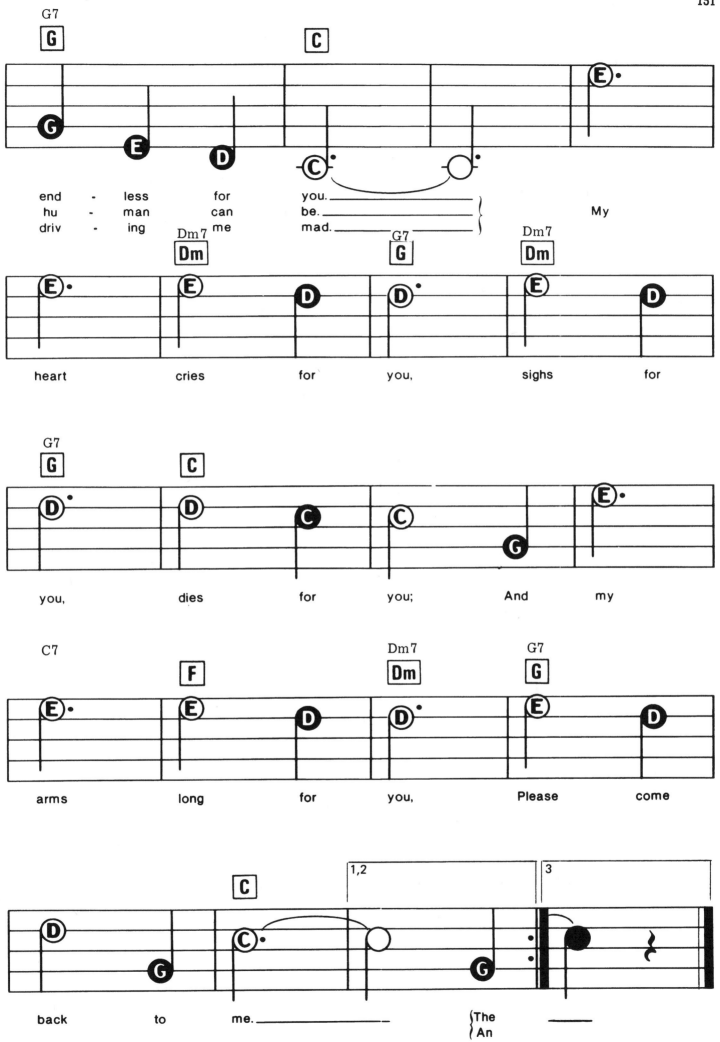

My Heart Is an Open Book

Registration 2
Rhythm: Fox Trot

Lyric by Hal David
Music by Lee Pockriss

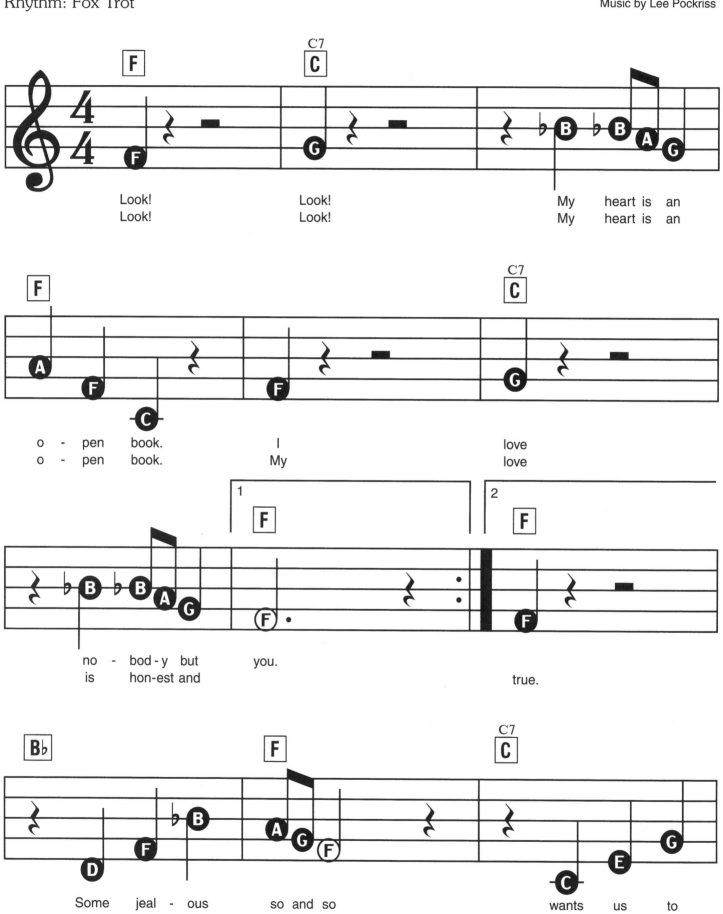

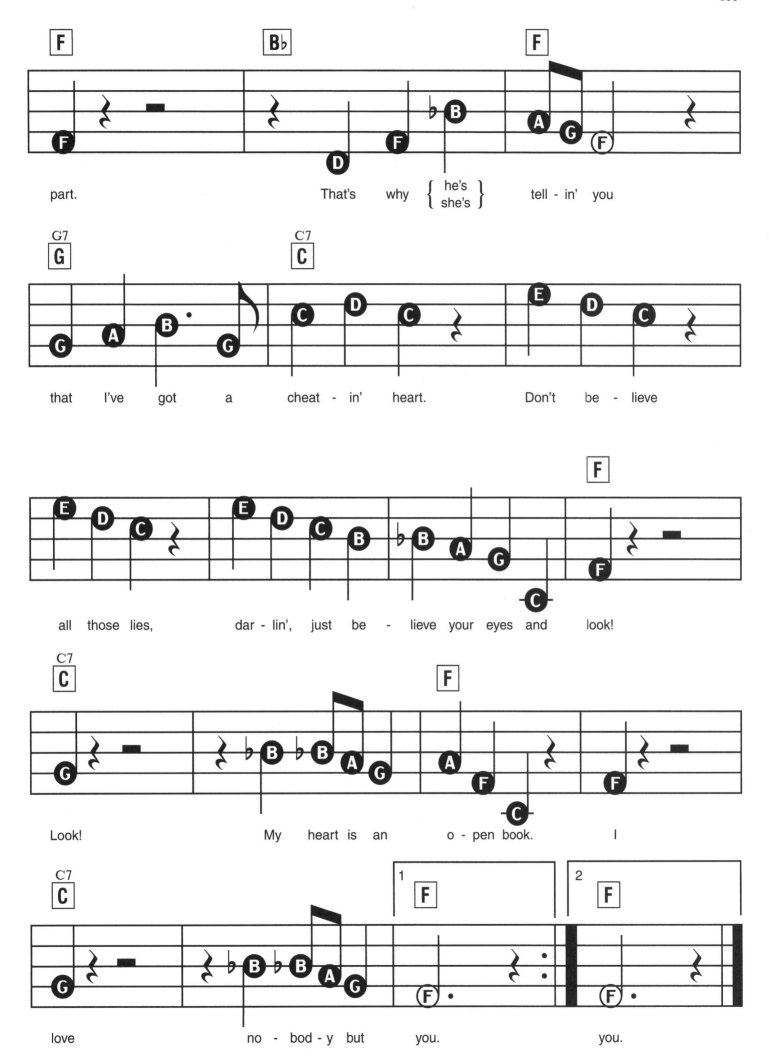

My Prayer

Registration 3
Rhythm: Fox Trot or Swing

Music by Georges Boulanger
Lyric and Musical Adaptation by Jimmy Kennedy

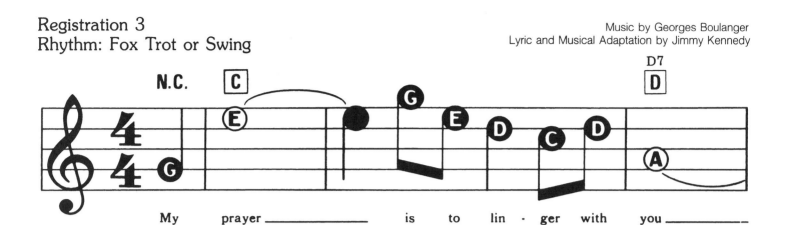

My   prayer _____ is to lin - ger with   you _____

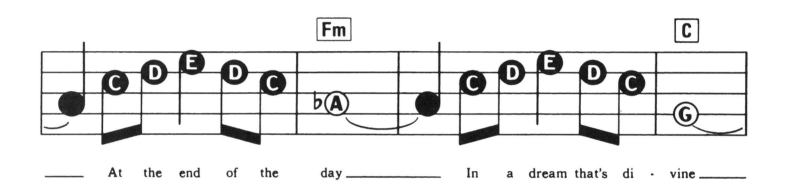

_____ At the end of the day _____ In a dream that's di - vine _____

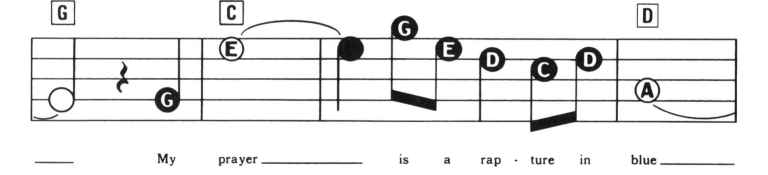

_____ My   prayer _____ is a rap - ture in   blue _____

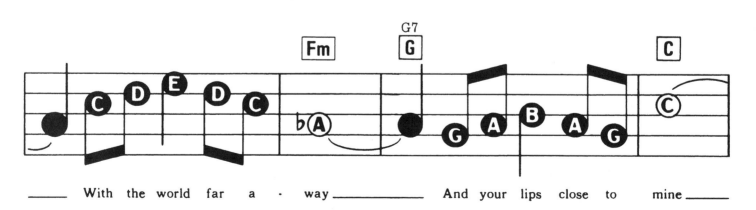

_____ With the world far a - way _____ And your lips close to   mine _____

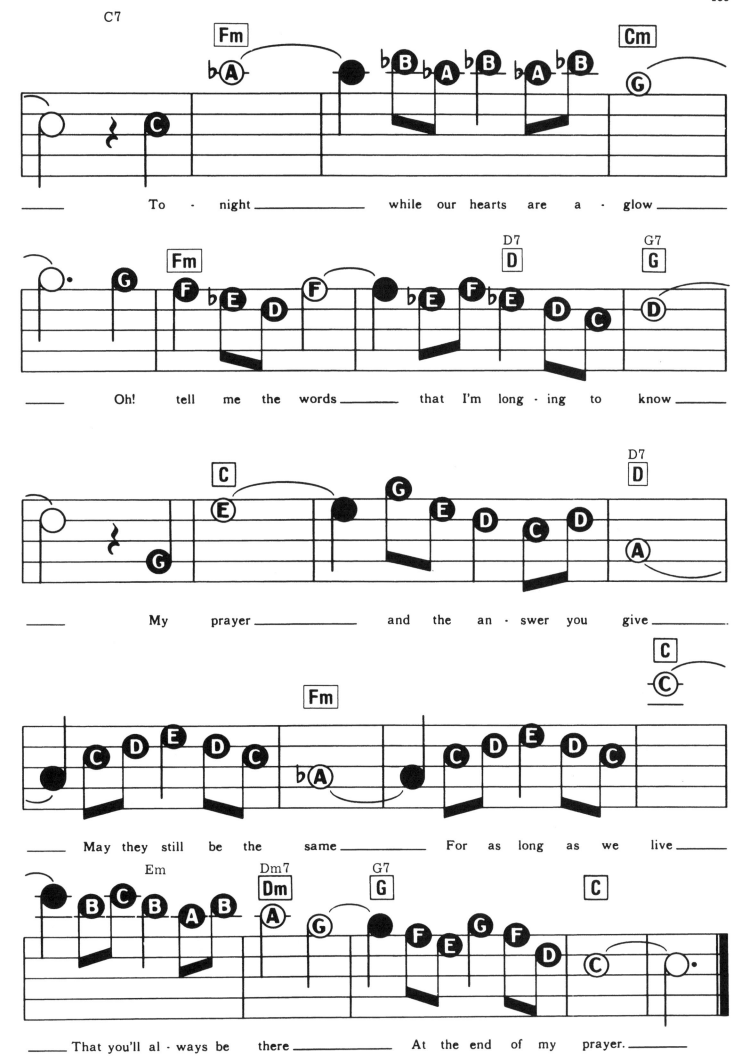

Oh! My Pa-Pa
(O Mein Papa)

Registration 7
Rhythm: Swing

English Words by John Turner and Geoffrey Parsons
Music and Orginal Lyric by Paul Burkhard

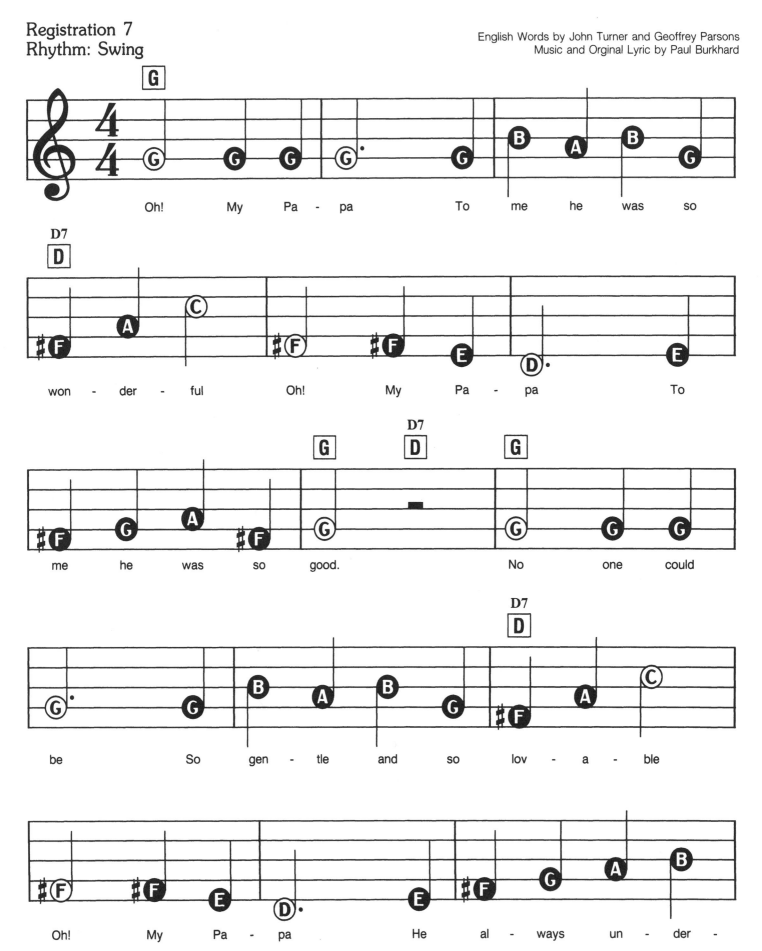

157

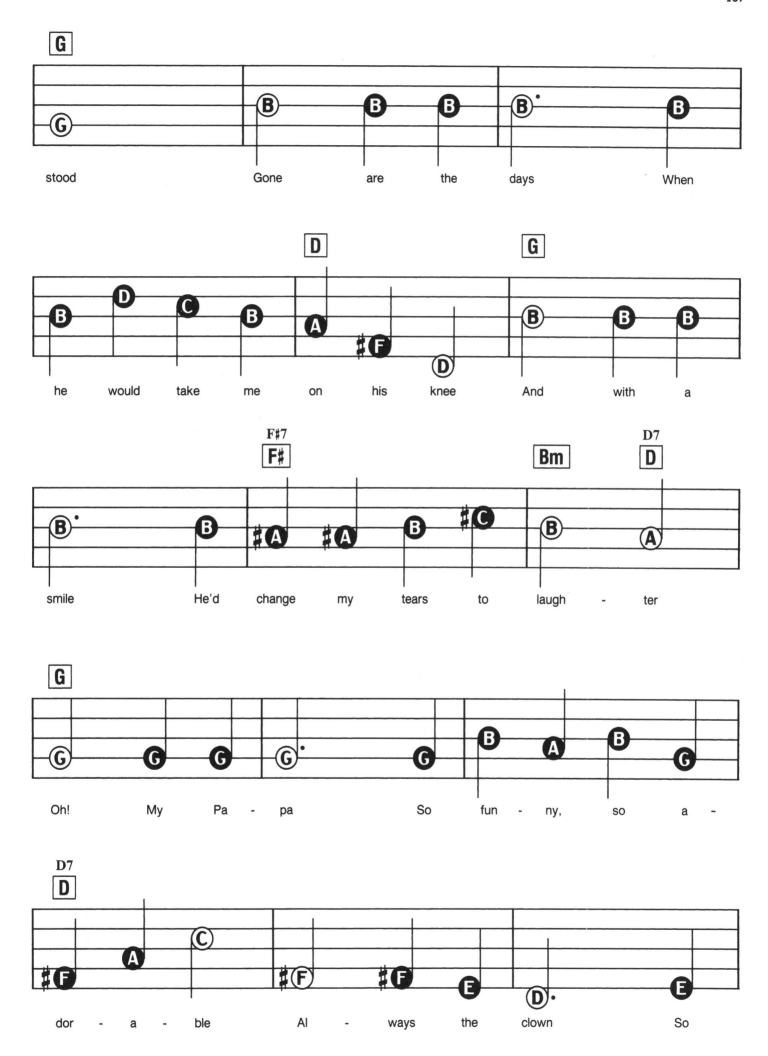

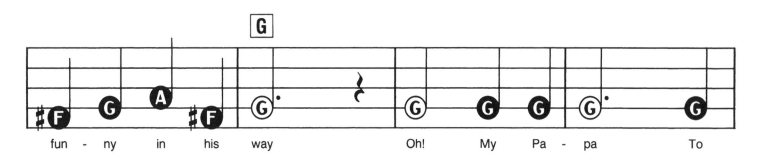

fun - ny in his way   Oh!   My   Pa - pa   To

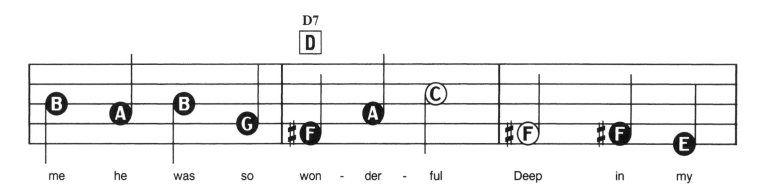

me   he   was   so   won - der - ful   Deep   in   my

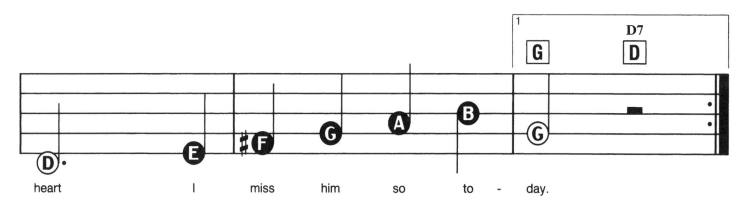

heart   I   miss   him   so   to - day.

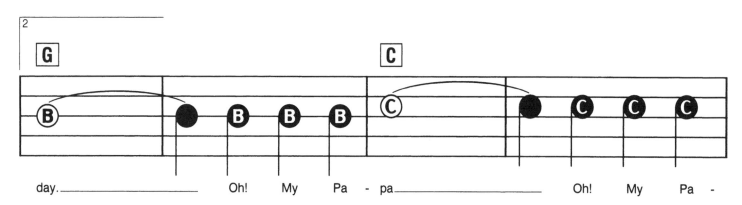

day.____   Oh!   My   Pa - pa____   Oh!   My   Pa -

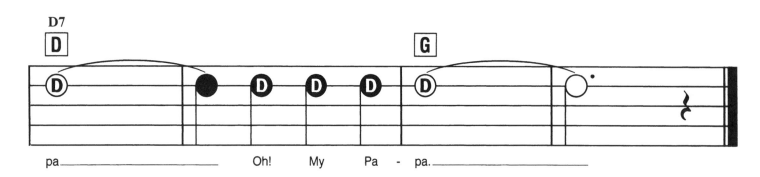

pa_____   Oh!   My   Pa - pa.____

Party Doll

Registration 8
Rhythm: Shuffle or Rock 'n' Roll

Words and Music by James Bowen
and Buddy Knox

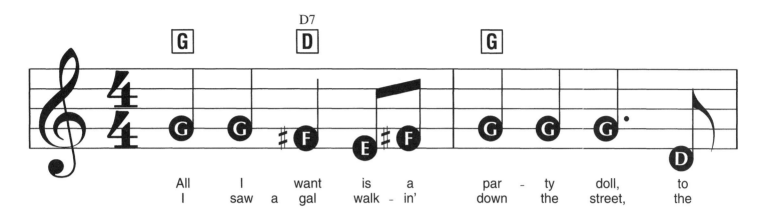

All I want is a par - ty doll, to
I saw a gal walk - in' down the street, to the

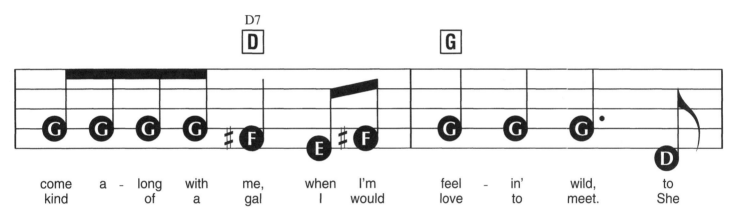

come a - long with me, when I'm feel - in' wild, to
kind of a gal I would love to meet. She

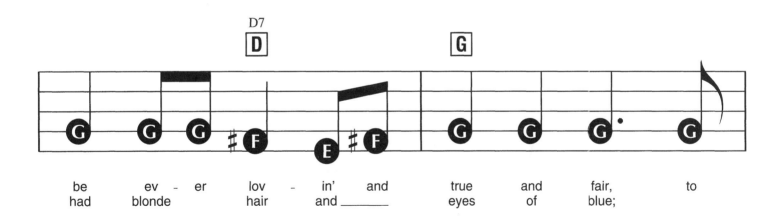

be ev - er lov - in' and true and fair, to
had blonde hair and _____ eyes of blue;

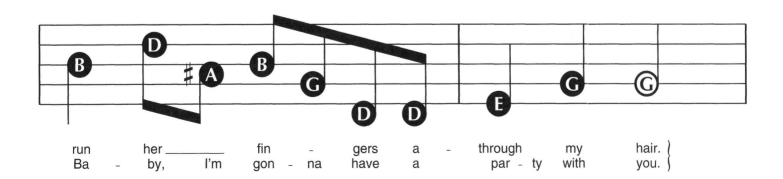

run her _____ fin - gers a - through my hair.
Ba - by, I'm gon - na have a par - ty with you.

160

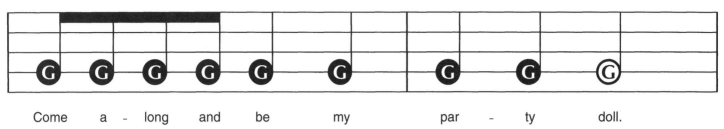

Come a - long and be my par - ty doll.

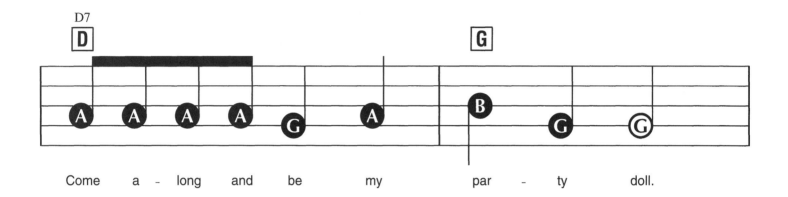

Come a - long and be my par - ty doll.

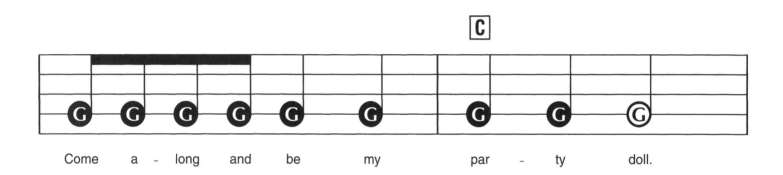

Come a - long and be my par - ty doll.

To Coda ⊕

I'll make love to you, to you.

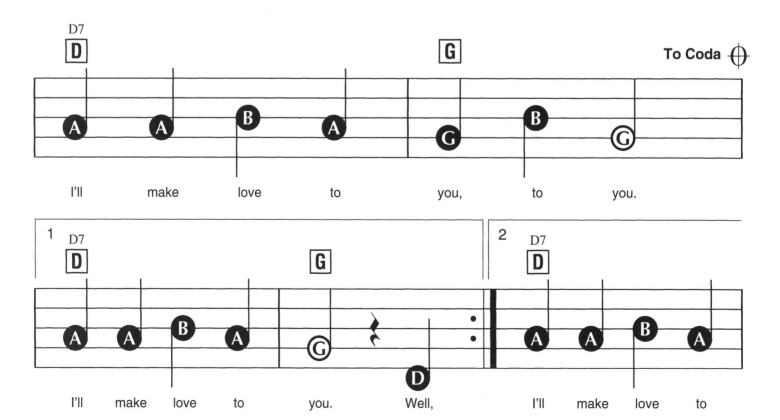

I'll make love to you. Well, I'll make love to

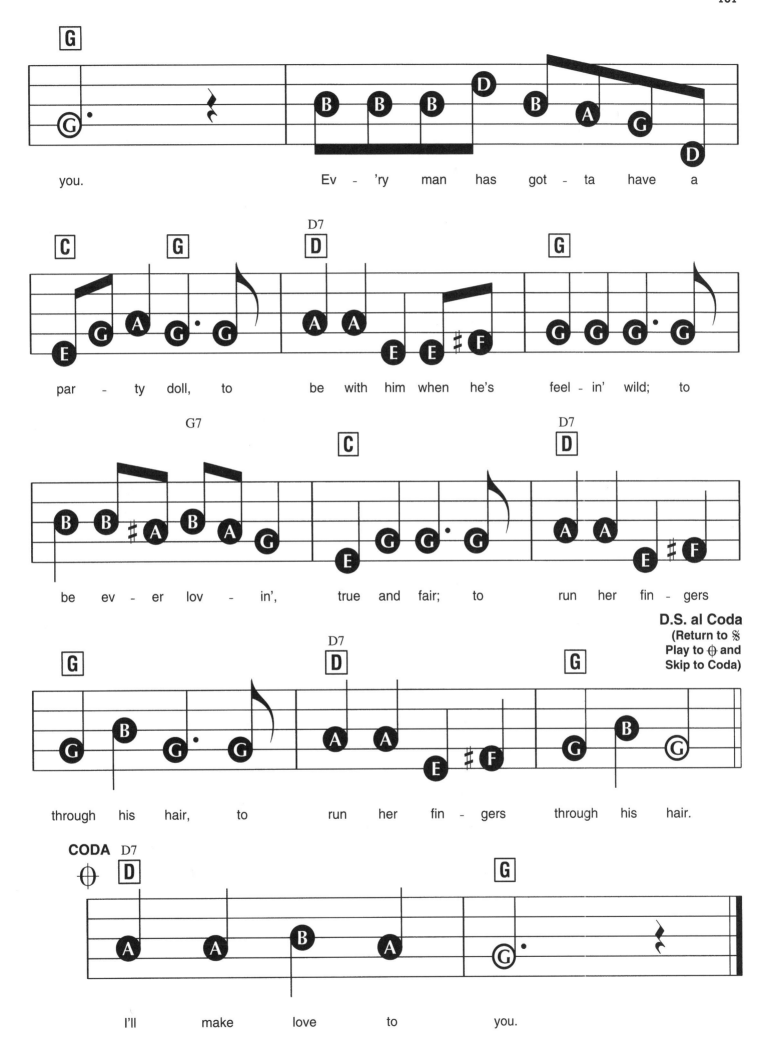

(You've Got)
Personality

Registration 5
Rhythm: Shuffle or Swing

Words and Music by Lloyd Price
and Harold Logan

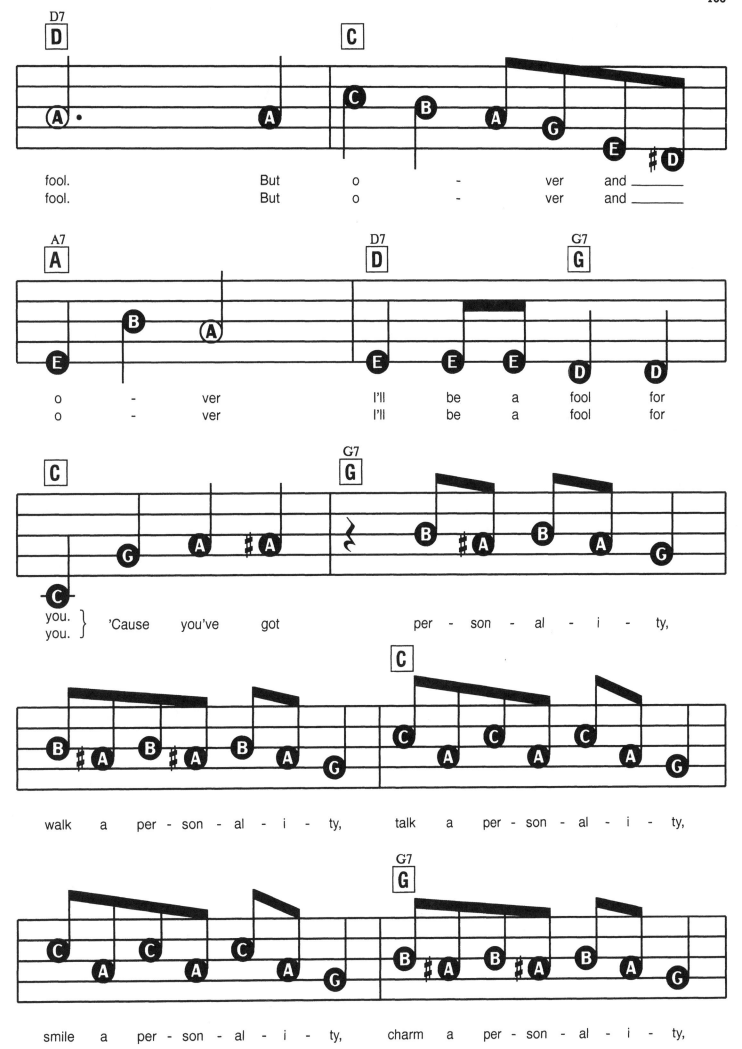

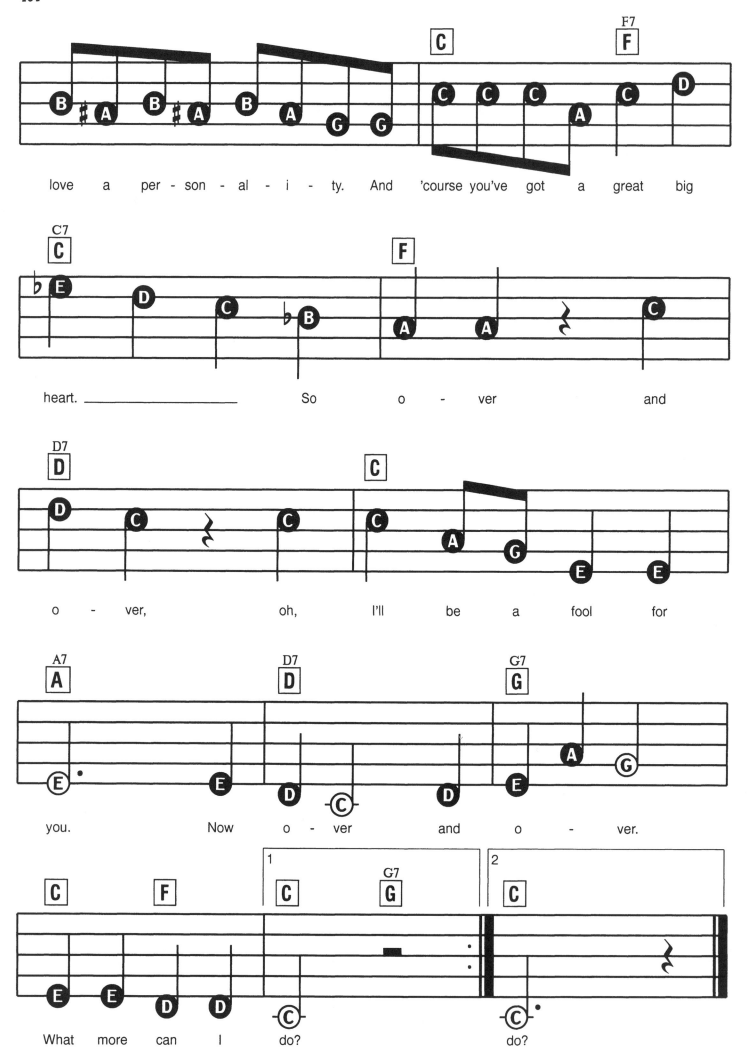

Primrose Lane

Registration 4
Rhythm: Swing or Jazz

Words and Music by Wayne Shanklin
and George Callender

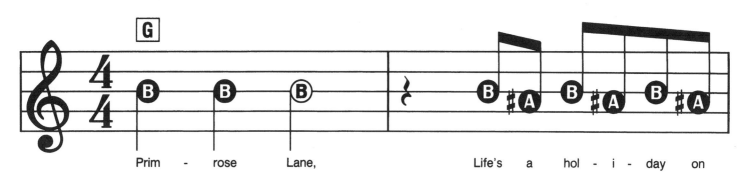

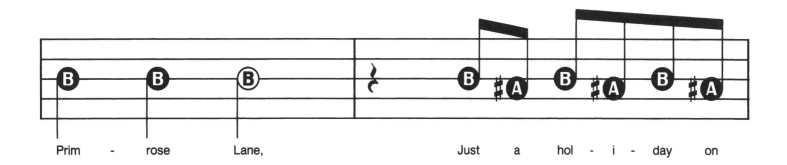

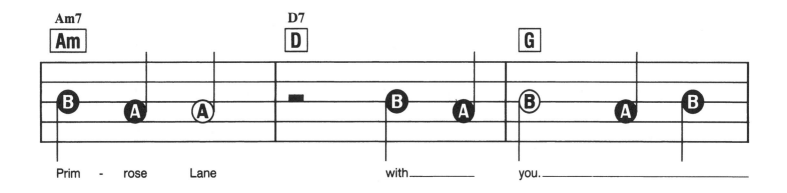

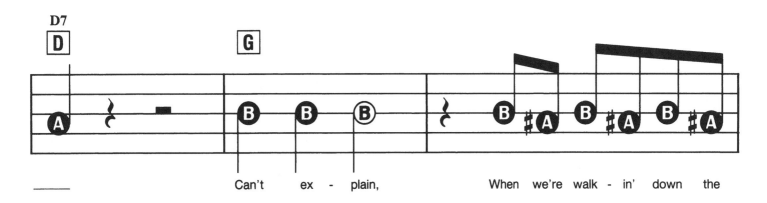

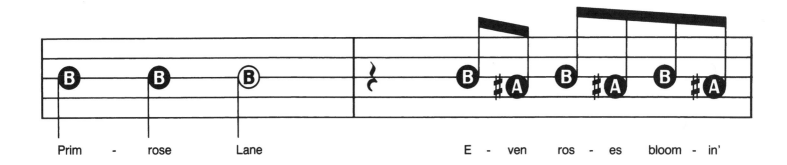

Prim - rose Lane   E - ven ros - es bloom - in'

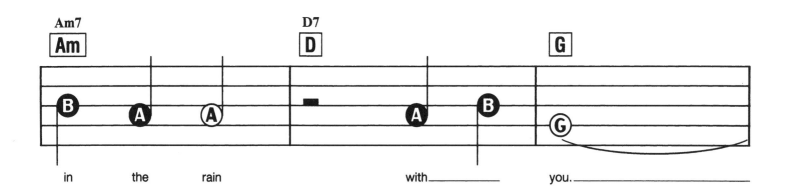

in the rain   with_____ you._____

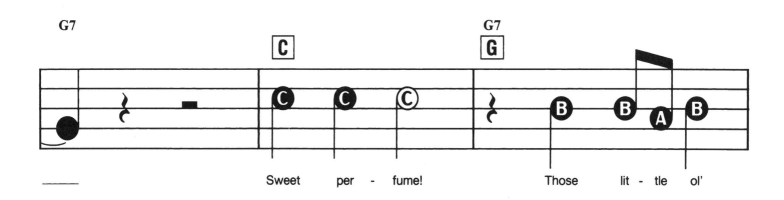

_____   Sweet per - fume!   Those lit - tle ol'

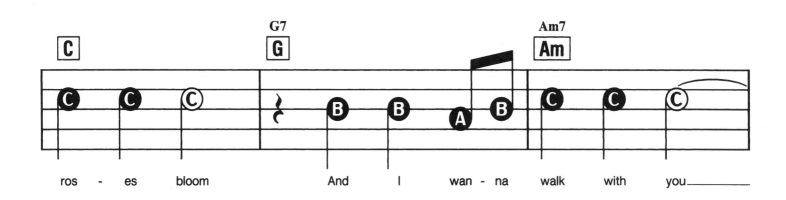

ros - es bloom   And I wan - na walk with you_____

167

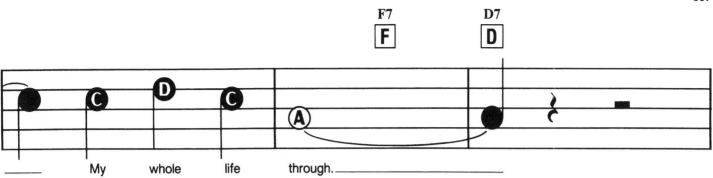

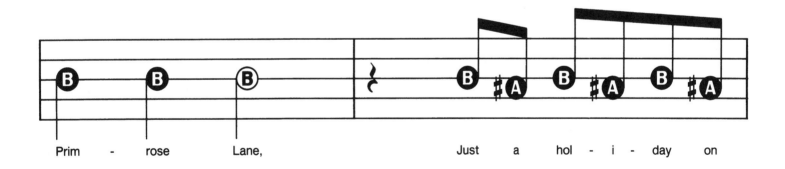

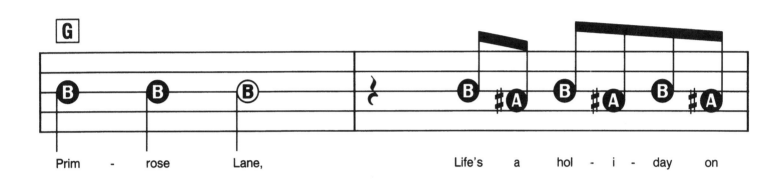

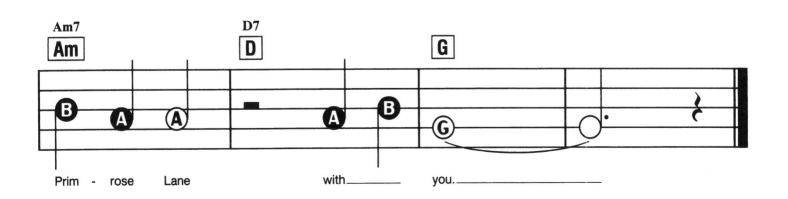

Poor Little Fool

Registration 8
Rhythm: Rock or 8 Beat

Words and Music by
Sharon Sheeley

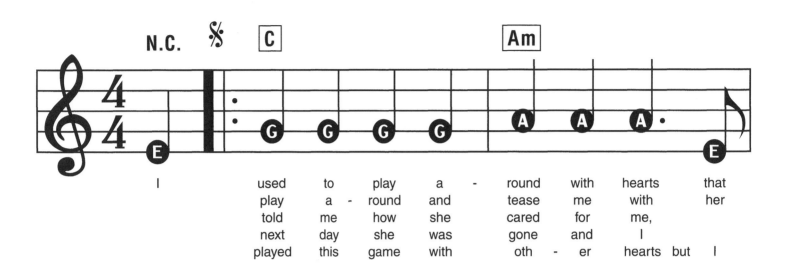

I	used	to	play	a -	round	with	hearts	that
	play	a -	round	and	tease	me	with	her
	told	me	how	she	cared	for	me,	
	next	day	how	she	was	gone	and	I
	played	this	game	with	oth -	er	hearts	but I

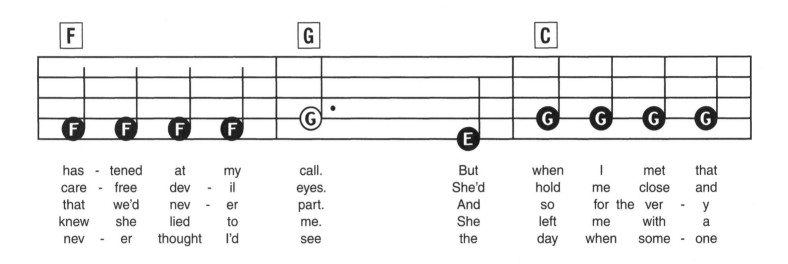

has -	tened	at	my	call.	But	when	I	met	that
care -	free	dev -	il	eyes.	She'd	hold	me	close	and
that	we'd	nev -	er	part.	And	so	for the	ver -	y
knew	she	lied	to	me.	She	left	me	with	a
nev -	er	thought	I'd	see	the	day	when	some -	one

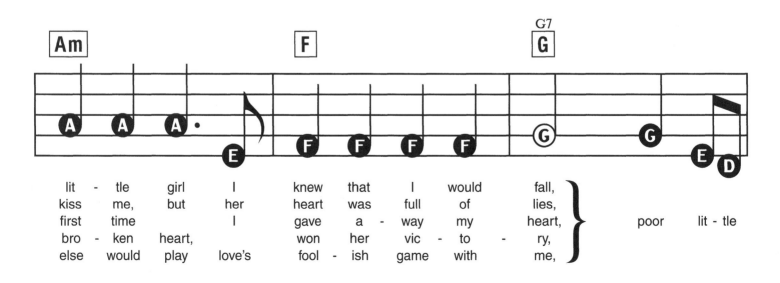

lit -	tle	girl	I	knew	that	I	would	fall,	poor	lit - tle
kiss	me,	but	her	heart	was	full	of	lies,		
first	time	I	gave	a -	way	my	heart,			
bro -	ken	heart,	won	her	vic -	to -	ry,			
else	would	play	love's	fool -	ish	game	with	me,		

169

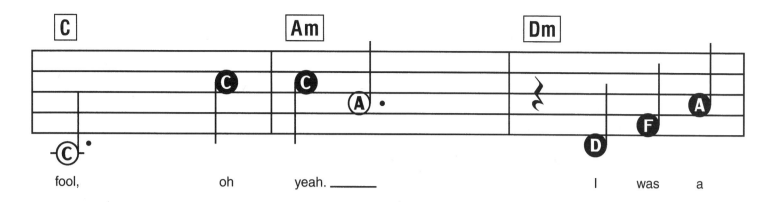

fool, oh yeah. _____ I was a

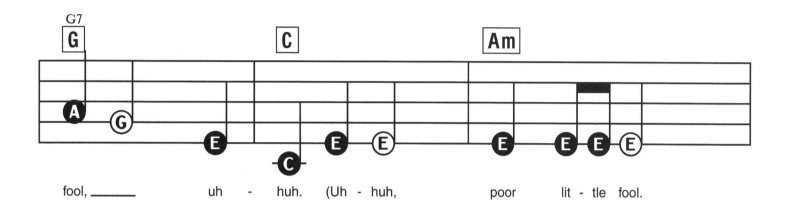

fool, _____ uh - huh. (Uh - huh, poor lit - tle fool.

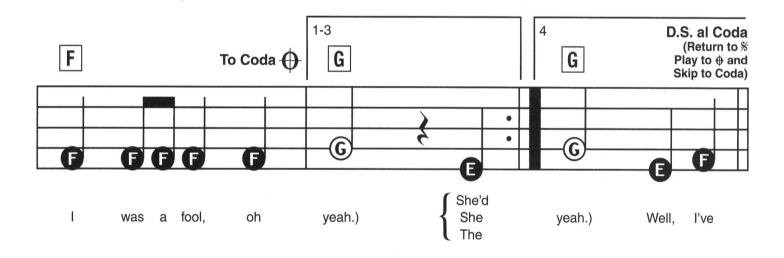

I was a fool, oh yeah.) She'd / She / The yeah.) Well, I've

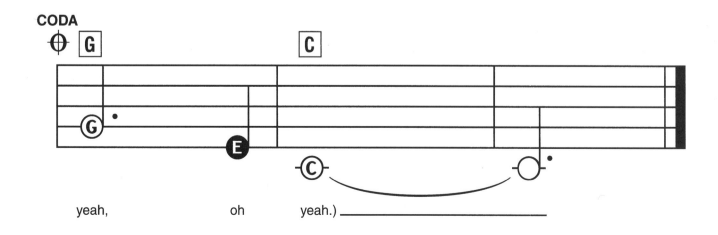

yeah, oh yeah.) _____

Put Your Head on My Shoulder

Registration 2
Rhythm: Slow Rock or Ballad

Words and Music by
Paul Anka

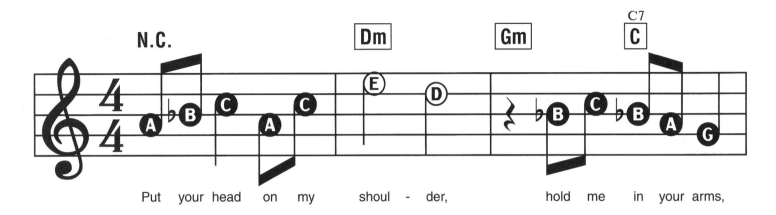

Put your head on my shoul - der, hold me in your arms,

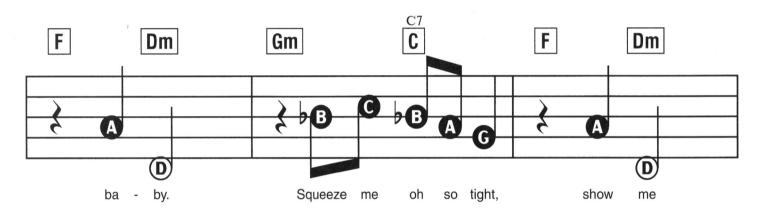

ba - by. Squeeze me oh so tight, show me

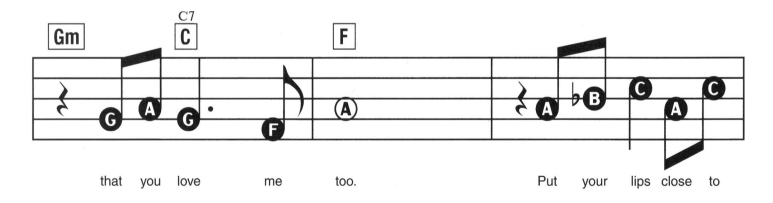

that you love me too. Put your lips close to

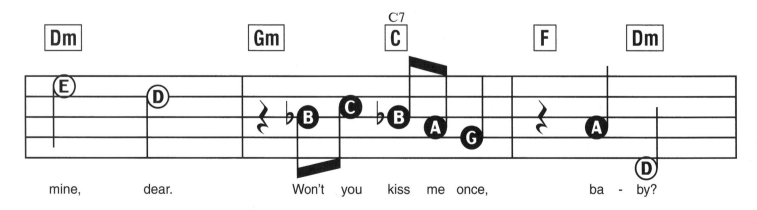

mine, dear. Won't you kiss me once, ba - by?

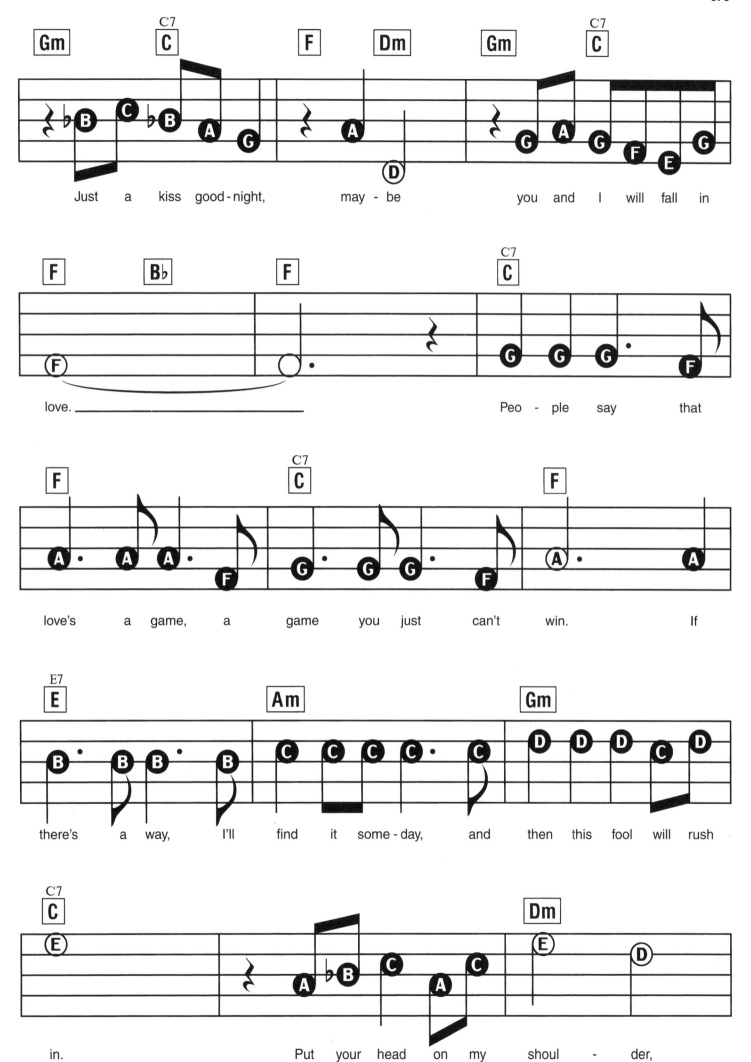

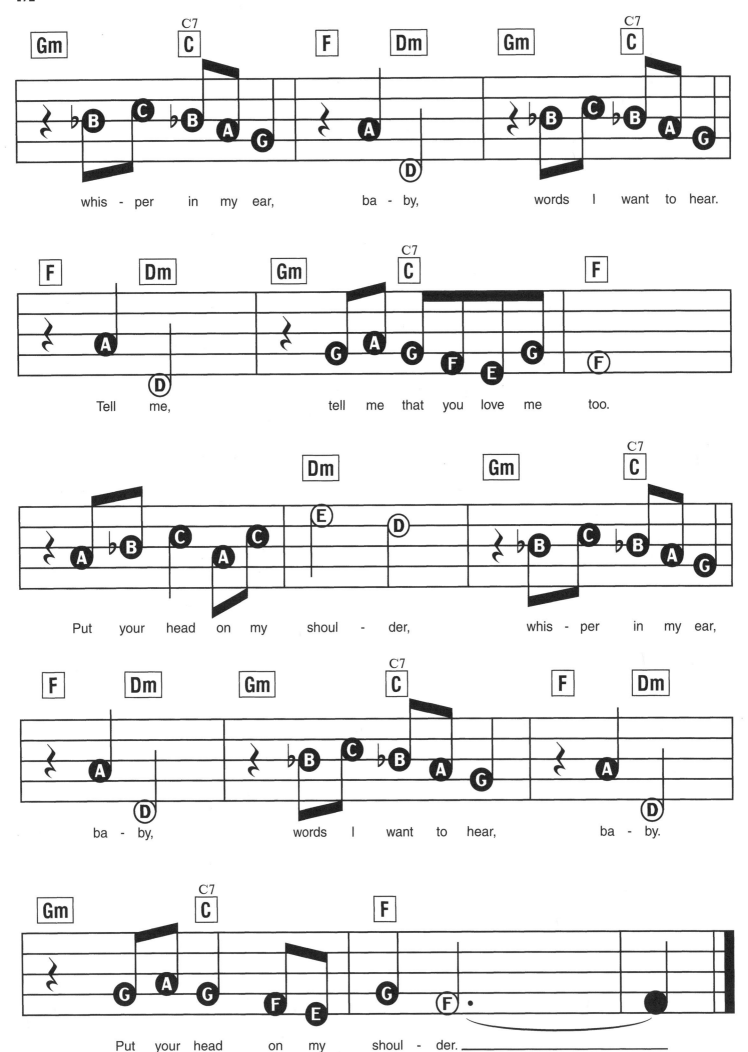

See You Later, Alligator

Registration 2
Rhythm: Shuffle or Swing

Words and Music by
Robert Guidry

N.C.

C

Well, I saw my ba - by
told me,
dad - dy,
'ga - tor,

with an - oth - er man to - day. _____
near - ly made me lose my head. _____
you know my love is just for you. _____
I know you meant it just for play. _____

F7

F

Well, I saw my ba - by
When I thought of what she
She said, I'm sor - ry, pret - ty
I said, wait a min - ute,

walk - ing
told me,
dad - dy,
'ga - tor,

C

with an - oth - er man to - day. _____
near - ly made me lose my head. _____
you know my love is just for you. _____
I know you meant it just for play. _____

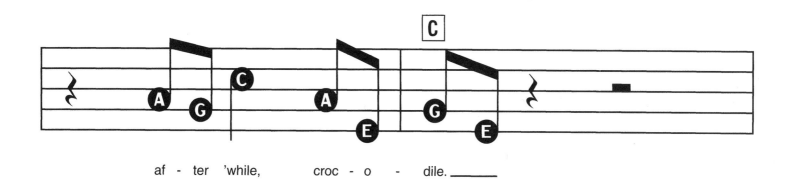

af - ter 'while, croc - o - dile. _____

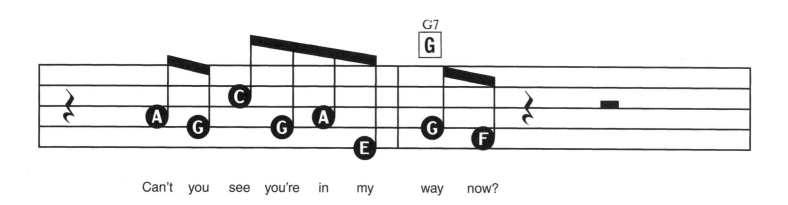

Can't you see you're in my way now?

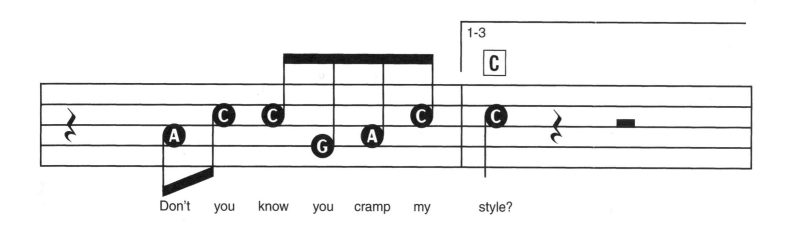

Don't you know you cramp my style?

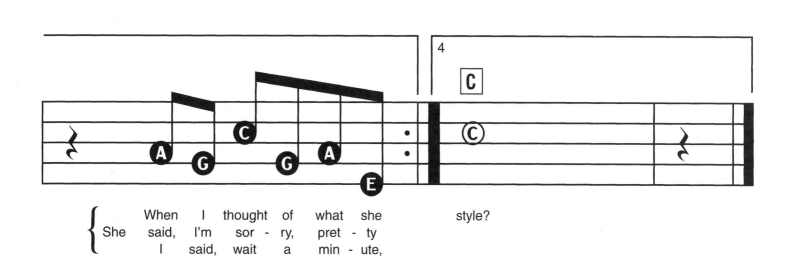

{ When I thought of what she   style?
She said, I'm sor - ry, pret - ty
I said, wait a min - ute,

Rock Around the Clock

Registration 8
Rhythm: Rock 'n' Roll

Words and Music by Max C. Freedman
and Jimmy DeKnight

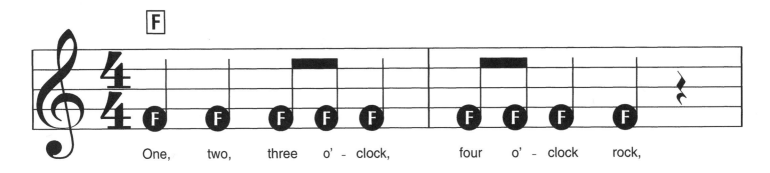

One,   two,   three o' - clock,   four o' - clock rock,

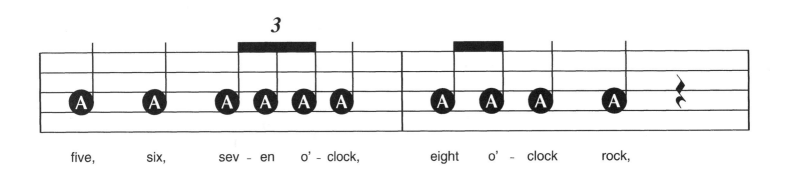

five,   six,   sev - en o' - clock,   eight o' - clock rock,

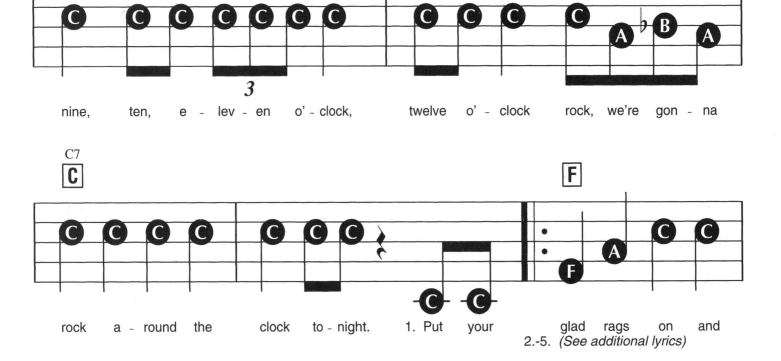

nine,   ten,   e - lev - en o' - clock,   twelve o' - clock   rock, we're gon - na

rock   a - round   the   clock   to - night.   1. Put   your   glad   rags   on   and

2.-5. (See additional lyrics)

join me, Hon. We'll have some fun when the clock strikes one. We're gon - na

rock a - round the clock to - night. We're gon - na rock, rock, rock 'til

broad day - light. We're gon - na rock, gon - na rock a - round the clock to -

night. _____ When the night. _____

Additional Lyrics

2. When the clock strikes two, and three and four,
   If the band slows down we'll yell for more,
   We're gonna rock around the clock tonight,
   We're gonna rock, rock, rock, etc....

3. When the chimes ring five and six and seven,
   We'll be rockin' up in seventh heav'n.
   We're gonna rock around the clock tonight,
   We're gonna rock, rock, rock, etc....

4. When it's eight, nine, ten, eleven, too,
   I'll be goin' strong and so will you,
   We're gonna rock around the clock tonight,
   We're gonna rock, rock, rock, etc....

5. When the clock strikes twelve, we'll cool off, then,
   Start a rockin' 'round the clock again,
   We're gonna rock around the clock tonight,
   We're gonna rock, rock, rock, etc....

Sea of Love

Registration 7
Rhythm: Slow Rock

Words and Music by George Khoury
and Philip Baptiste

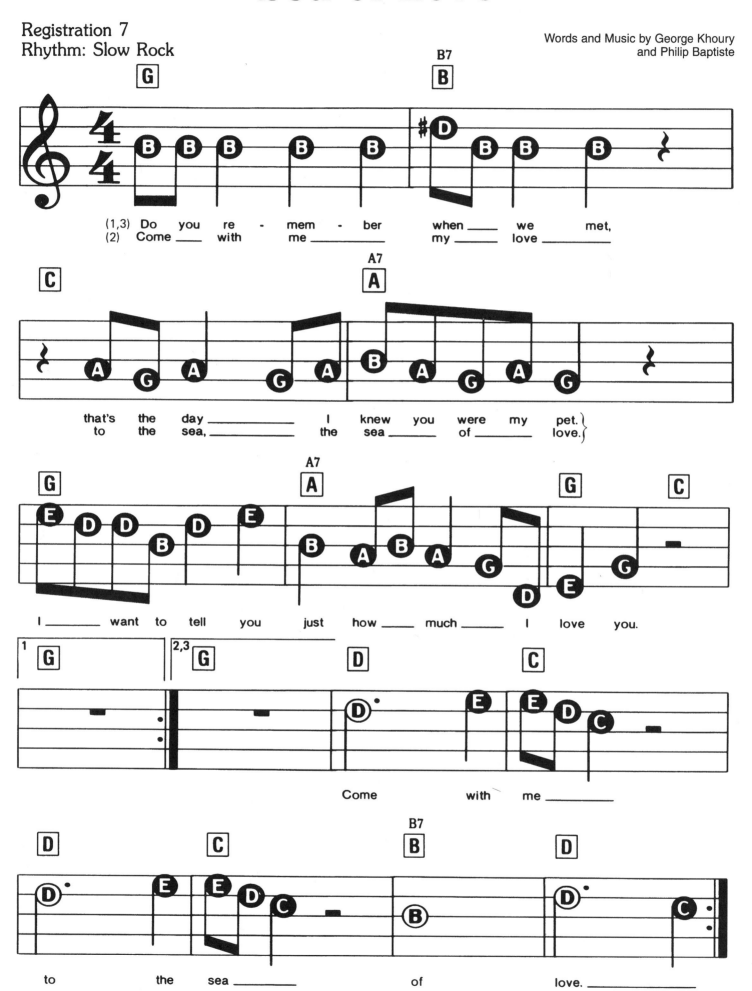

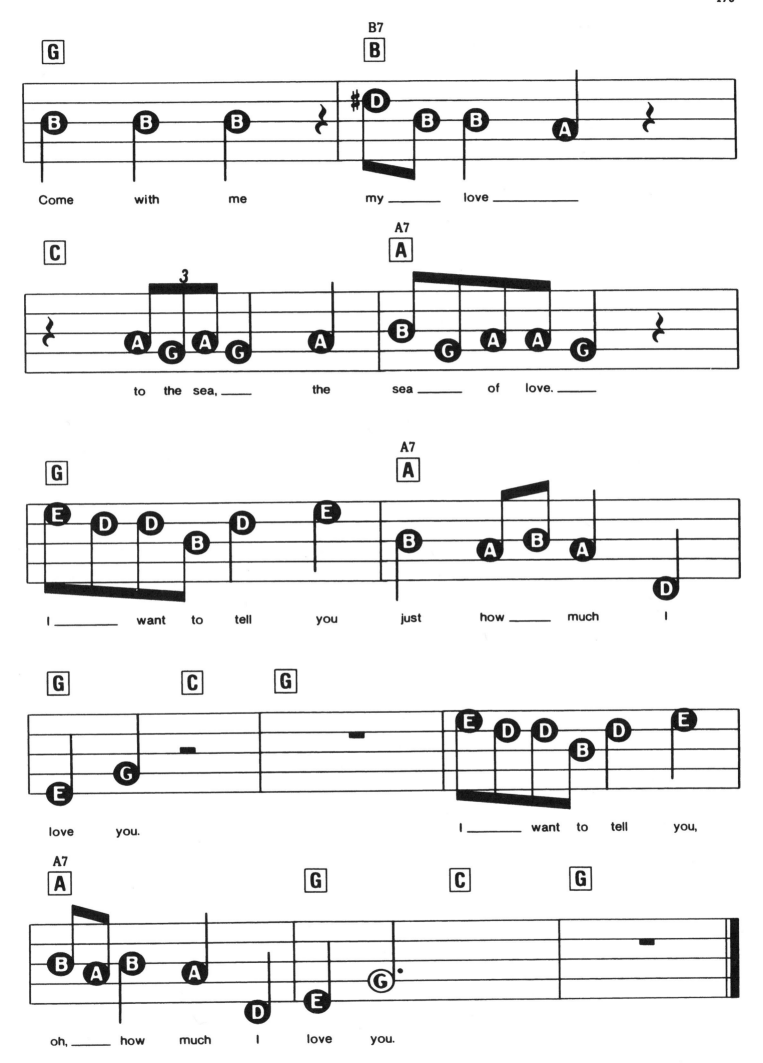

Searchin'

Registration 1
Rhythm: Fox Trot or Swing

Words and Music by Jerry Leiber
and Mike Stoller

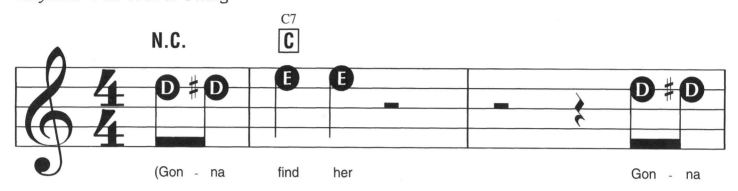

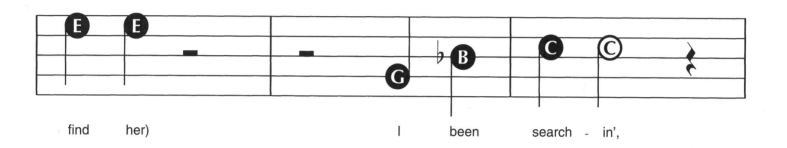

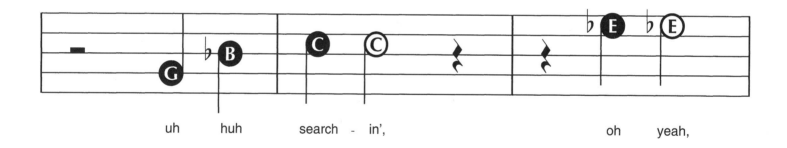

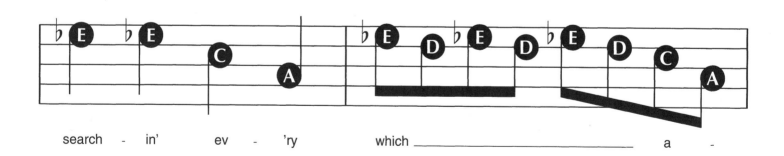

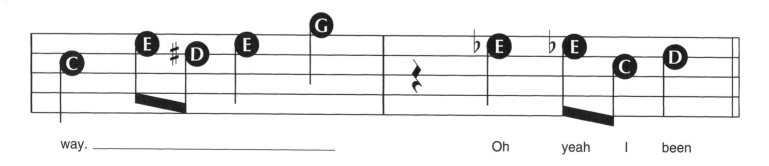

181

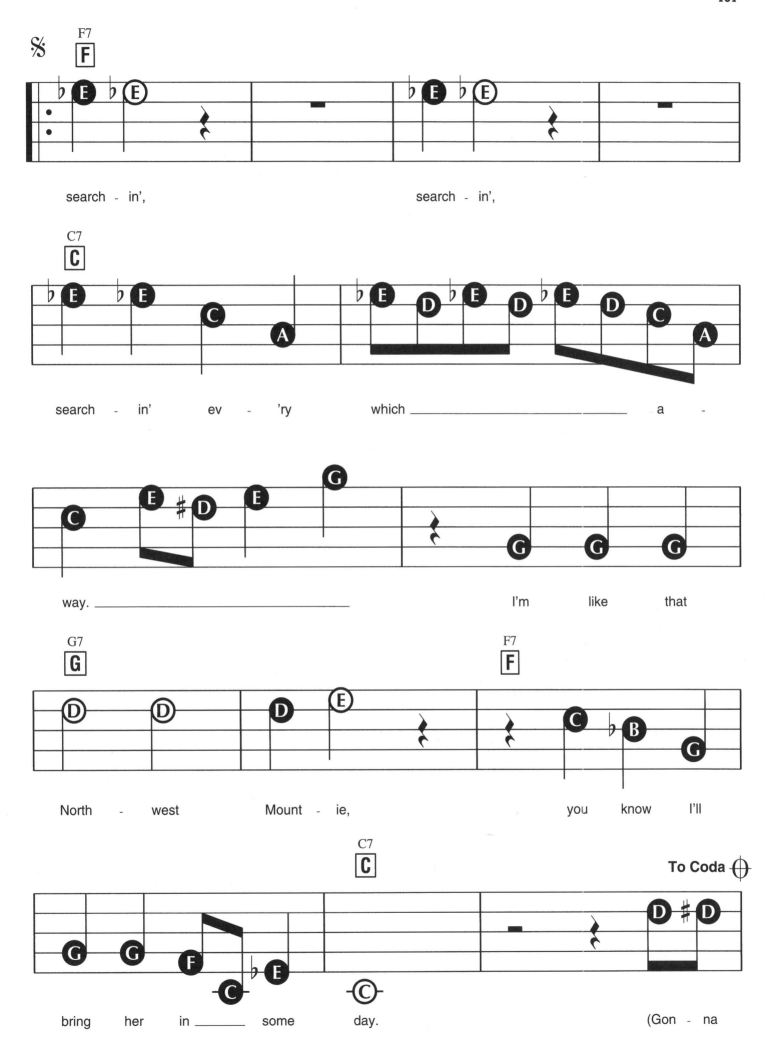

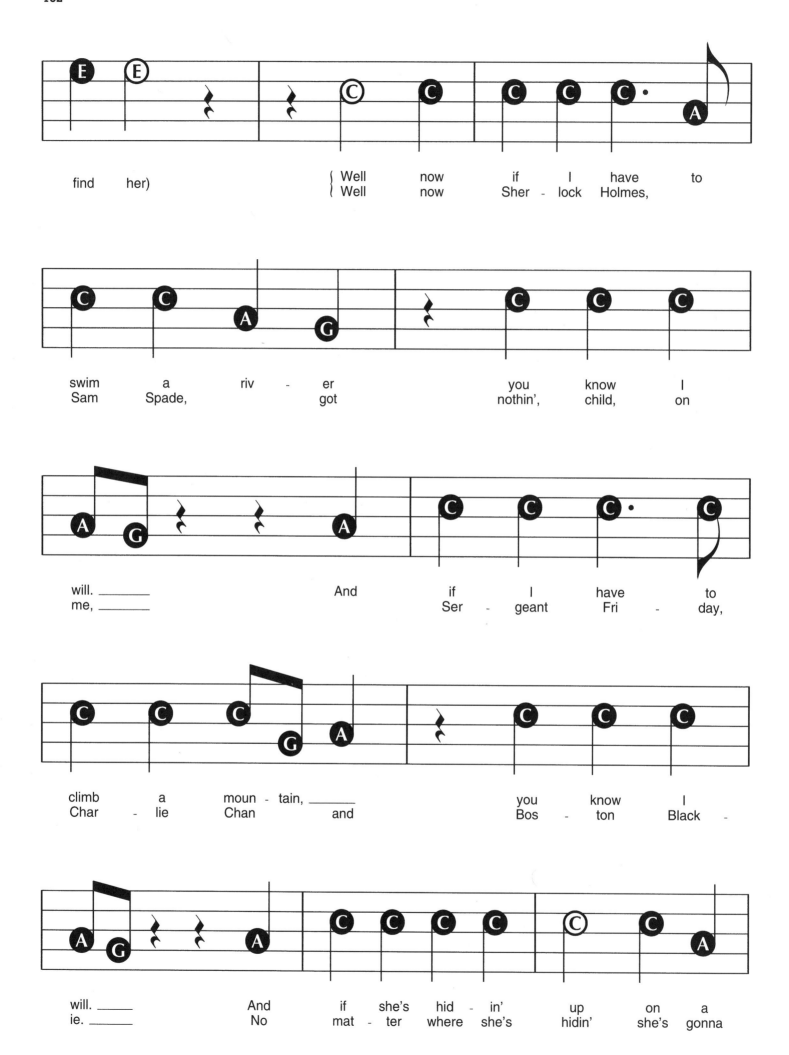

183

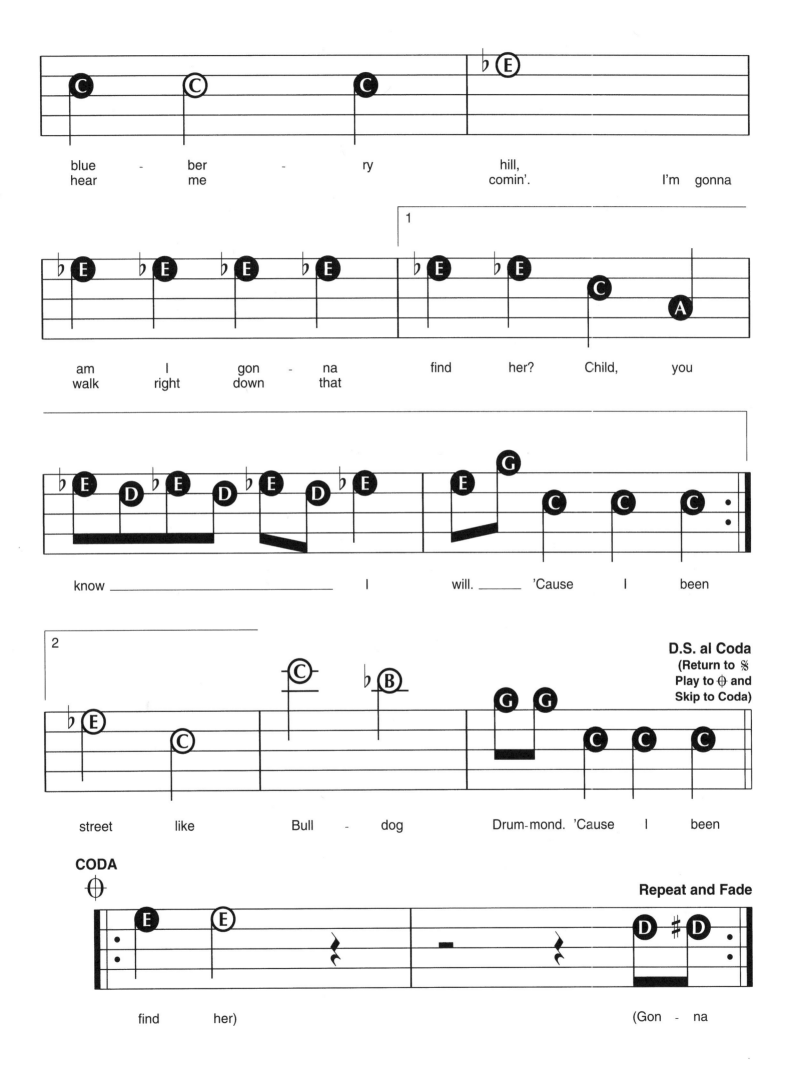

See Saw

Registration 1
Rhythm: R&B or Rock

Words and Music by Steve Cropper
and Don Covay

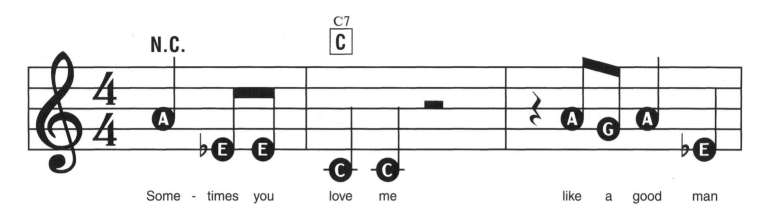

Some - times you love me like a good man

ought - a. Some - times you hurt me so bad _____

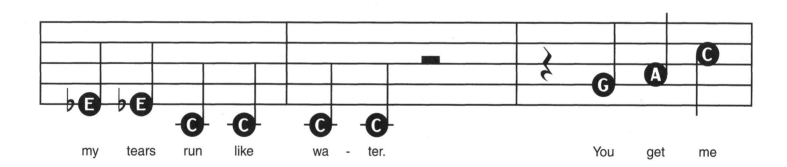

my tears run like wa - ter. You get me

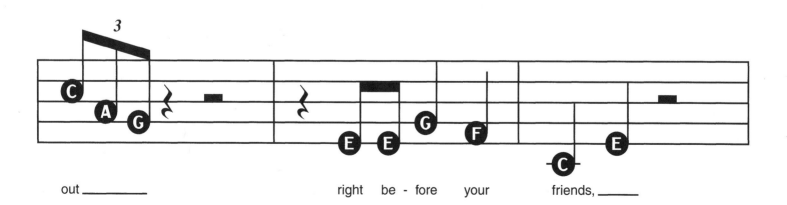

out _____ right be - fore your friends, _____

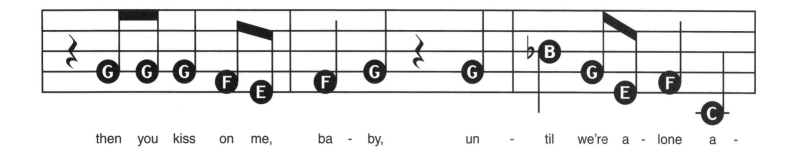

then you kiss on me, ba - by, un - til we're a - lone a -

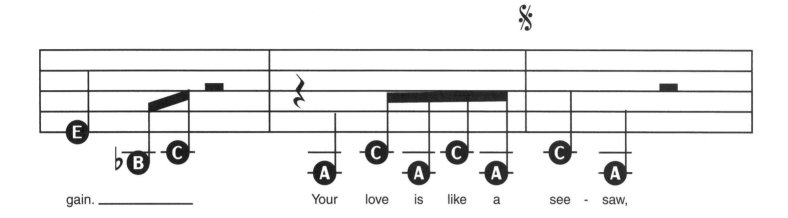

gain. _____ Your love is like a see - saw,

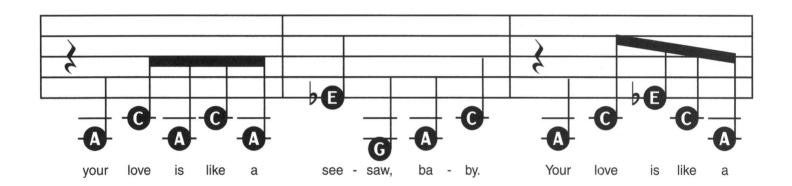

your love is like a see - saw, ba - by. Your love is like a

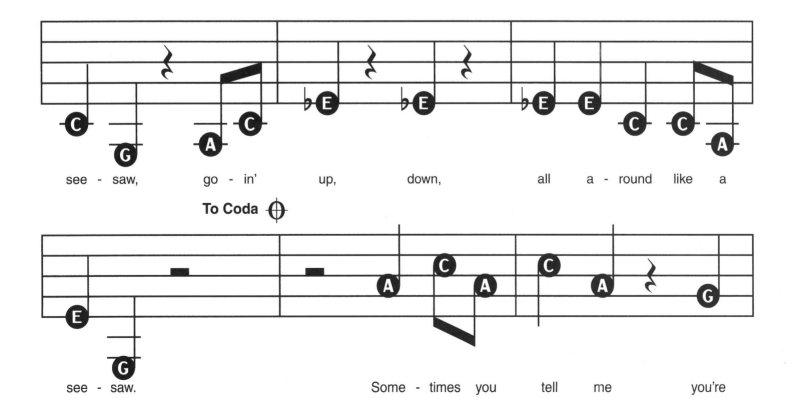

see - saw, go - in' up, down, all a - round like a

To Coda ⊕

see - saw. Some - times you tell me you're

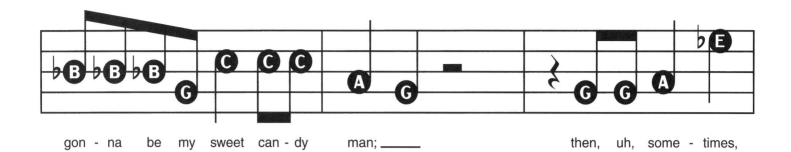

gon - na be my sweet can - dy man; _____ then, uh, some - times,

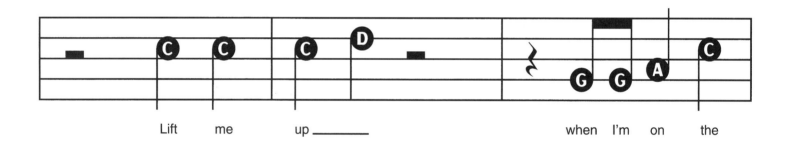

ba - by, don't know where I stand. _____

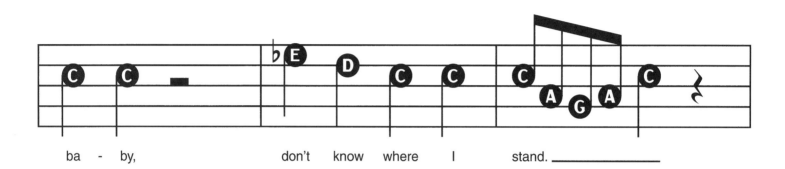

Lift me up _____ when I'm on the

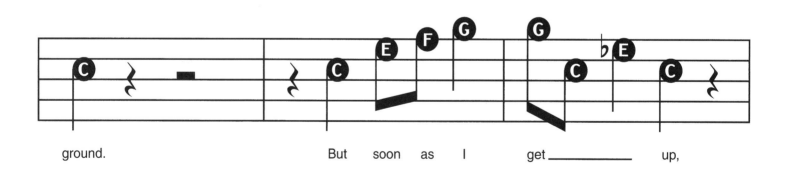

ground. But soon as I get _____ up,

D.S. al Coda
(Return to %
Play to ⊕ and
Skip to Coda)

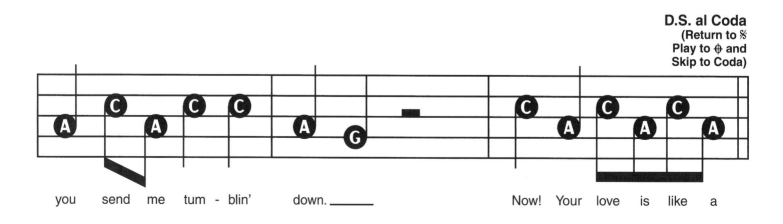

you send me tum - blin' down. _____ Now! Your love is like a

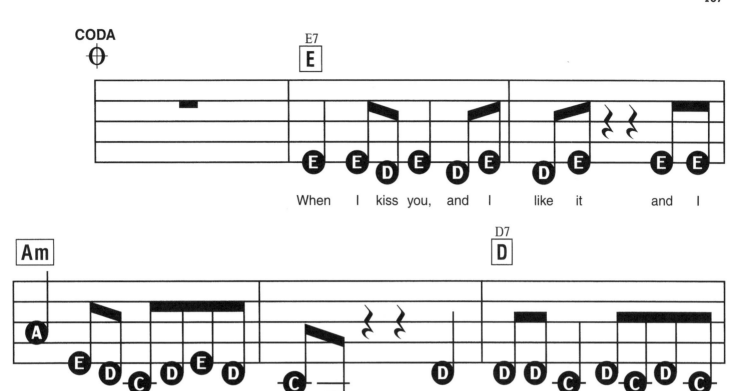

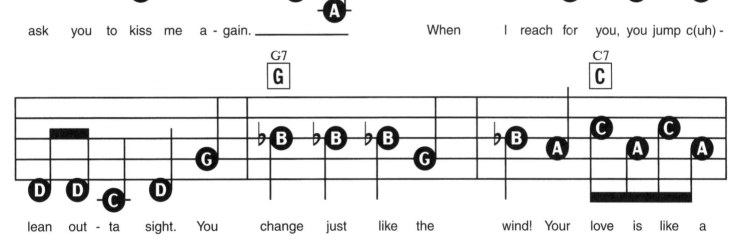

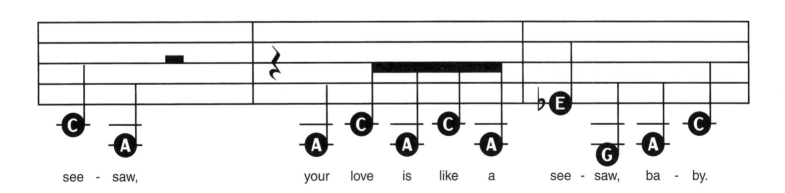

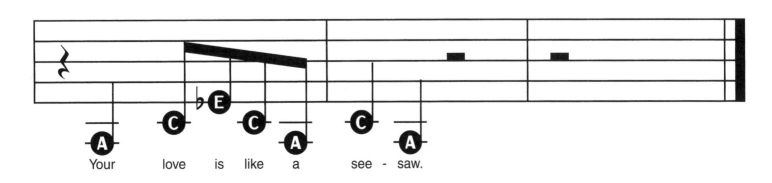

Since I Don't Have You

Registration 1
Rhythm: Rock

Words and Music by James Beaumont,
Janet Vogel, Joseph Verscharen, Walter Lester,
Lennie Martin, Joseph Rock and John Taylor

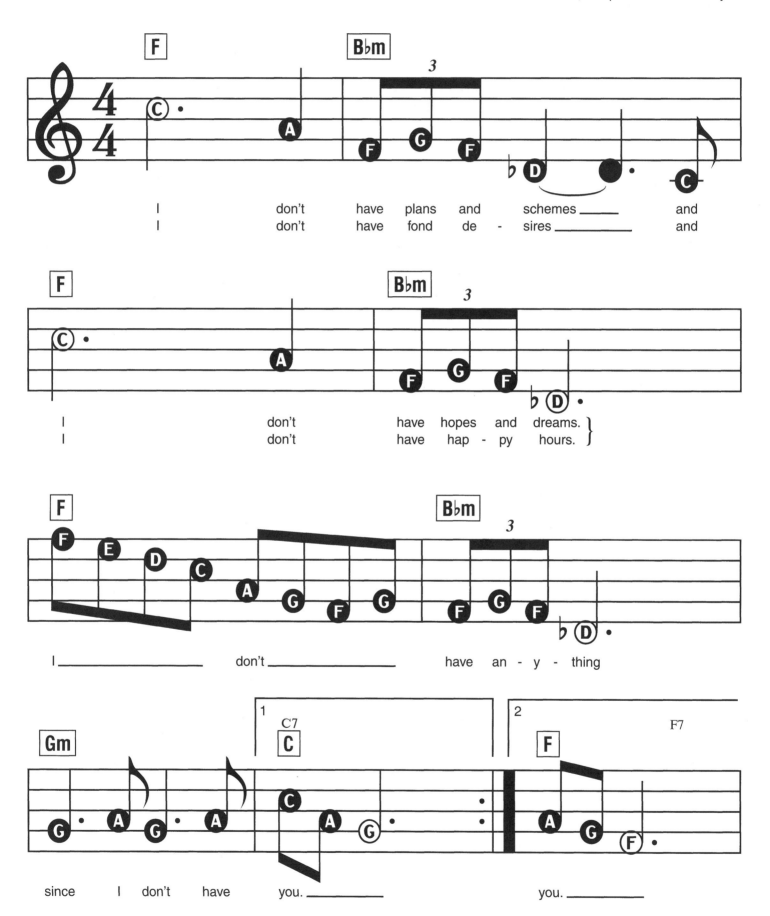

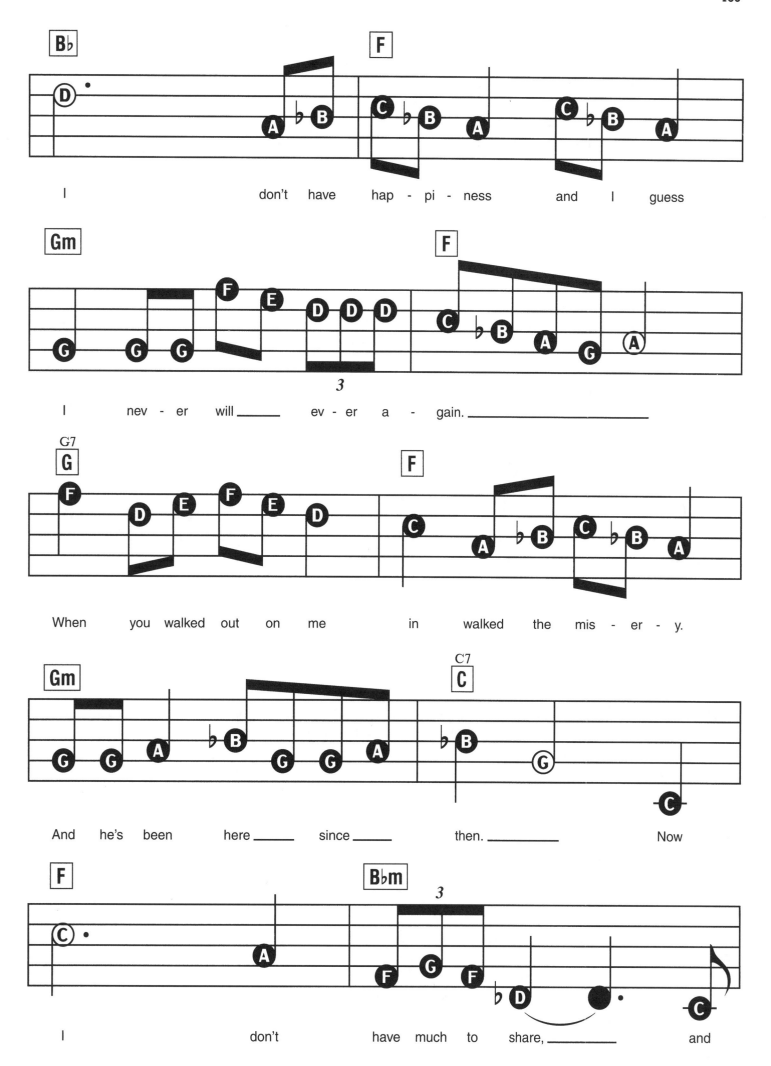

190

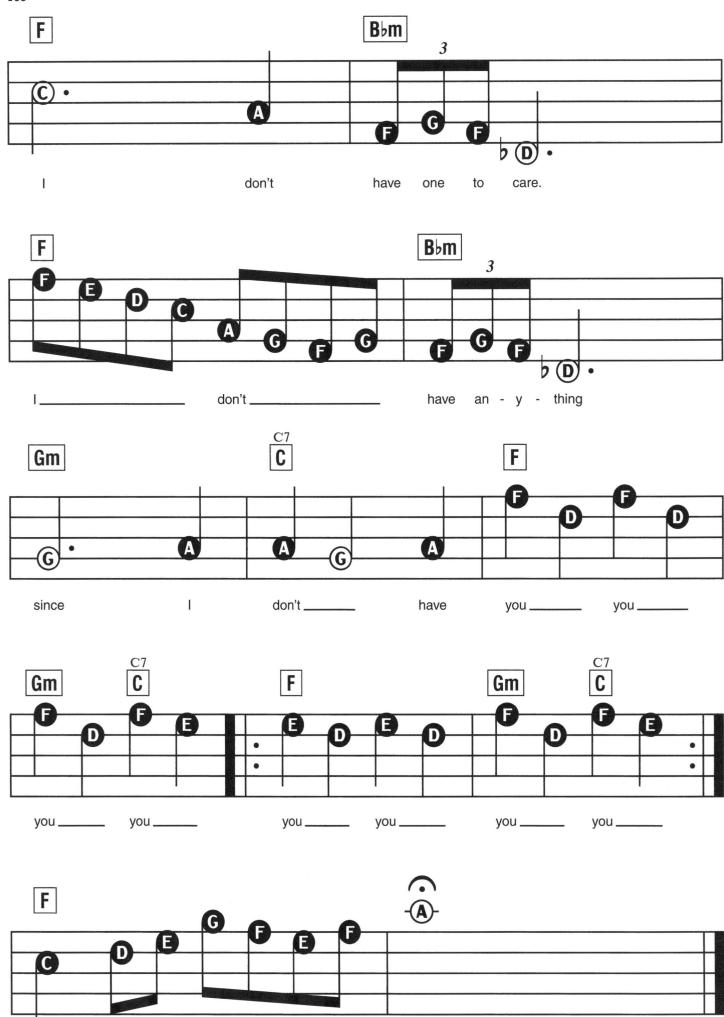

Sincerely

Registration 8
Rhythm: Ballad or Broadway

Words and Music by Alan Freed
and Harvey Fuqua

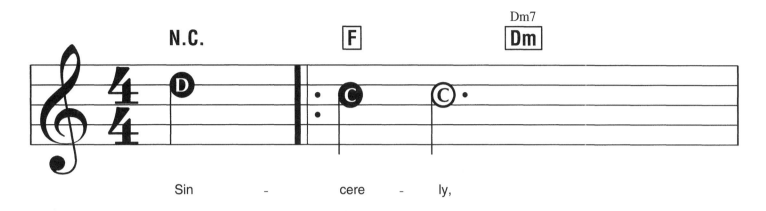

Sin - cere - ly,

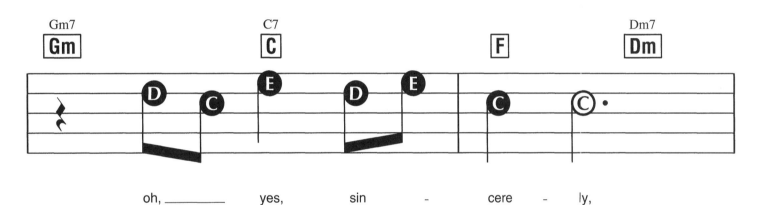

oh, _____ yes, sin - cere - ly,

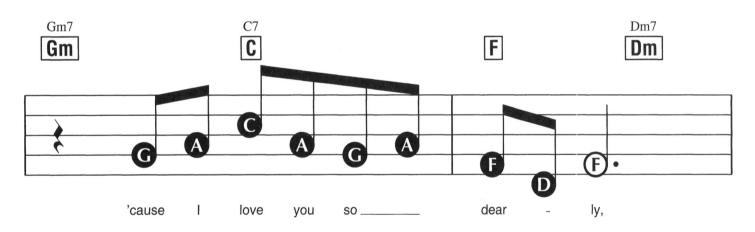

'cause I love you so _____ dear - ly,

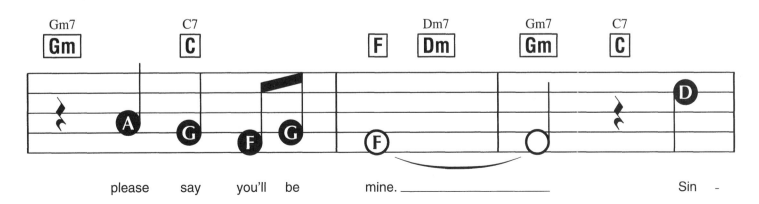

please say you'll be mine. _____ Sin -

192

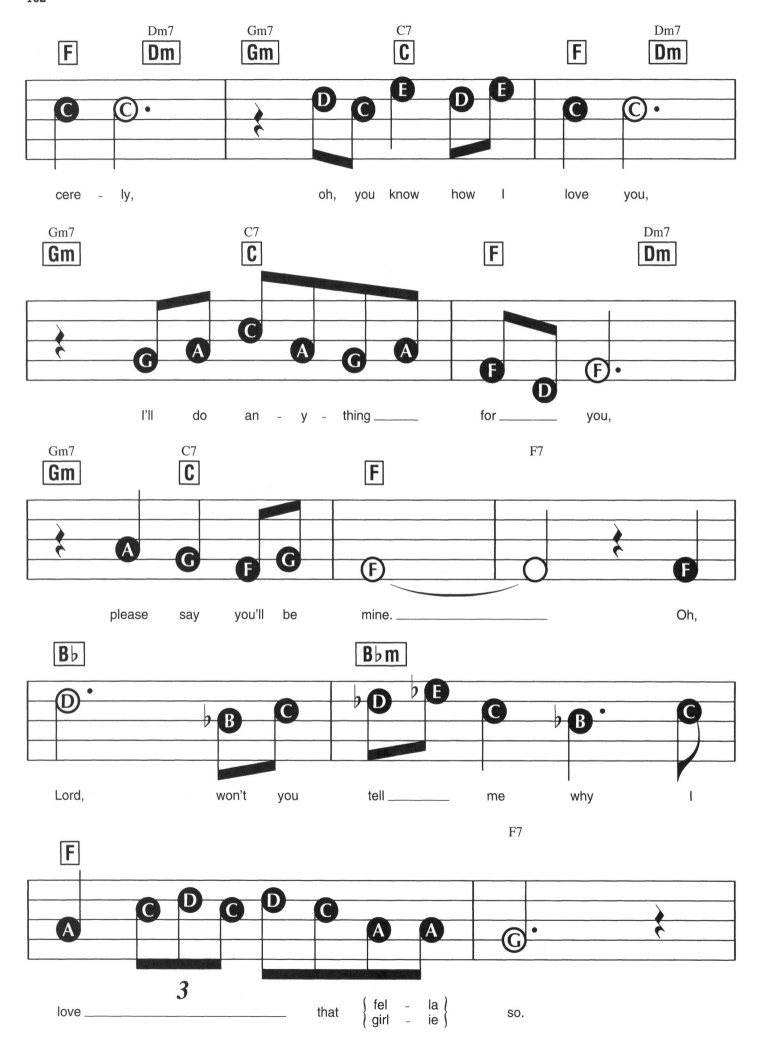

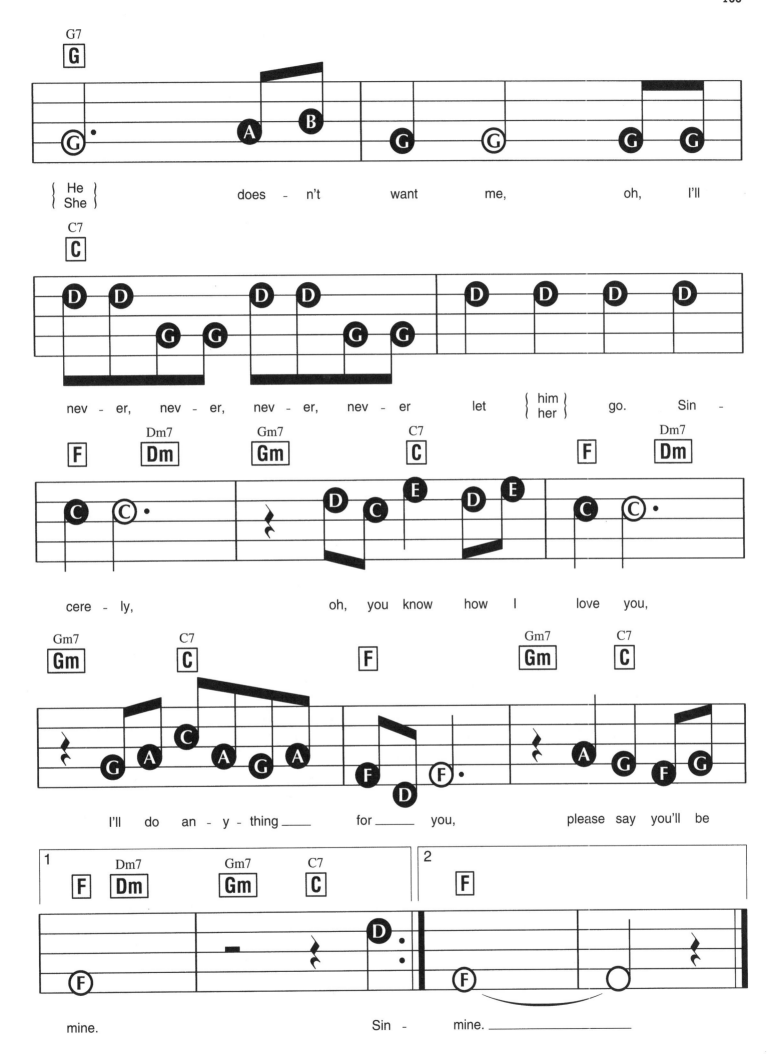

Singing the Blues

Registration 9
Rhythm: Shuffle

Words and Music by
Melvin Endsley

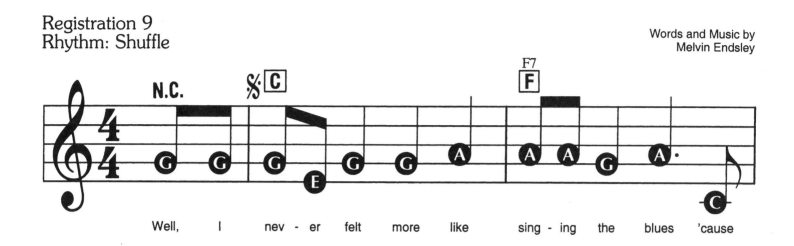

Well, I nev - er felt more like sing - ing the blues 'cause

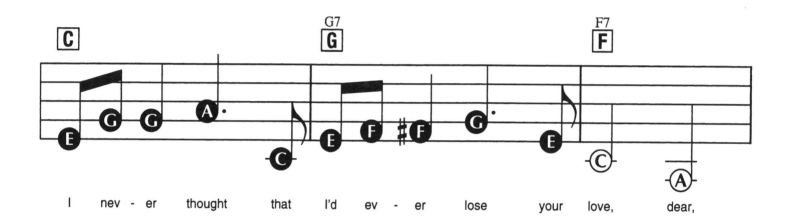

I nev - er thought that I'd ev - er lose your love, dear,

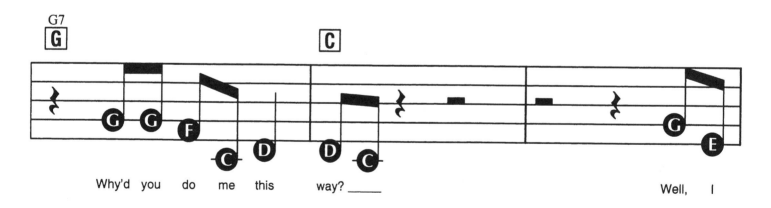

Why'd you do me this way? _____ Well, I

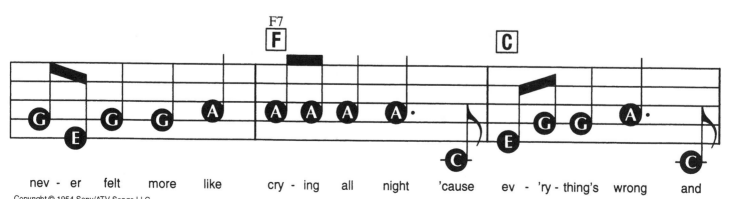

nev - er felt more like cry - ing all night 'cause ev - 'ry - thing's wrong and

195

Stagger Lee

Registration 8
Rhythm: Rock or Swing

Words and Music by Lloyd Price
and Harold Logan

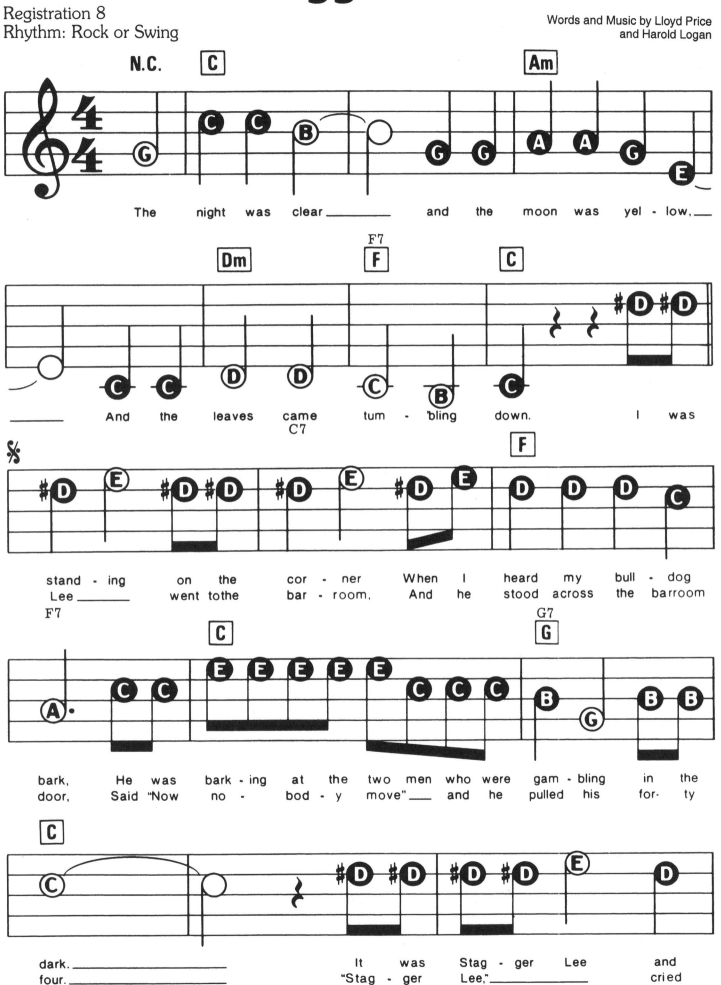

198

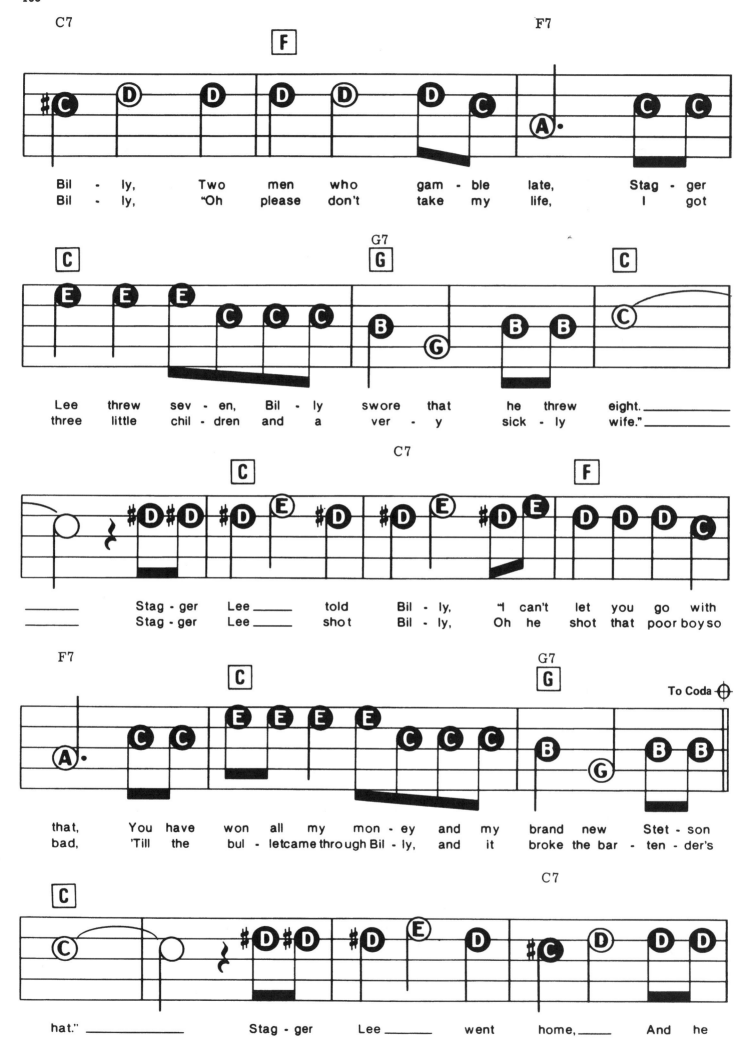

199

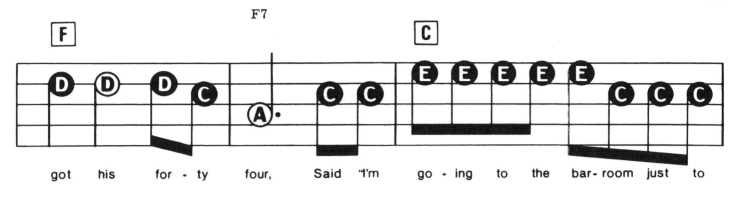

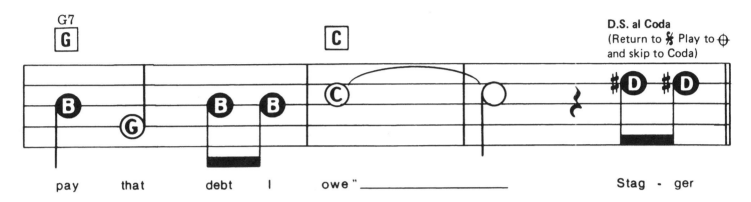

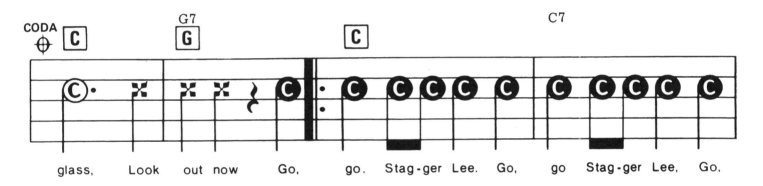

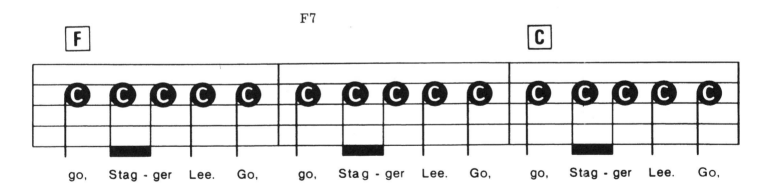

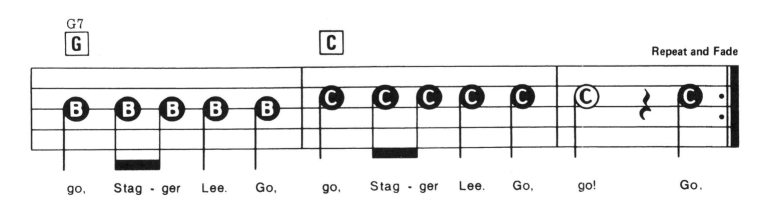

Sixteen Candles

Registration 8
Rhythm: Slow Rock or Ballad

Words and Music by Luther Dixon
and Allyson R. Khent

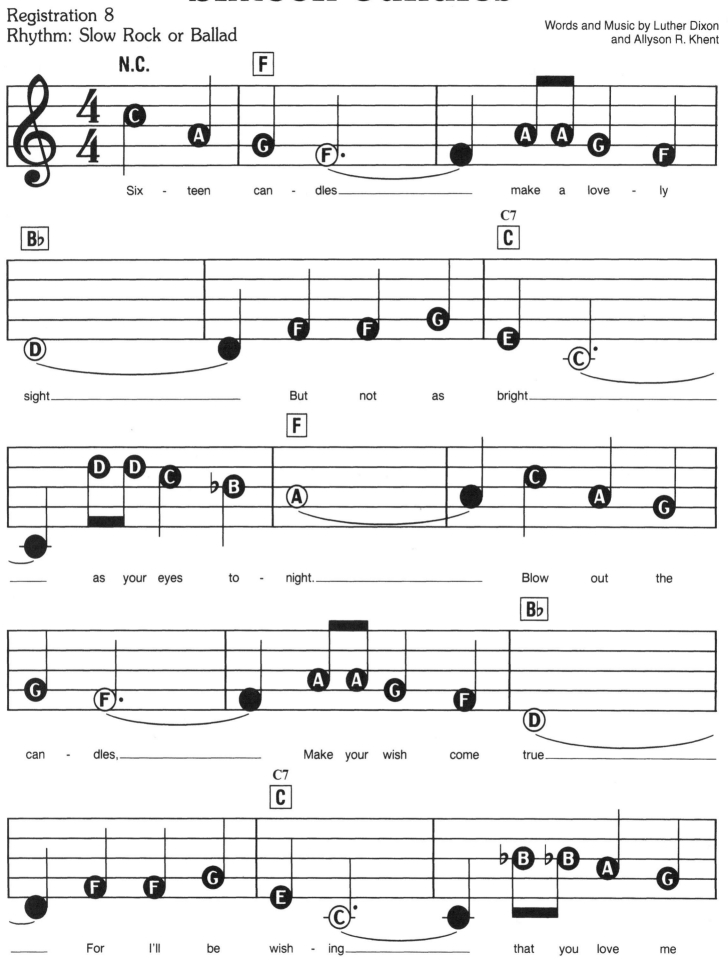

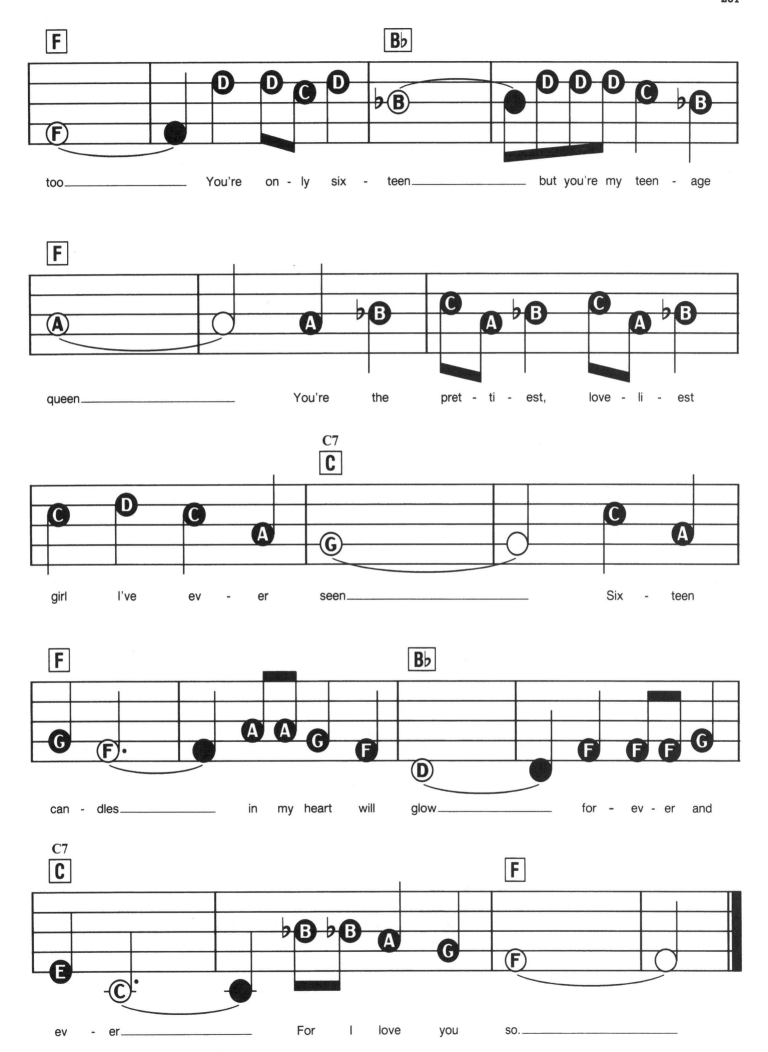

Sixteen Tons

Registration 9
Rhythm: Rock

Words and Music by
Merle Travis

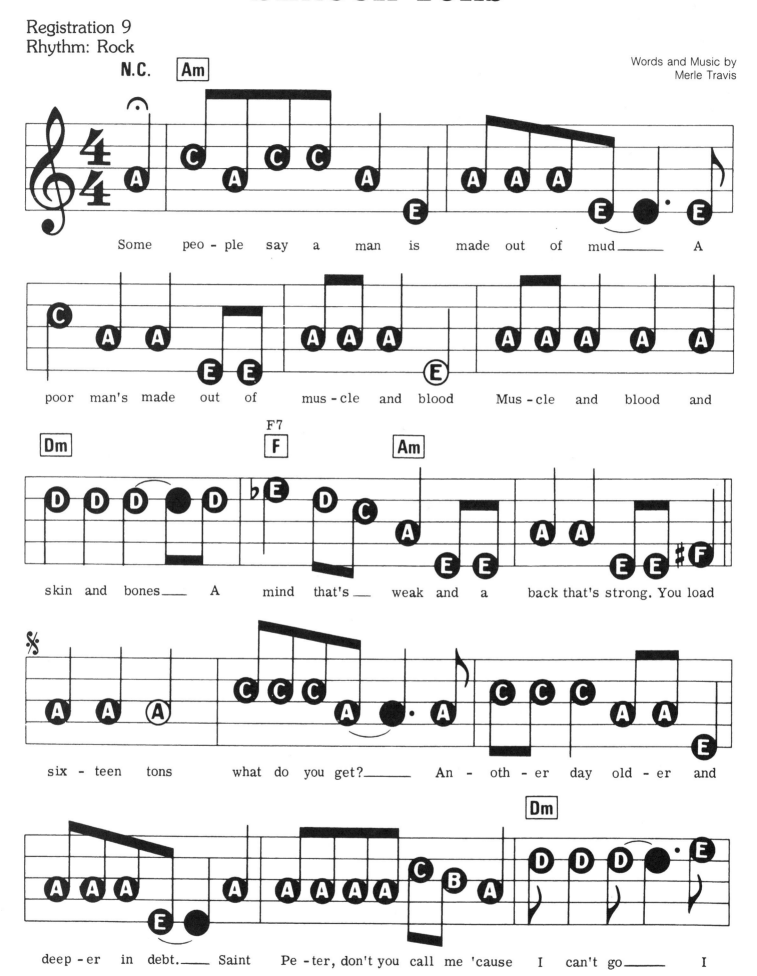

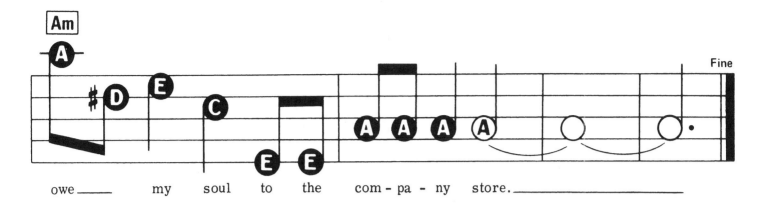

owe____ my soul to the com-pa-ny store._____

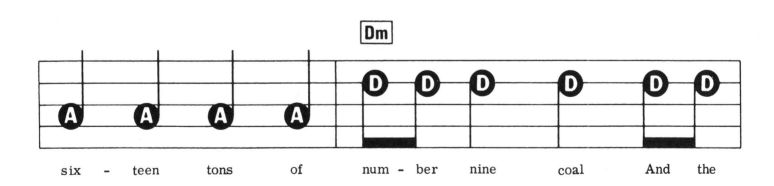

I was born____ one morn-in' when the sun did-n't shine____ I

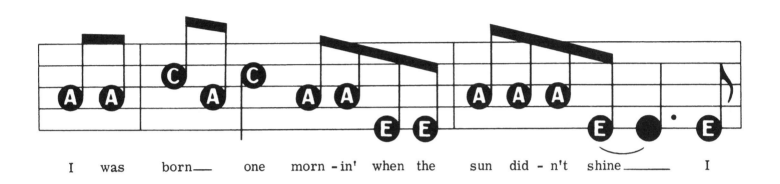

picked up my shov-el and I walked to the mine, I load-ed

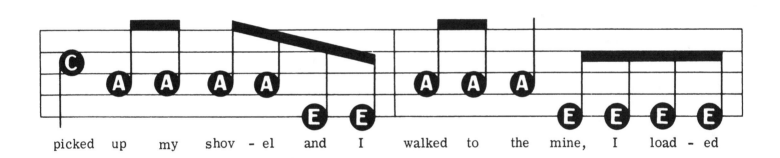

six-teen tons of num-ber nine coal And the

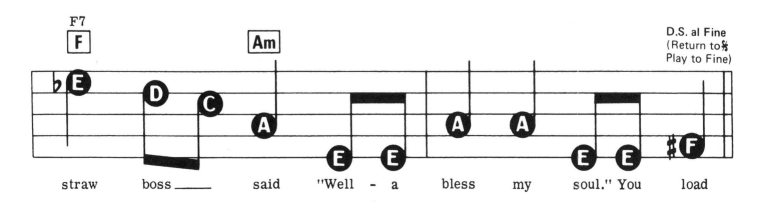

straw boss____ said "Well-a bless my soul." You load

Smoke Gets in Your Eyes
from ROBERTA

Registration 10
Rhythm: Ballad or Swing

Words by Otto Harbach
Music by Jerome Kern

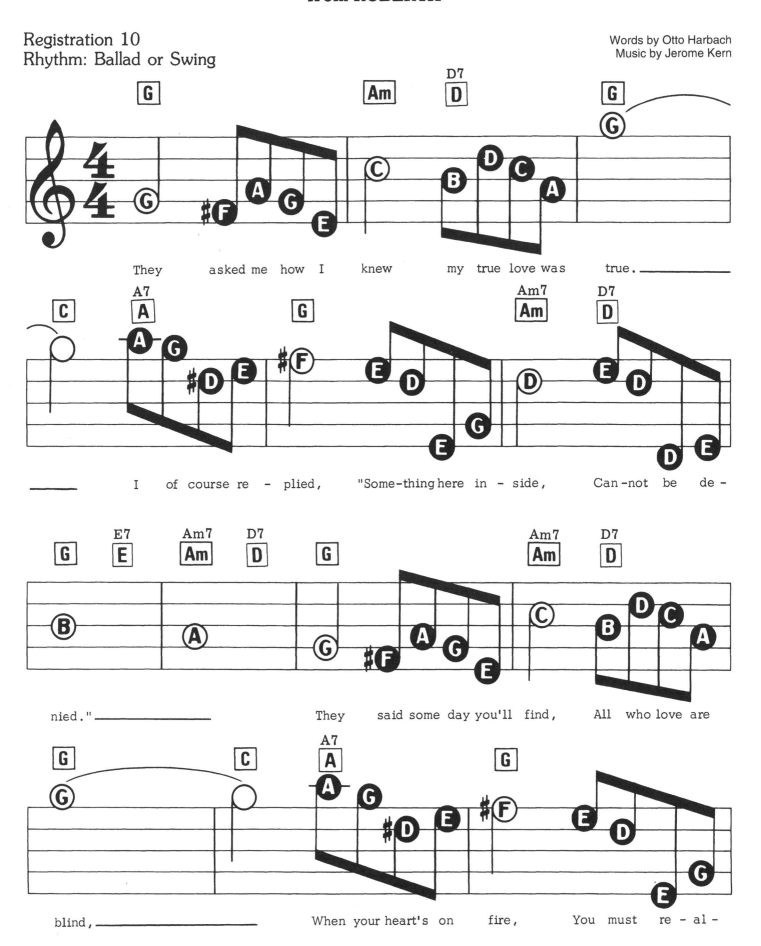

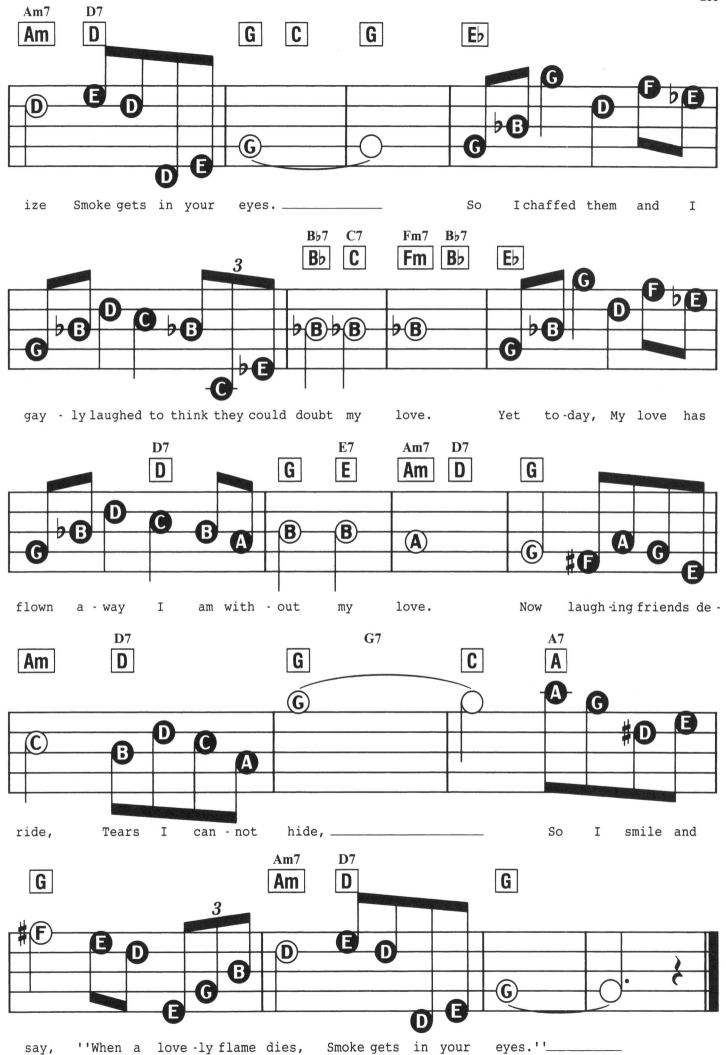

The Stroll

Registration 2
Rhythm: Rock

Words and Music by Clyde Otis
and Nancy Lee

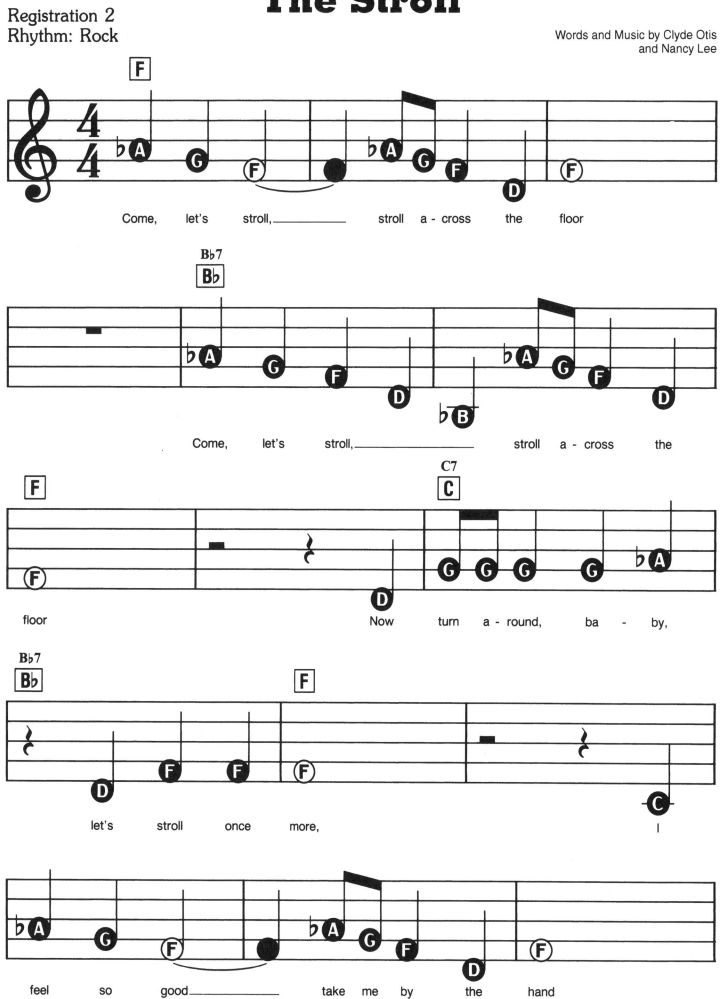

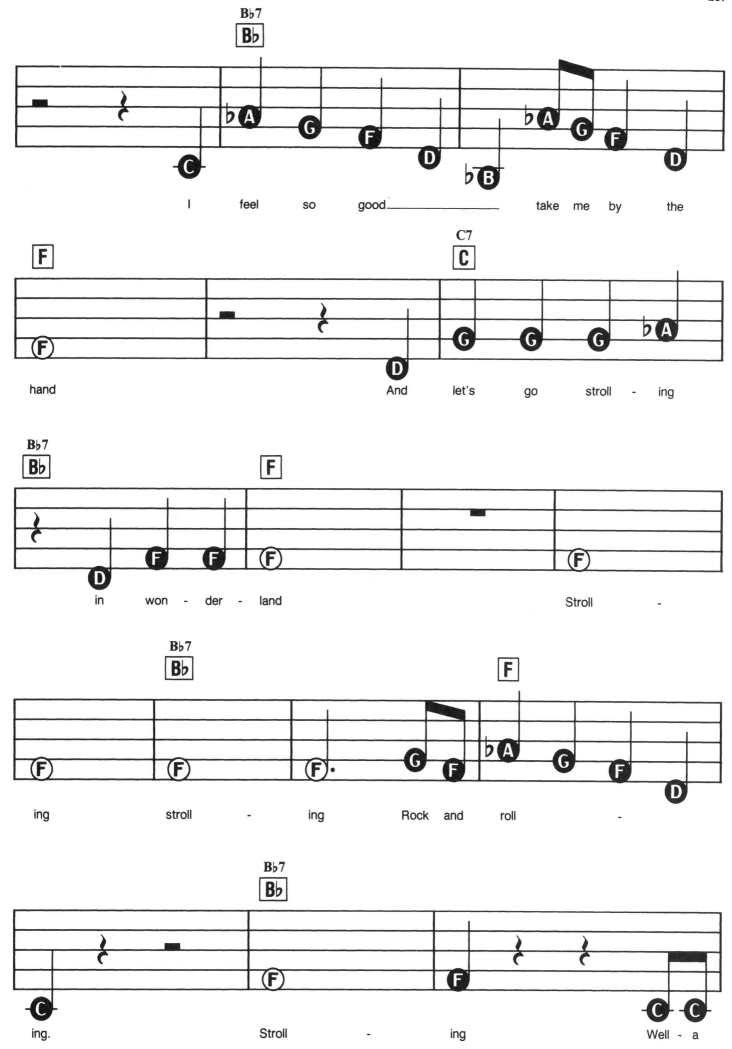

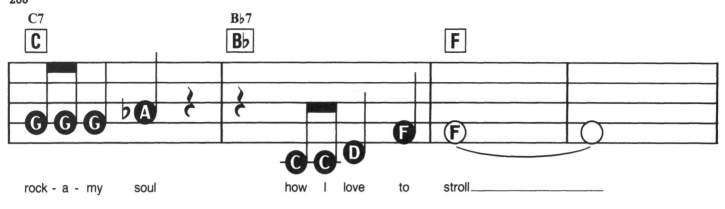

rock - a - my soul   how I love to stroll_____

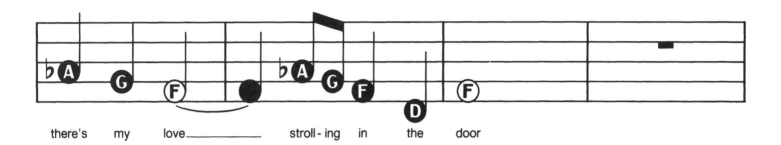

there's   my   love_____   stroll - ing   in   the   door

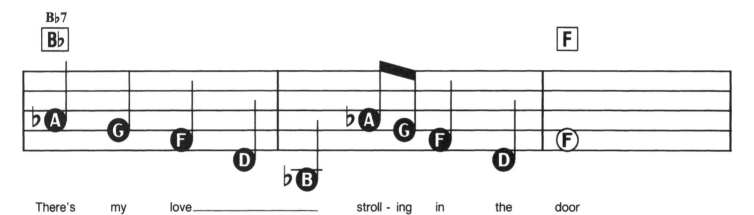

There's   my   love_____   stroll - ing   in   the   door

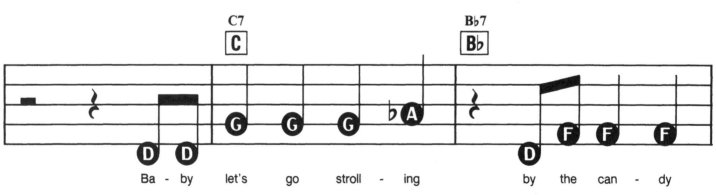

Ba - by   let's   go   stroll - ing   by   the   can - dy

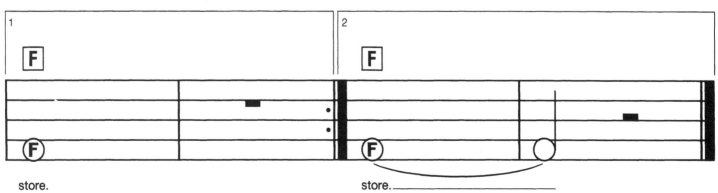

store.   store._____

Tequila

Registration 8
Rhythm: Latin Rock or Rock

By Chuck Rio

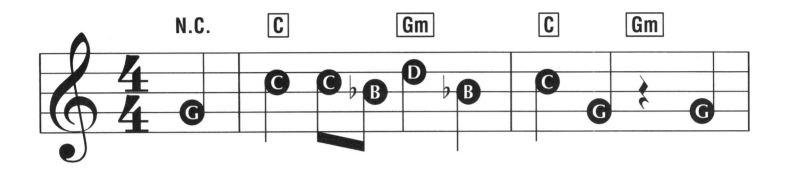

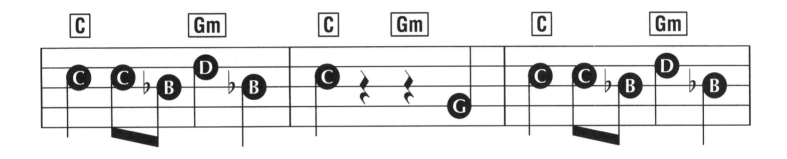

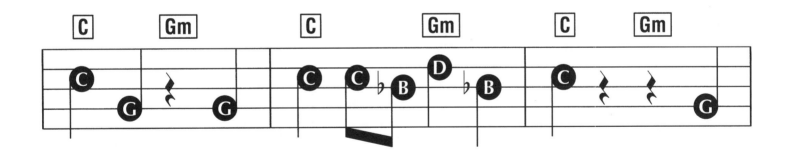

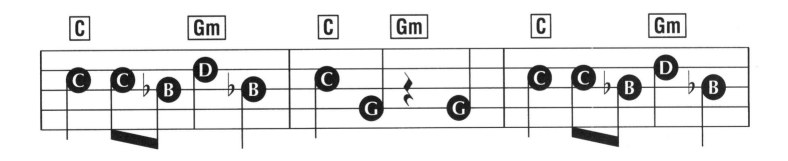

210

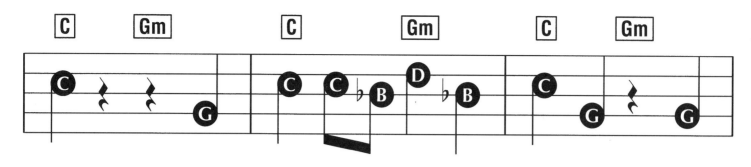

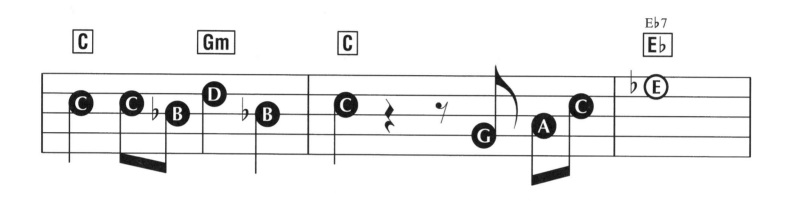

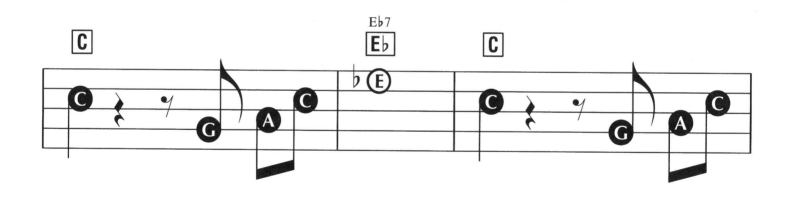

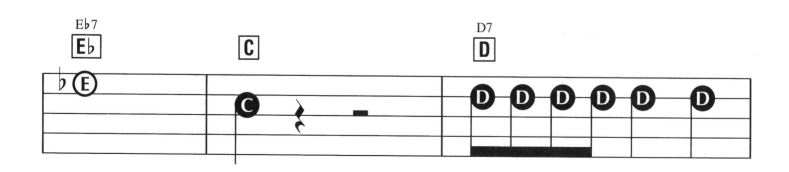

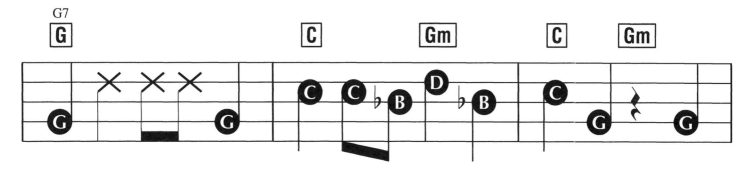

(Spoken:) Te - qui - la!

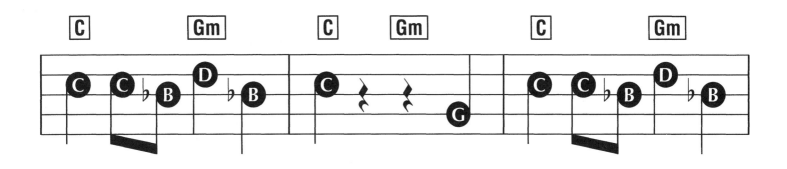

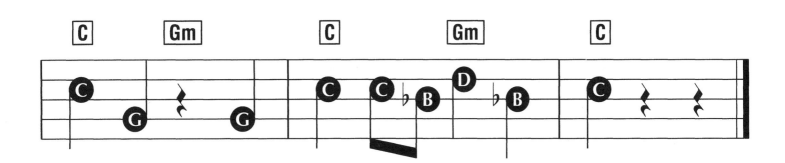

Tammy

Registration 3
Rhythm: Waltz

Words and Music by Jay Livingston
and Ray Evans

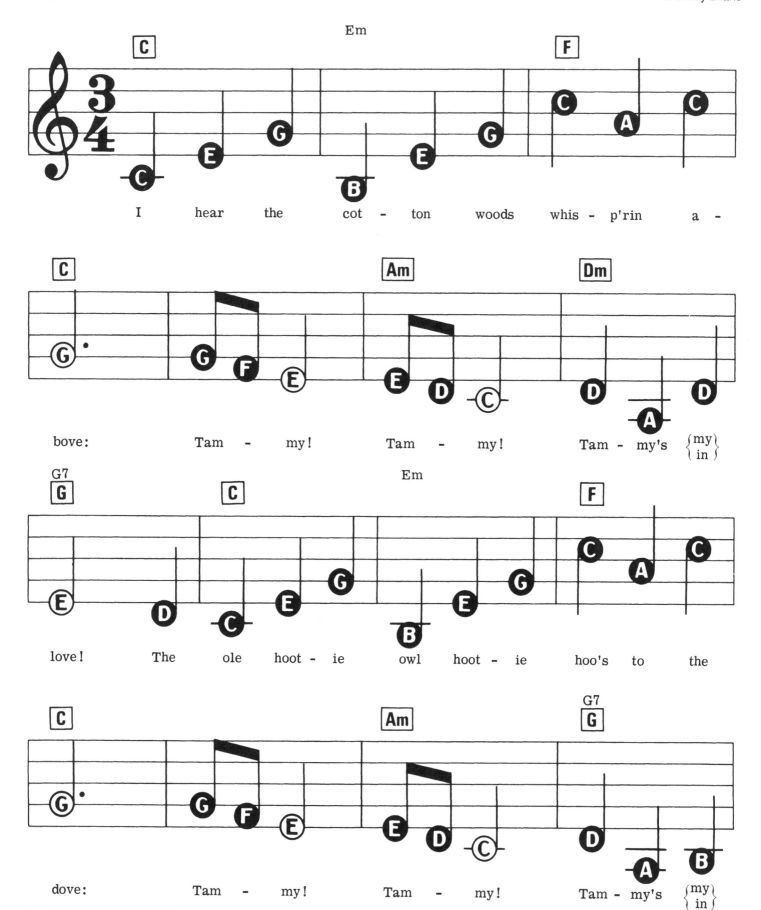

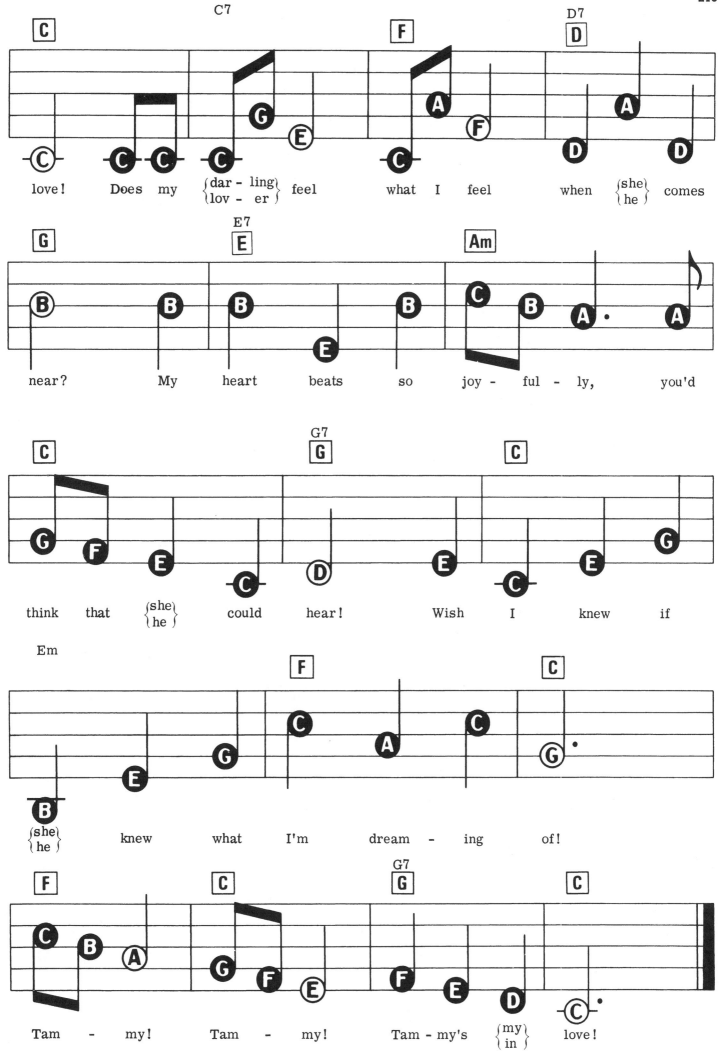

Teach Me Tonight

Registration 8
Rhythm: Fox Trot or Swing

Words by Sammy Cahn
Music by Gene DePaul

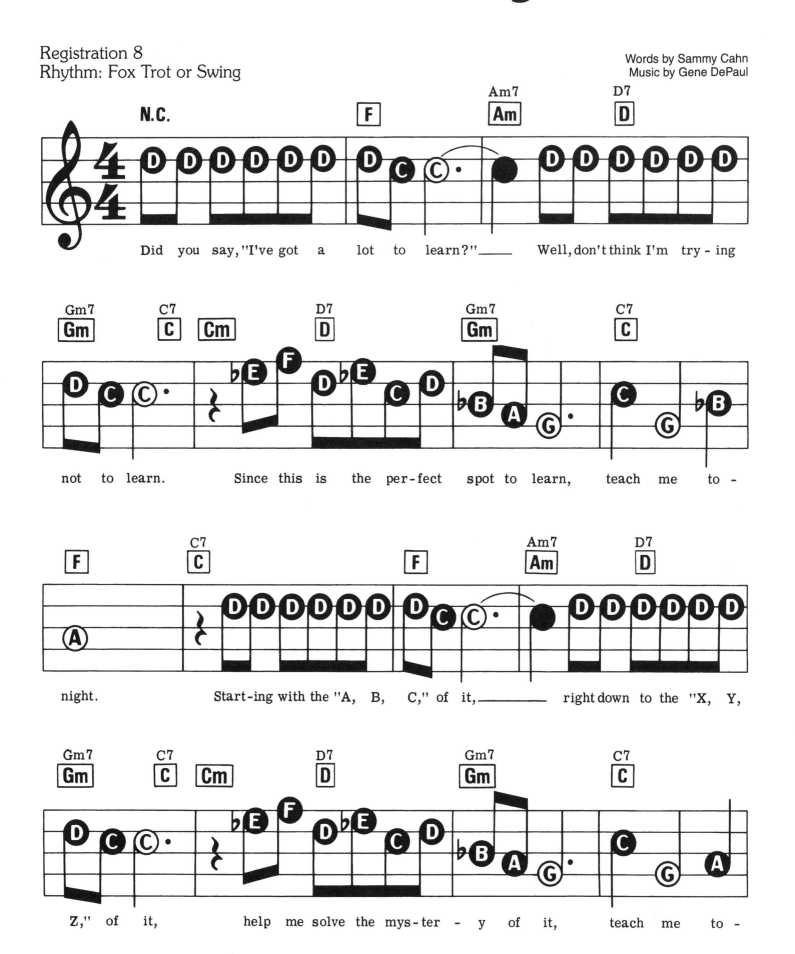

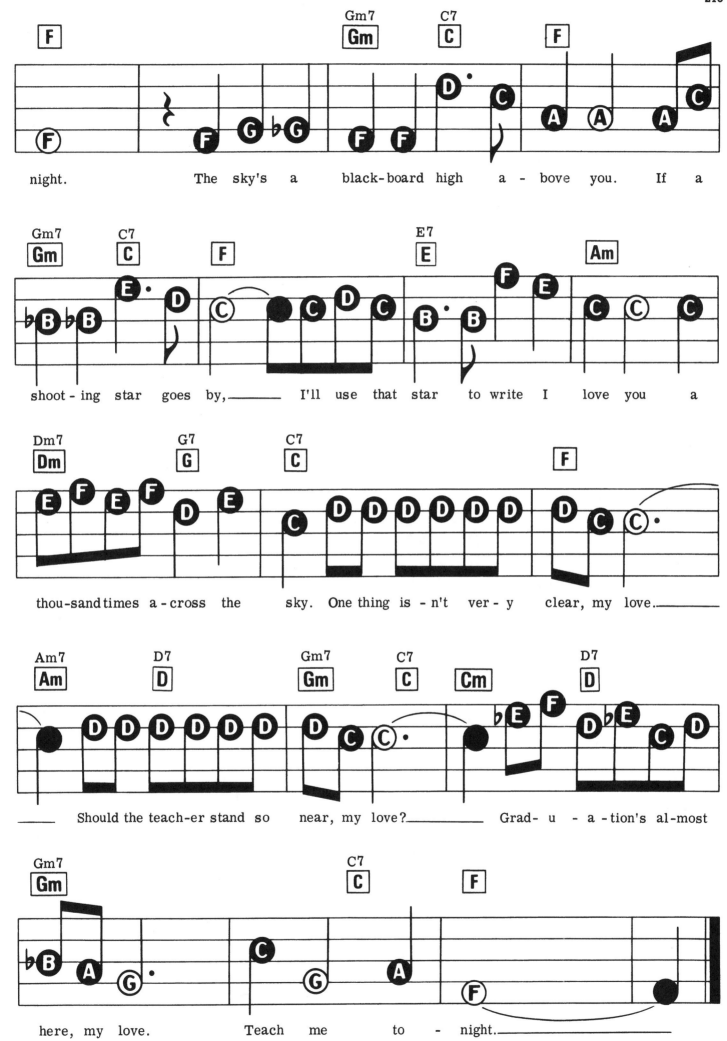

Tears on My Pillow

Registration 9
Rhythm: Slow Rock or Shuffle

Words and Music by Sylvester Bradford
and Al Lewis

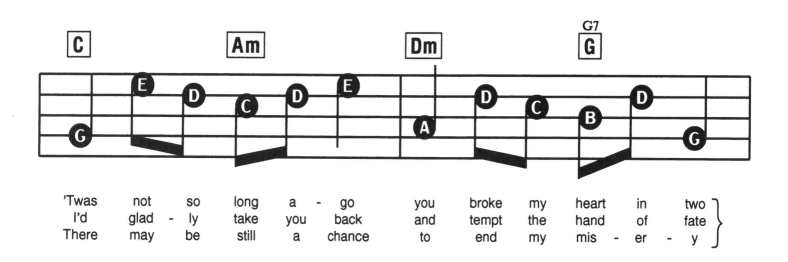

You   don't   re - mem - ber   me   but   I   re - mem - ber   you
If   we   could   start   a - new   I   would - n't   hes - i - tate
Be - fore   you   go   a - way   my   dar - ling   think   of   me

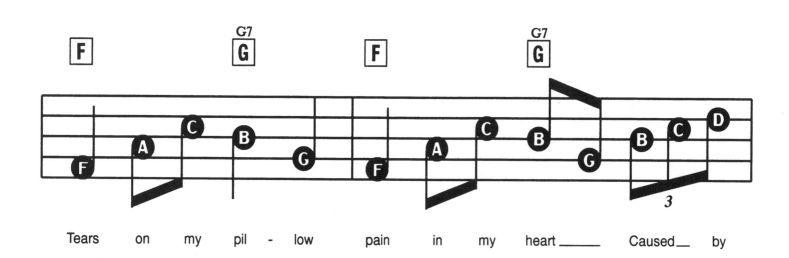

'Twas   not   so   long   a - go   you   broke   my   heart   in   two
I'd   glad - ly   take   you   back   and   tempt   the   hand   of   fate
There   may   be   still   a   chance   to   end   my   mis - er - y

Tears   on   my   pil - low   pain   in   my   heart _____ Caused ___ by

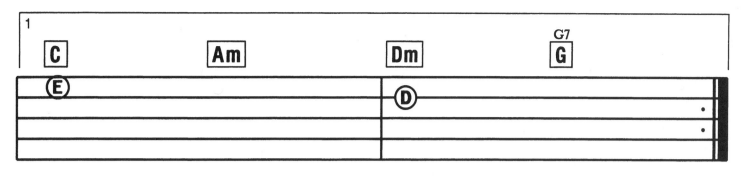

you.

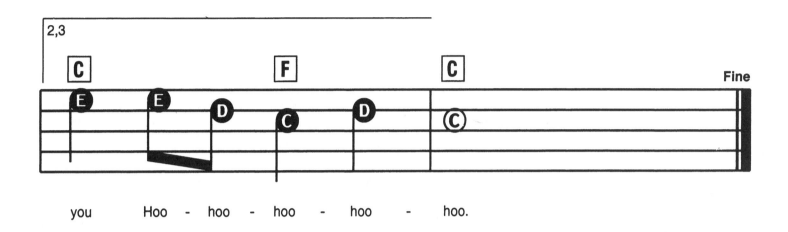

you Hoo - hoo - hoo - hoo - hoo.

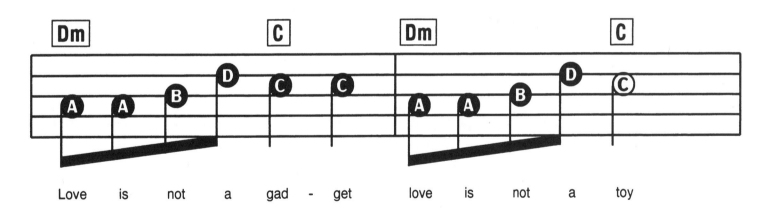

Love is not a gad - get love is not a toy

D.C. al Fine
(Return to beginning
Play to Fine)

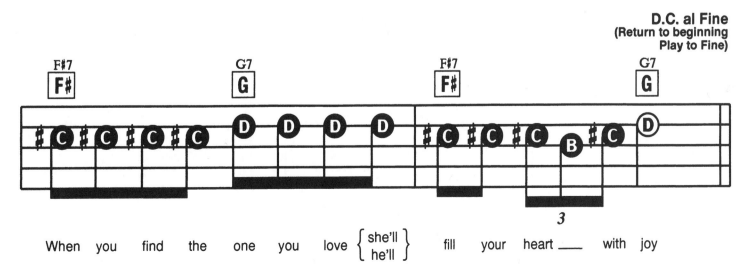

When you find the one you love { she'll / he'll } fill your heart ___ with joy

(Let Me Be Your)
Teddy Bear

Registration 1
Rhythm: Rock

Words and Music by Kal Mann
and Bernie Lowe

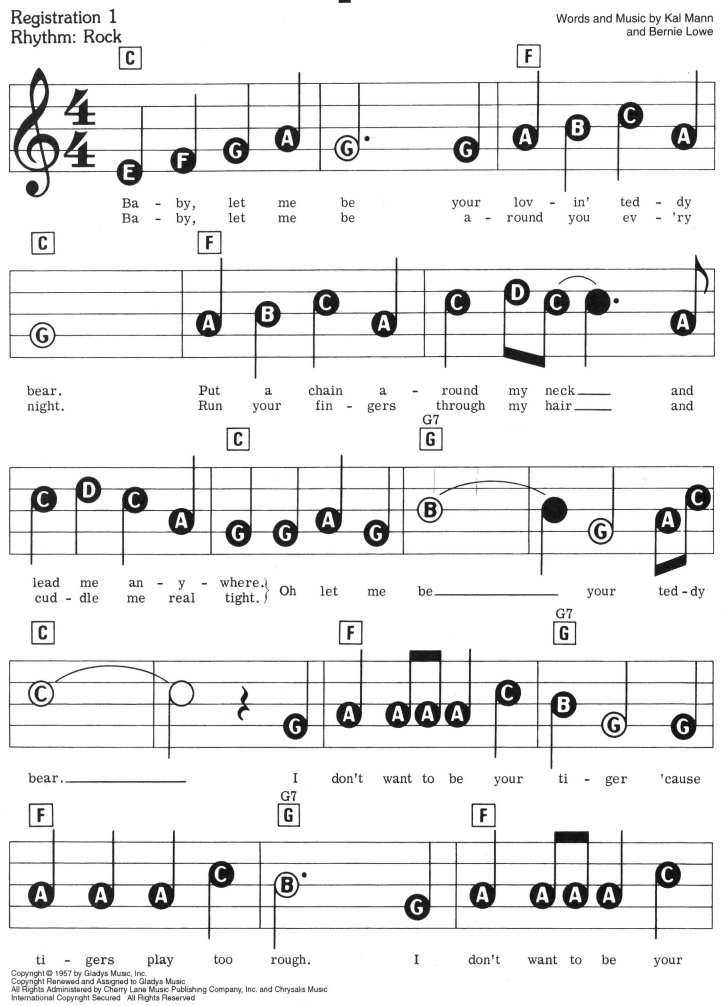

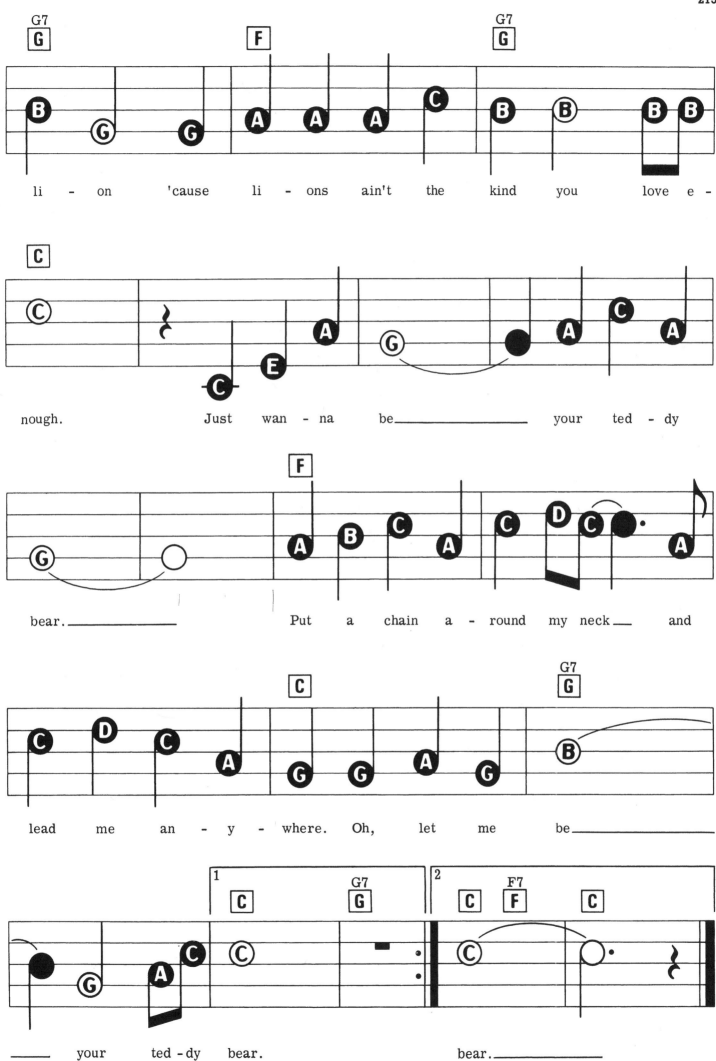

Tennessee Waltz

Registration 4
Rhythm: Waltz

Words and Music by Redd Stewart
and Pee Wee King

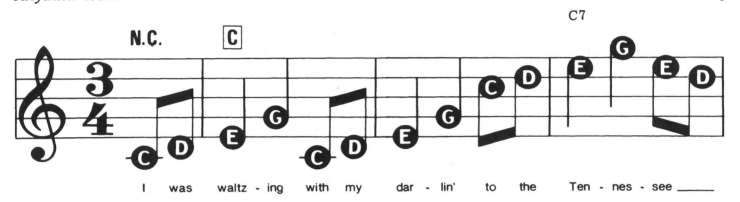

I was waltz - ing with my dar - lin' to the Ten - nes - see _____

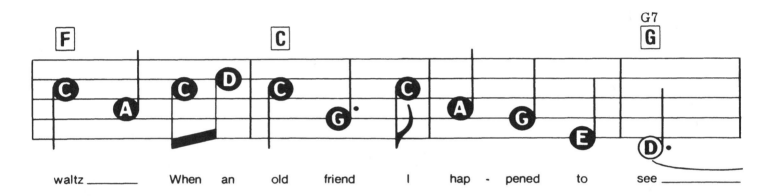

waltz _____ When an old friend I hap - pened to see _____

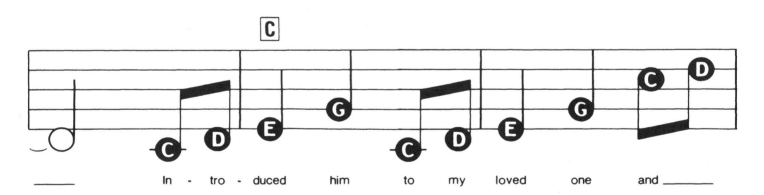

_____ In - tro - duced him to my loved one and _____

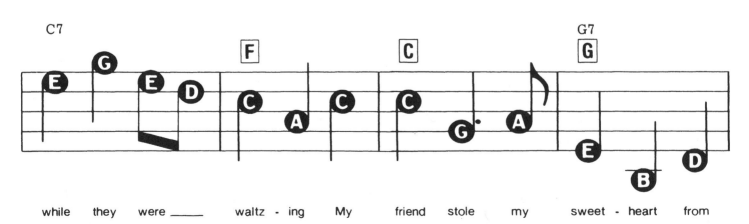

while they were _____ waltz - ing My friend stole my sweet - heart from

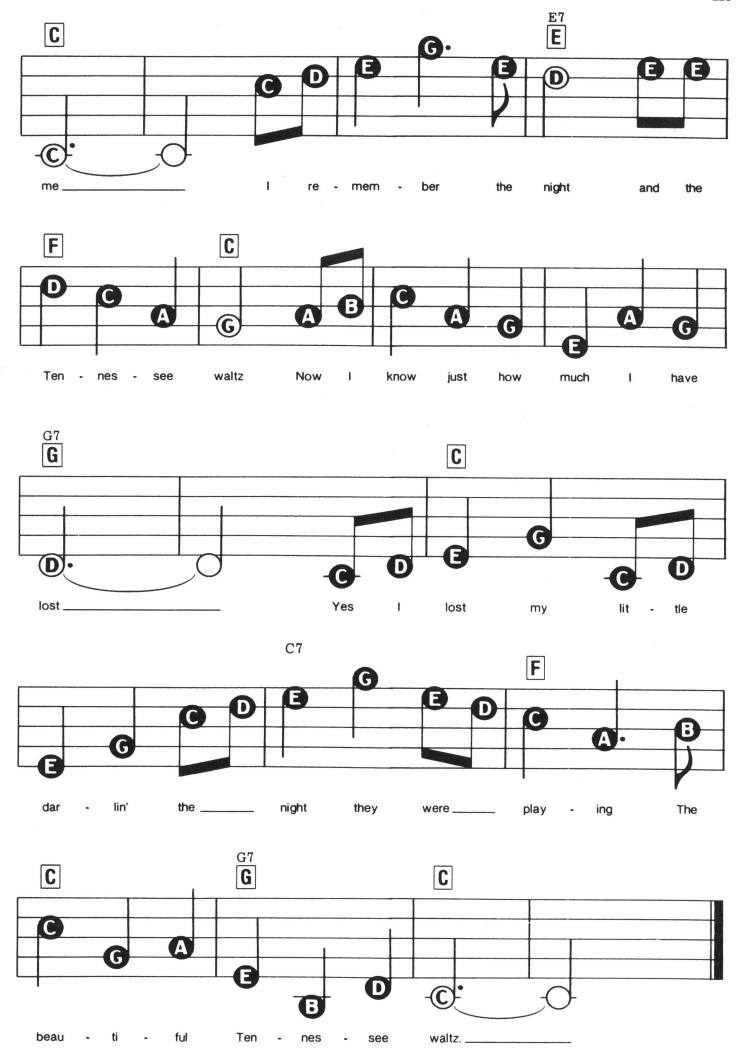

That's Amoré
(That's Love)
from the Paramount Picture THE CADDY

Registration 3
Rhythm: Waltz

Words by Jack Brooks
Music by Harry Warren

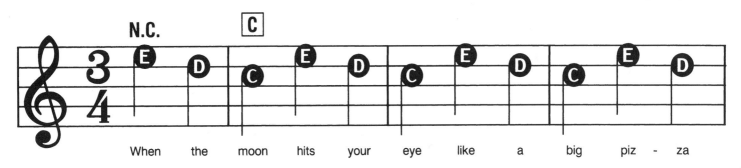

When the moon hits your eye like a big piz - za

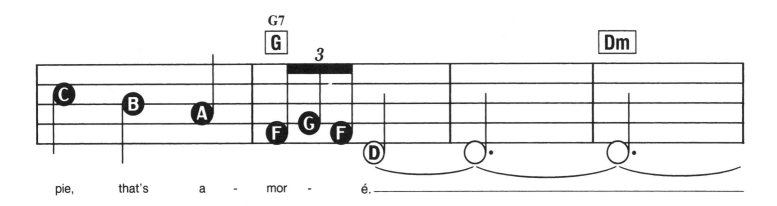

pie, that's a - mor - é. _____

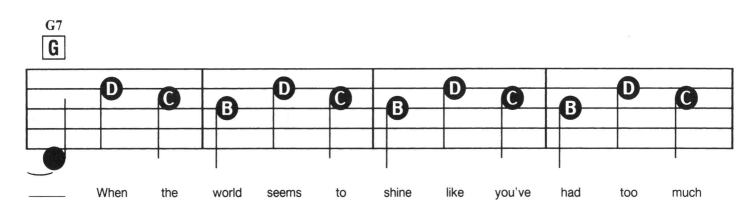

_____ When the world seems to shine like you've had too much

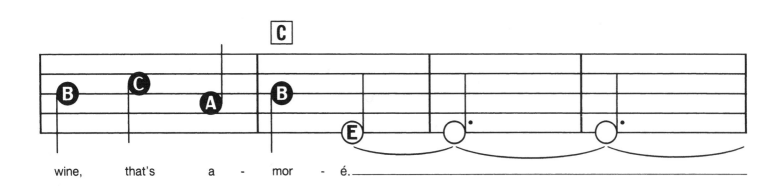

wine, that's a - mor - é. _____

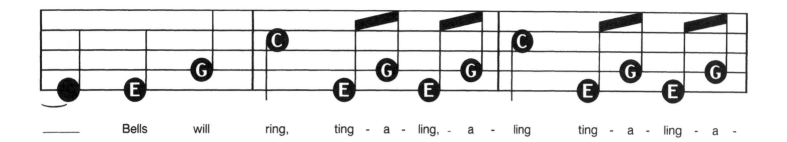

Bells will ring, ting - a - ling, - a - ling ting - a - ling - a -

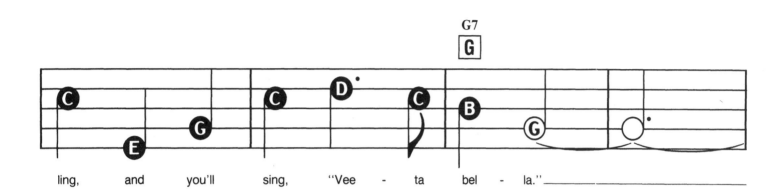

ling, and you'll sing, "Vee - ta bel - la." _____

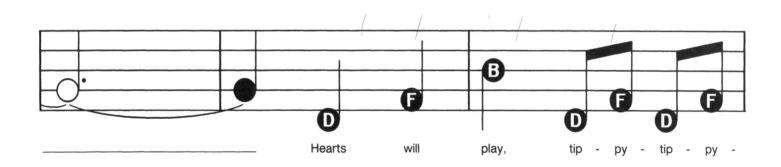

_____ Hearts will play, tip - py - tip - py -

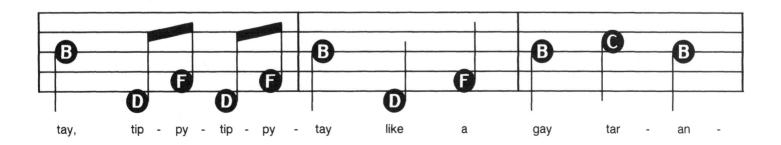

tay, tip - py - tip - py - tay like a gay tar - an -

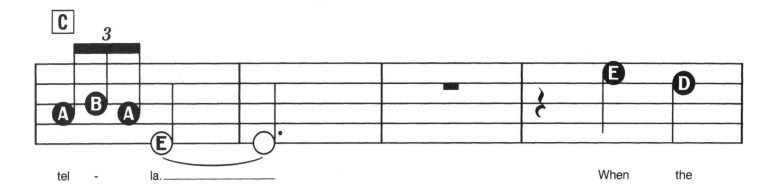

tel - la._____ When the

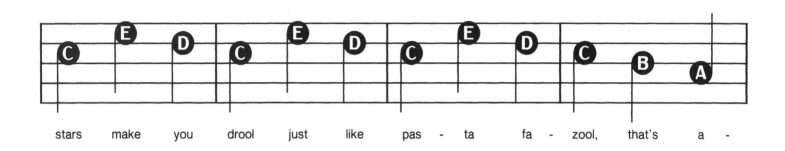

stars make you drool just like pas - ta fa - zool, that's a -

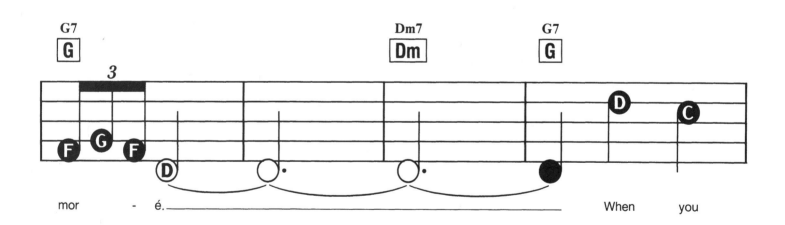

mor - é._____ When you

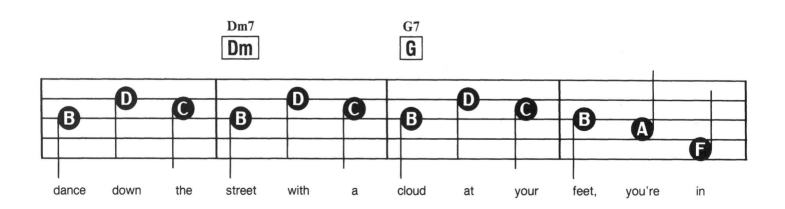

dance down the street with a cloud at your feet, you're in

225

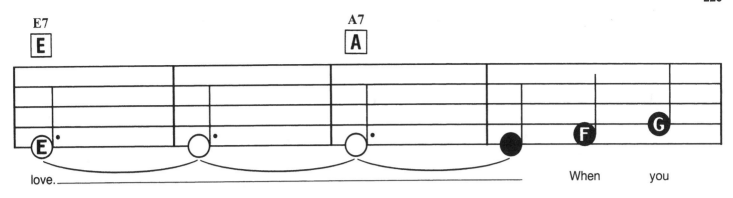

love._____ When you

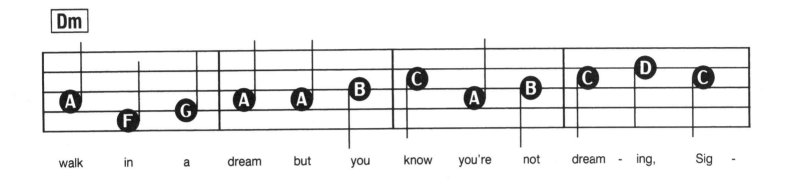

walk in a dream but you know you're not dream - ing, Sig -

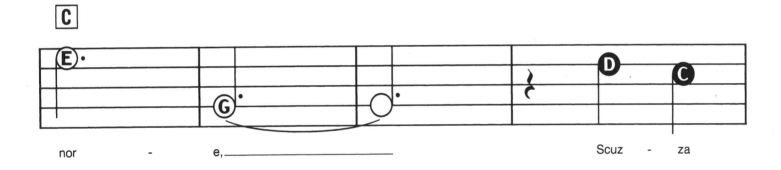

nor - e,_____ Scuz - za

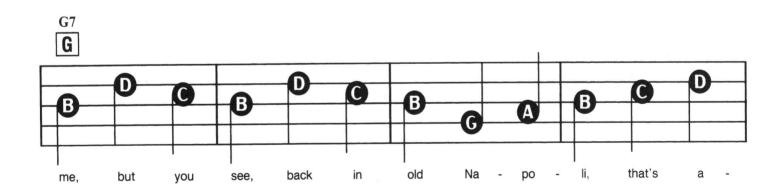

me, but you see, back in old Na - po - li, that's a -

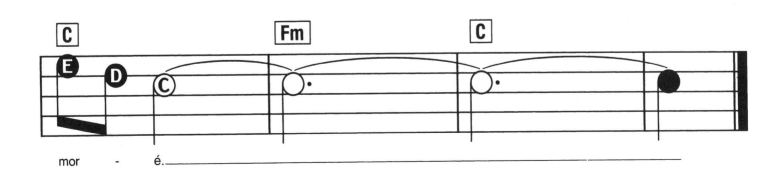

mor - é._____

There Goes My Baby

Registration 2
Rhythm: Rock

Words and Music by Jerry Leiber, Mike Stoller,
Ben E. Nelson, Lover Patterson and George Treadwell

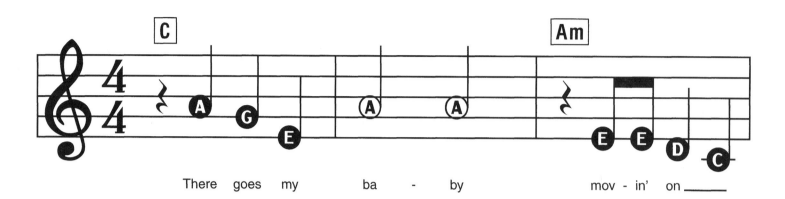

There goes my ba - by mov - in' on ____

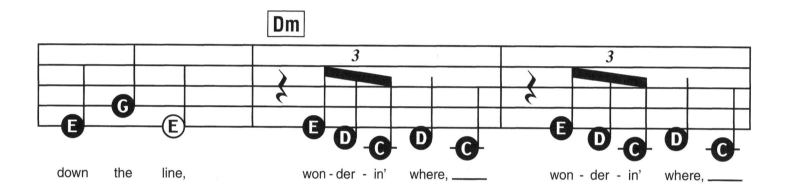

down the line, won - der - in' where, ____ won - der - in' where, ____

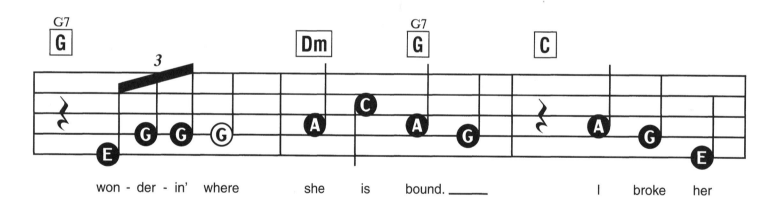

won - der - in' where she is bound. ____ I broke her

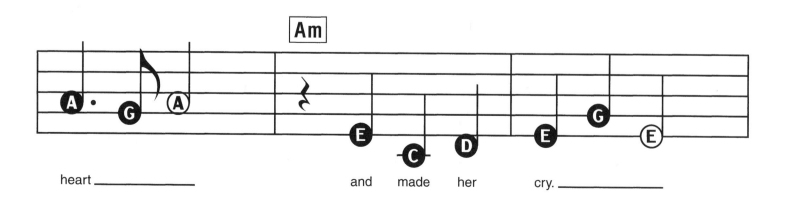

heart ____ and made her cry. ____

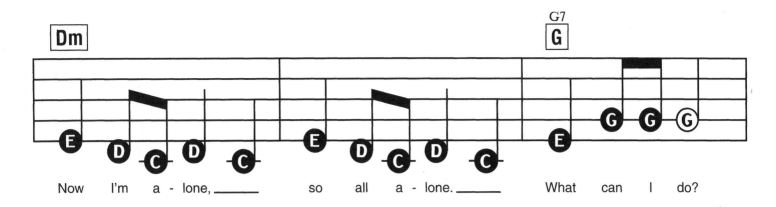

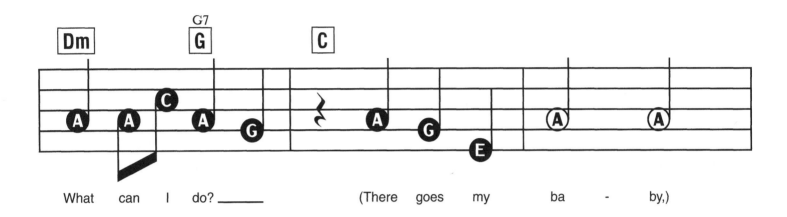

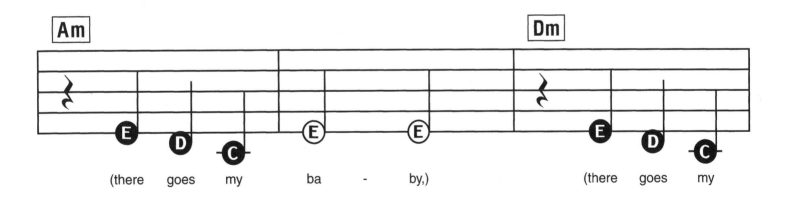

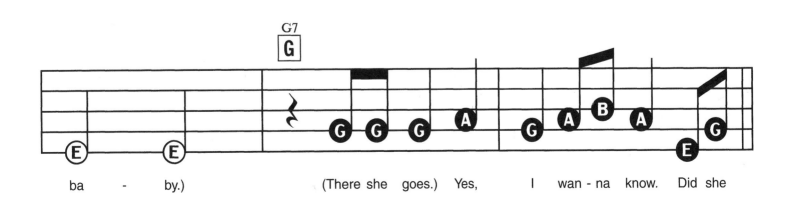

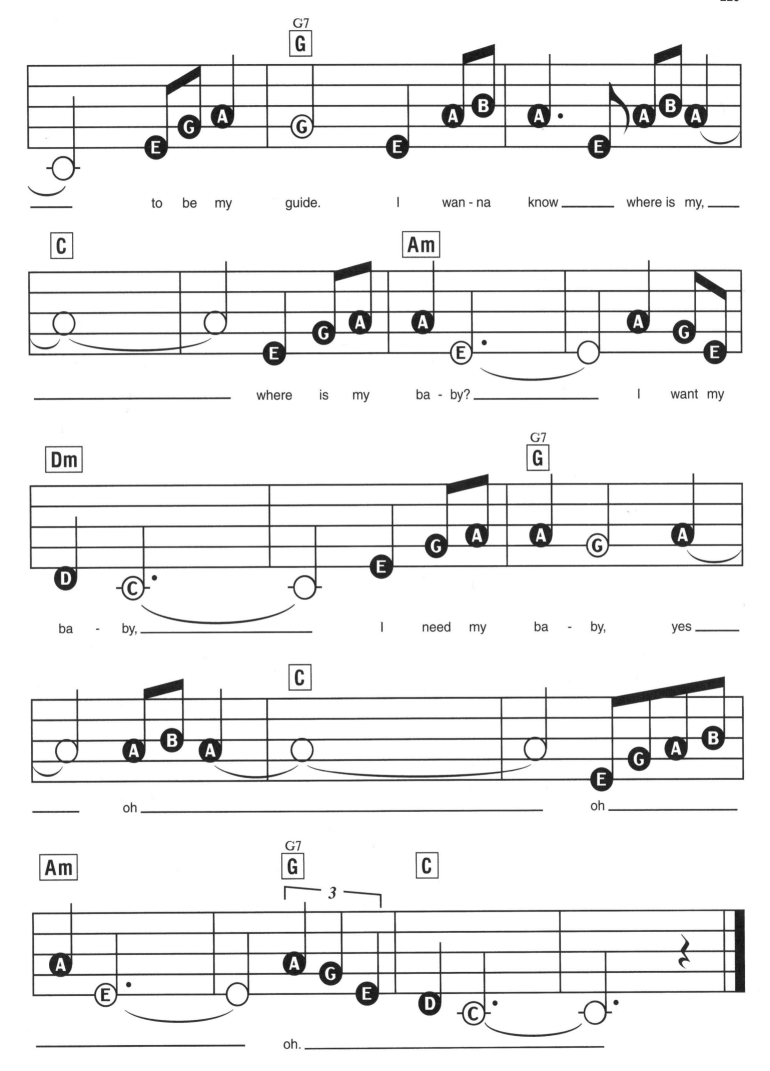

Tom Dooley

Registration 8
Rhythm: Ballad or Slow Rock

Words and Music Collected, Adapted and Arranged by Frank Warner,
John A. Lomax and Alan Lomax
From the singing of Frank Proffitt

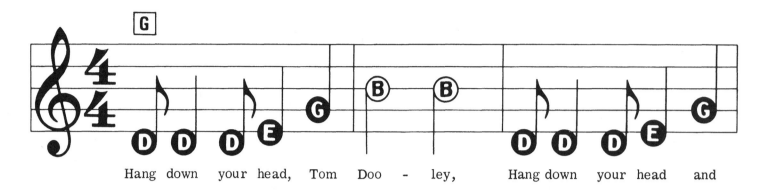

Hang down your head, Tom Doo - ley, Hang down your head and

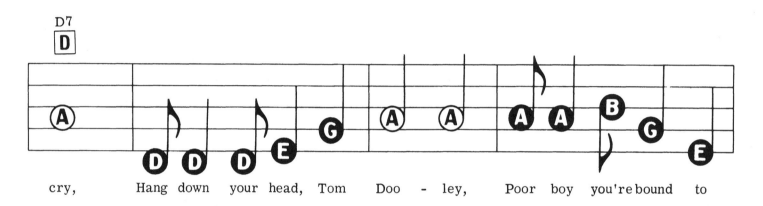

cry, Hang down your head, Tom Doo - ley, Poor boy you're bound to

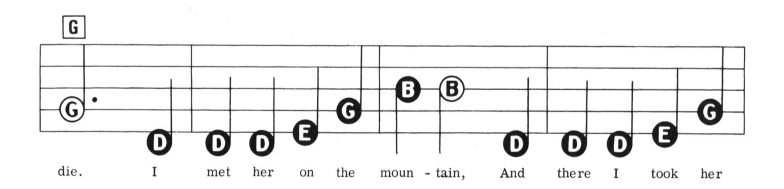

die. I met her on the moun - tain, And there I took her

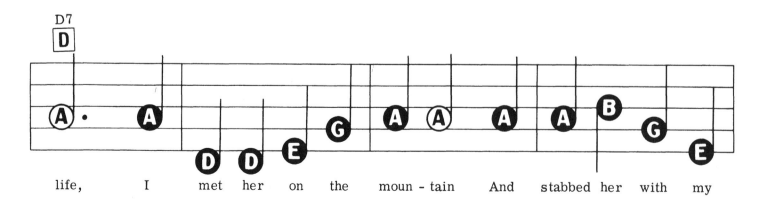

life, I met her on the moun - tain And stabbed her with my

Turn Me Loose

Registration 7
Rhythm: Rock

Words and Music by Doc Pomus
and Mort Shuman

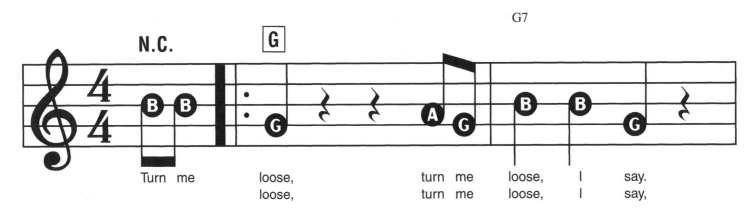

Turn me loose, turn me loose, I say.
loose, turn me loose, I say,

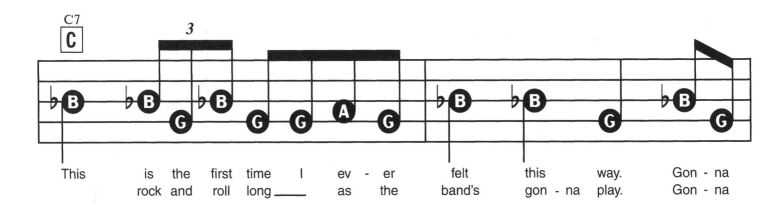

This is the first time I ev - er felt this way. Gon - na
rock and roll long ___ as the band's gon - na play. Gon - na

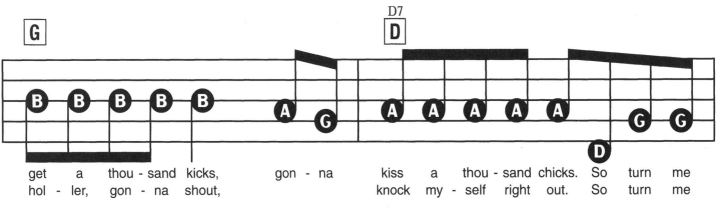

get a thou - sand kicks, gon - na kiss a thou - sand chicks. So turn me
hol - ler, gon - na shout, knock my - self right out. So turn me

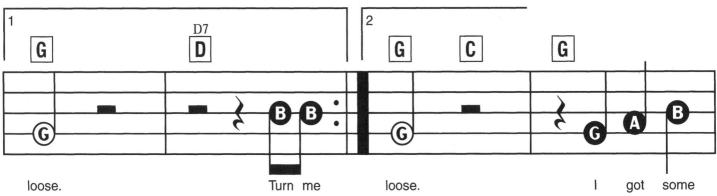

loose.
Turn me loose.
I got some

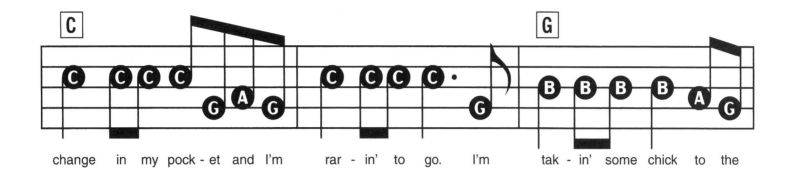

change in my pock-et and I'm rar-in' to go. I'm tak-in' some chick to the

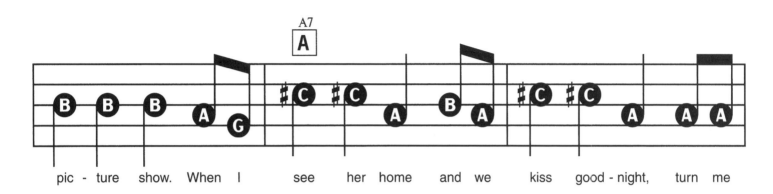

pic-ture show. When I see her home and we kiss good-night, turn me

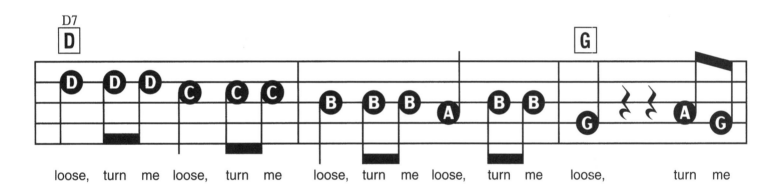

loose, turn me loose, turn me loose, turn me loose, turn me loose, turn me

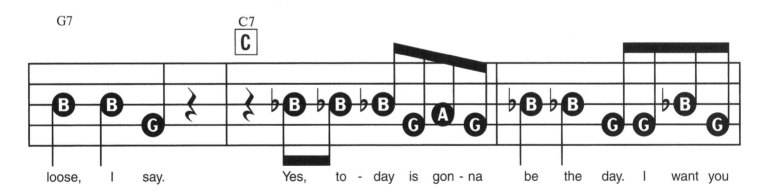

loose, I say. Yes, to-day is gon-na be the day. I want you

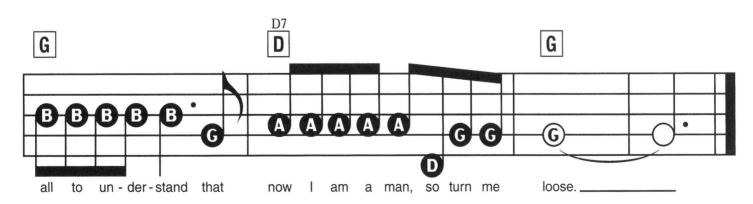

all to un-der-stand that now I am a man, so turn me loose. _____

Twilight Time

Lyric by Buck Ram
Music by Morty Nevins and Al Nevins

Registration 9
Rhythm: Slow Rock or Shuffle

The Walk

Registration 8
Rhythm: Rock

Words and Music by
Jimmy McCracklin

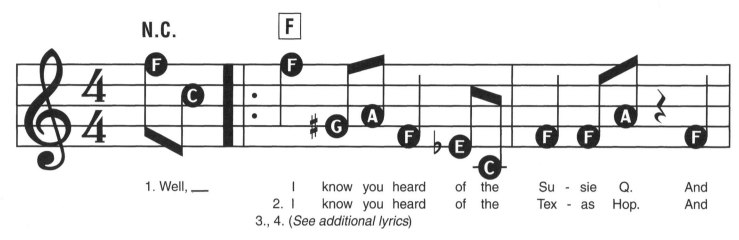

1. Well, ___ I know you heard of the Su - sie Q. And
2. I know you heard of the Tex - as Hop. And
3., 4. (*See additional lyrics*)

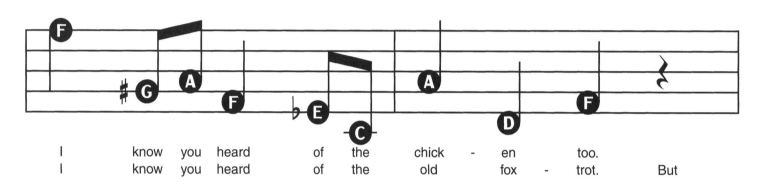

I know you heard of the chick - en too.
I know you heard of the old fox - trot. But

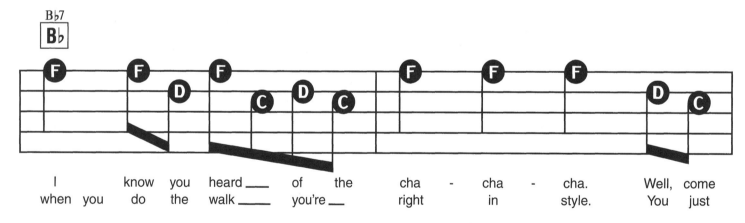

I know you heard ___ of the cha - cha - cha. Well, come
when you do the walk ___ you're ___ right in style. You just

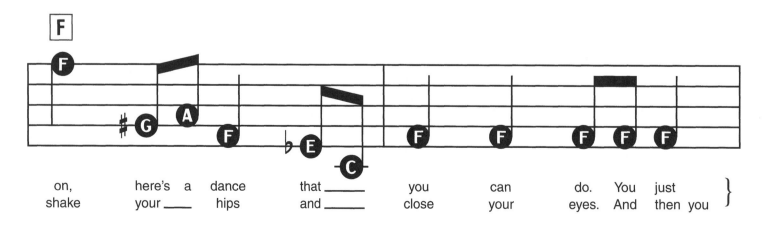

on, here's a dance that ___ you can do. You just
shake your ___ hips and ___ close your eyes. And then you

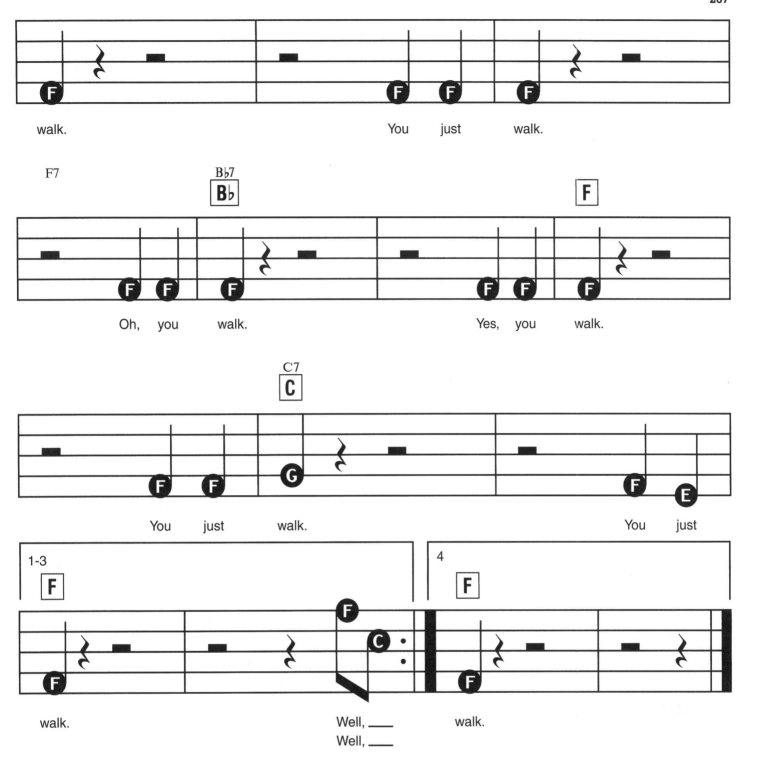

walk.   You   just   walk.

Oh,   you   walk.   Yes,   you   walk.

You   just   walk.   You   just

walk.   Well, ___   walk.
               Well, ___

Additional Lyrics

3. Well, I know you heard of the old mambo,
   And I know you heard of the old conga;
   But to really do the walk you start in close,
   And don't step on your partner's toes.
   You just walk. You just walk. Oh, you walk.
   Yes, you walk. Yeah, you walk. You just walk.

4. If you don't know what it's all about,
   Come to me and I'll show you how.
   We'll do it fast and we'll do it slow.
   Then you'll know the walk ev'rywhere you go.
   You just walk, then you walk.
   Now you walk, keep on walkin'.
   Keep on walkin'. That's the walk.

The Wayward Wind

Registration 4
Rhythm: Country or Shuffle

Words and Music by Herb Newman
and Stan Lebowsky

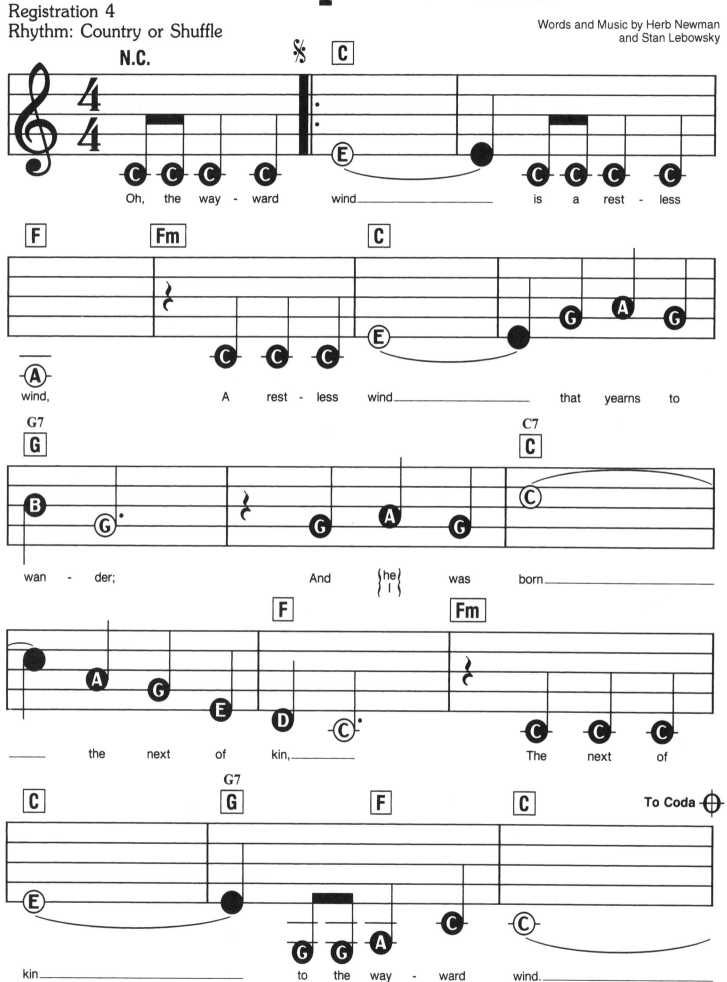

239

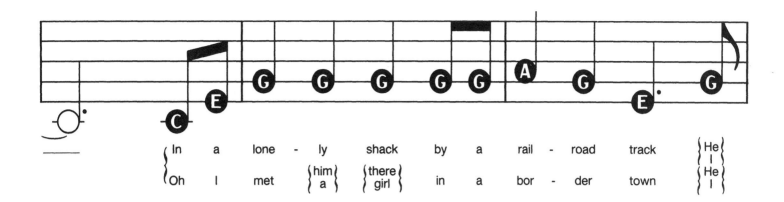

In a lone - ly shack by a rail - road track { He | He }
Oh I met { him a } { there girl } in a bor - der town { He | He }

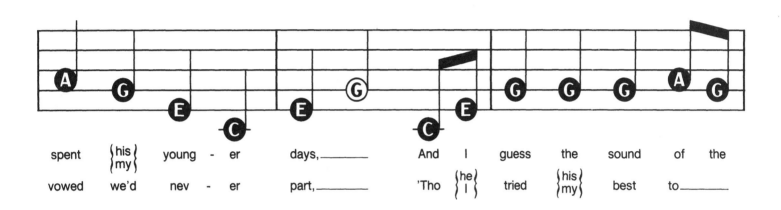

spent { his my } young - er days,_____ And I guess the sound of the
vowed we'd nev - er part,_____ 'Tho { he I } tried { his my } best to_____

G7
G

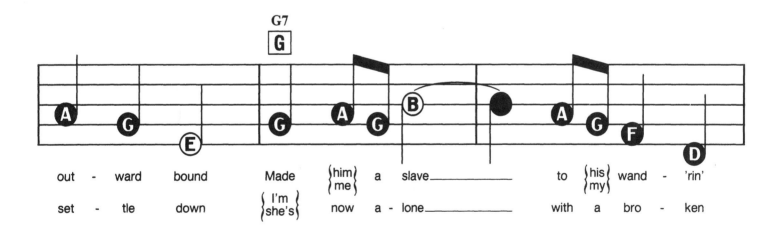

out - ward bound Made { him me } a slave_____ to { his my } wand - 'rin'
set - tle down { I'm she's } now a - lone_____ with a bro - ken

C

2nd time D.S. al Coda
(Return to %
Play to ⊕ and
skip to Coda)

CODA
⊕

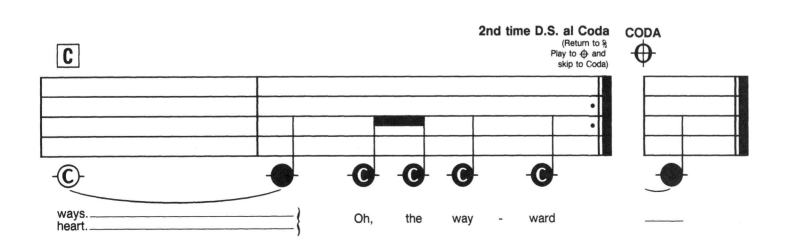

ways._____ { Oh, the way - ward
heart._____ }

Wear My Ring Around Your Neck

Registration 5
Rhythm: Rock

Words and Music by Bert Carroll
and Russell Moody

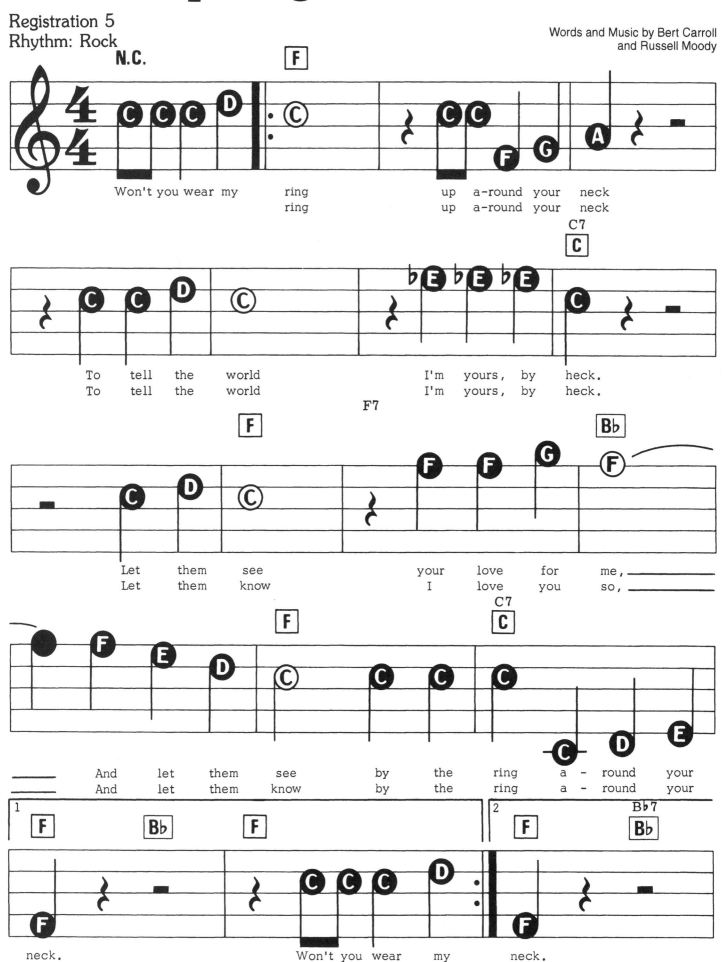

241

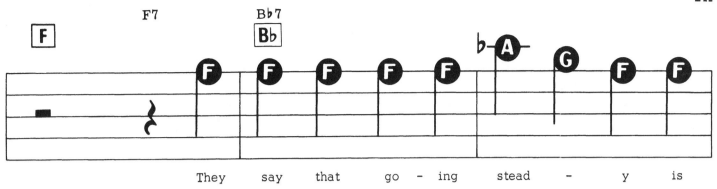

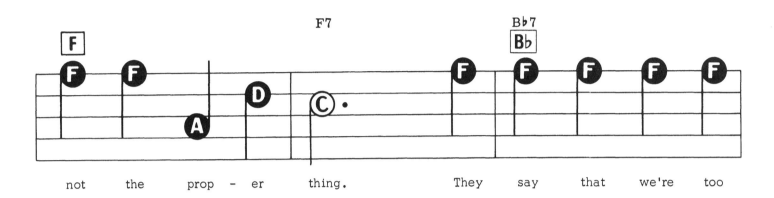

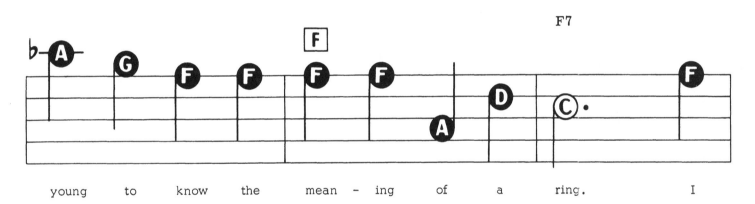

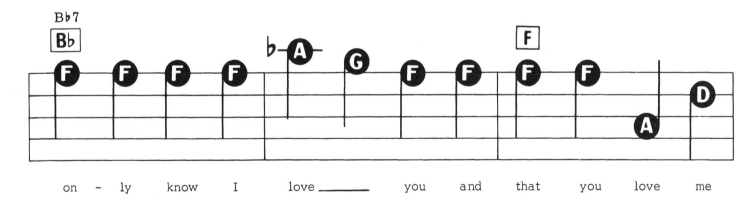

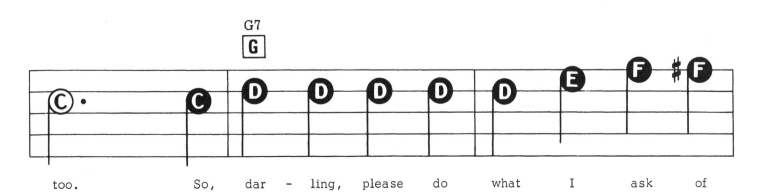

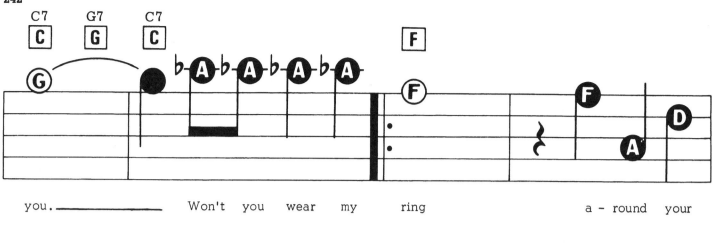

you._____ Won't you wear my ring a - round your

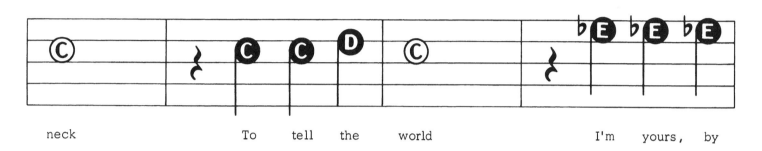

neck   To tell the world   I'm yours, by

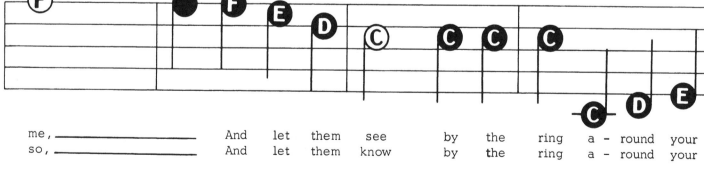

heck.   Let them see   your love for
Let them know   I love you

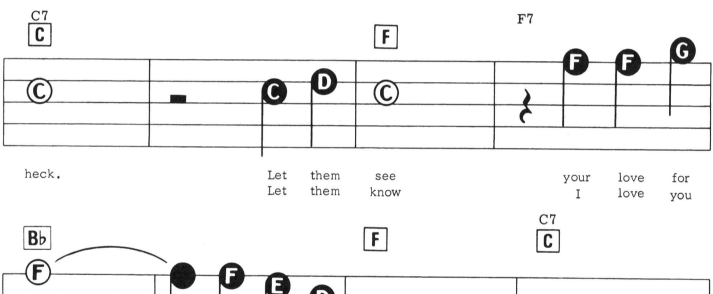

me,_____ And let them see by the ring a - round your
so,_____ And let them know by the ring a - round your

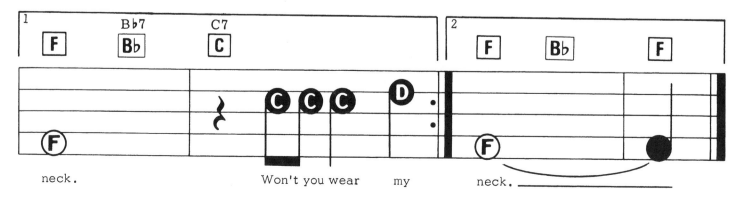

neck.   Won't you wear my   neck._____

What'd I Say

Registration 8
Rhythm: Shuffle or Swing

Words and Music by
Ray Charles

Hey, Ma - ma, don't you treat me wrong.
See the girl with the dia - mond ring.
Tell your Ma - ma, tell your Pa.

Come and love me all night long. Oh,
She knows how to twist that thing. Oh,
I'm gon - na ship you back to Ar - kan - sas. Oh,

oh, hey, hey, all
oh, hey, hey, all
yes, you don't do right, you don't do

right now.
right now.
right.

(Instrumental)

244

2

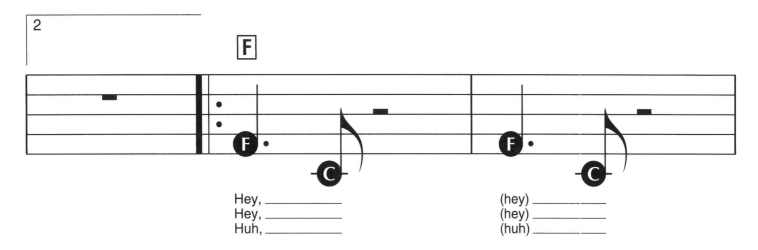

Hey, _____ (hey) _____
Hey, _____ (hey) _____
Huh, _____ (huh) _____

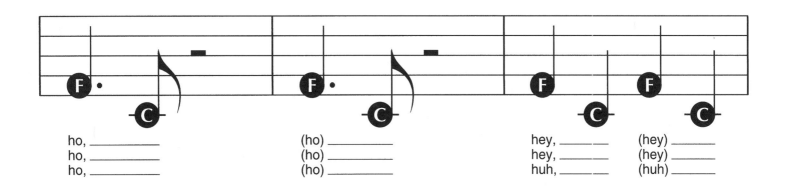

ho, _____ (ho) _____ hey, _____ (hey) _____
ho, _____ (ho) _____ hey, _____ (hey) _____
ho, _____ (ho) _____ huh, _____ (huh) _____

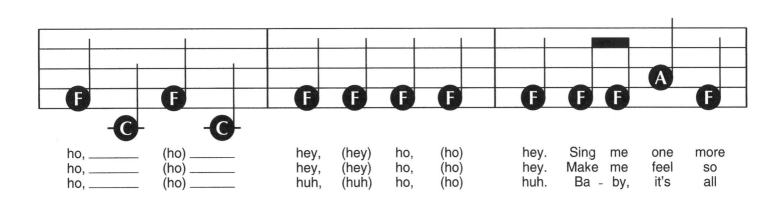

ho, _____ (ho) _____ hey, (hey) ho, (ho) hey. Sing me one more
ho, _____ (ho) _____ hey, (hey) ho, (ho) hey. Make me feel so
ho, _____ (ho) _____ huh, (huh) ho, (ho) huh. Ba - by, it's all

time.
good.
right.

Sing me one more time.
Make me feel so good.
Ba - by, it's all right, right now.

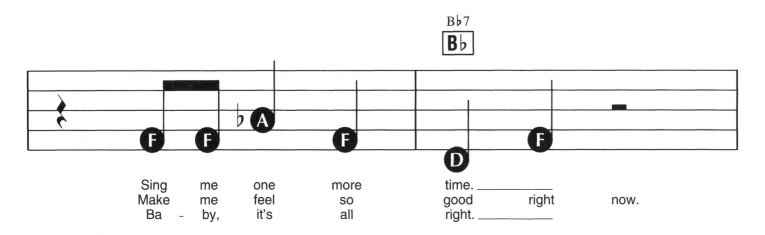

Sing me one more time. _____
Make me feel so good right now.
Ba - by, it's all right. _____

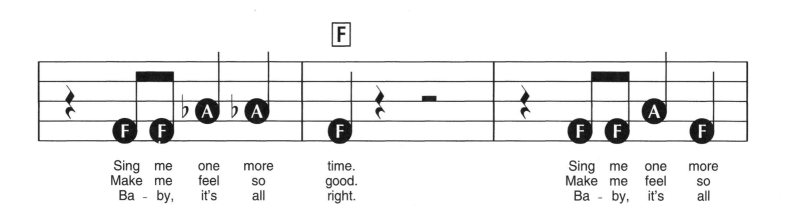

Sing me one more time.
Make me feel so good.
Ba - by, it's all right.

Sing me one more
Make me feel so
Ba - by, it's all

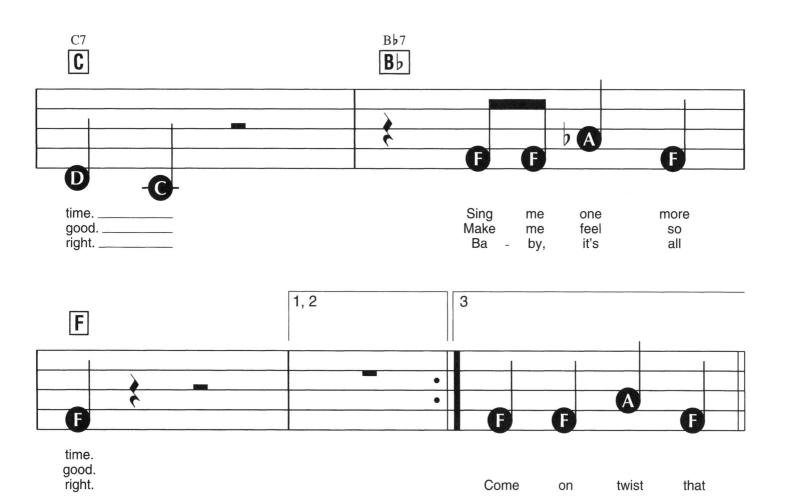

time. _____
good. _____
right. _____

Sing me one more
Make me feel so
Ba - by, it's all

time.
good.
right.

Come on twist that

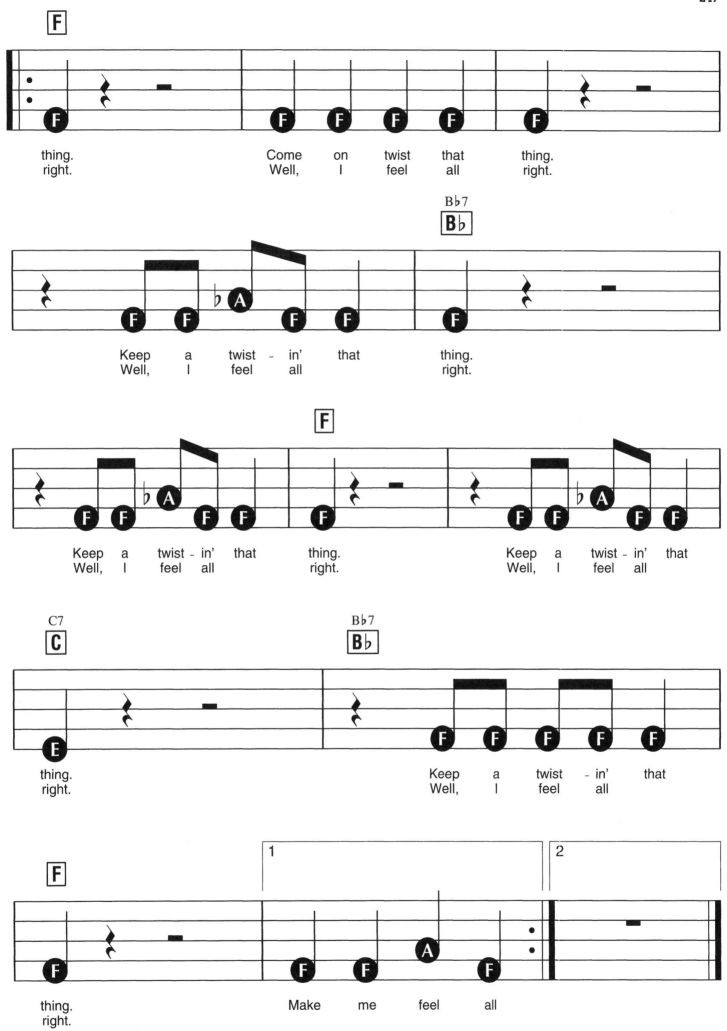

A White Sport Coat
(And a Pink Carnation)

Registration 8
Rhythm: Country or Fox Trot

Words and Music by
Marty Robbins

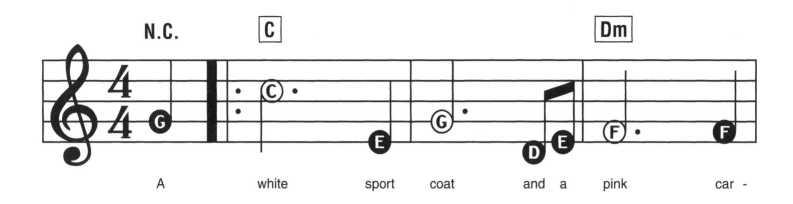

A white sport coat and a pink car -

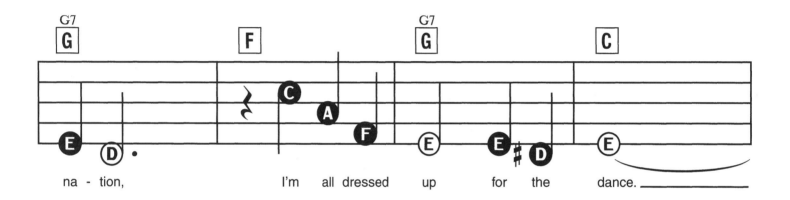

na - tion, I'm all dressed up for the dance. _____

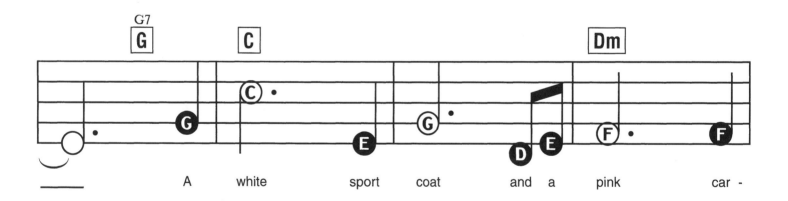

A white sport coat and a pink car -

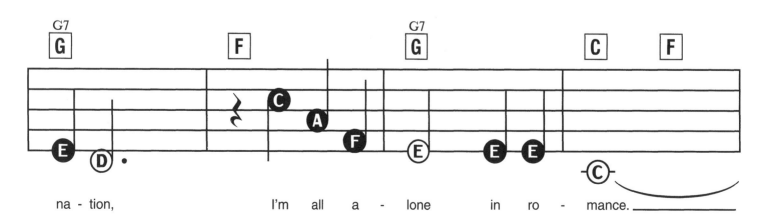

na - tion, I'm all a - lone in ro - mance. _____

249

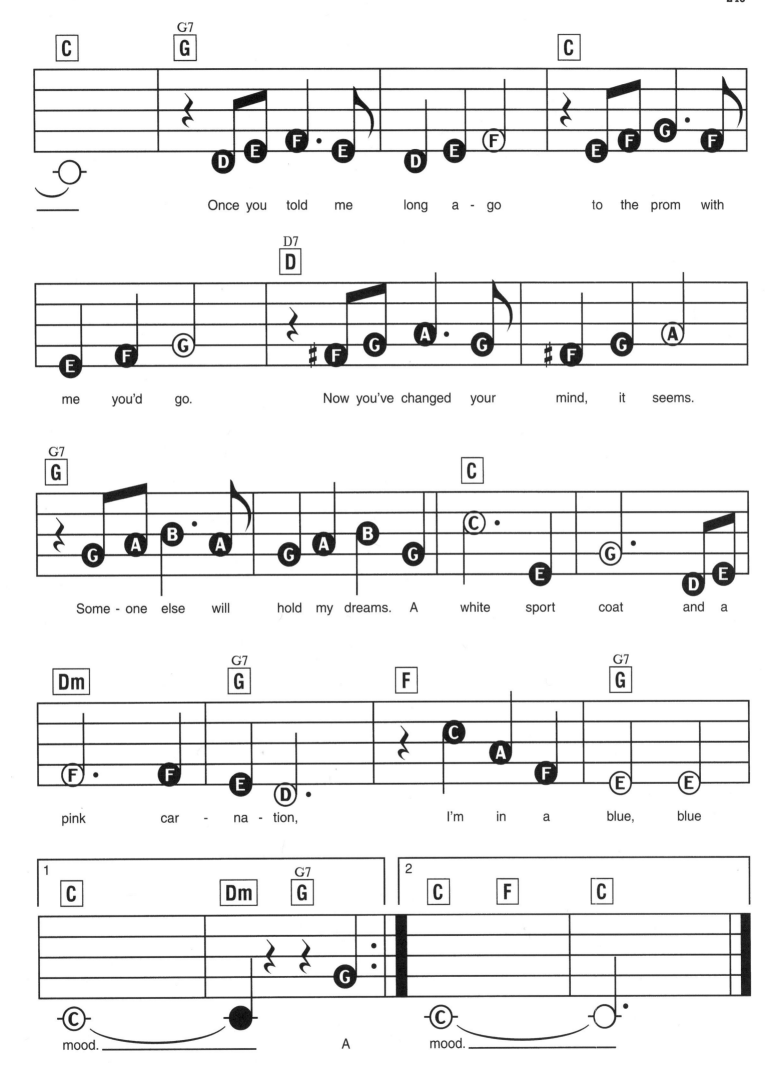

Why

Registration 7
Rhythm: Pops or Latin

Words and Music by Bob Marcucci
and Peter DeAngelis

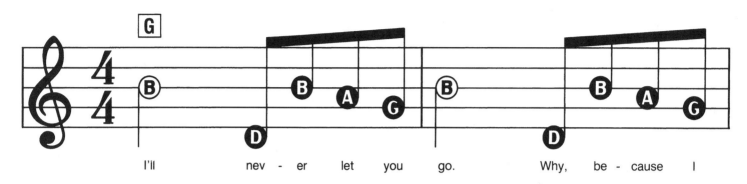

I'll nev - er let you go. Why, be - cause I

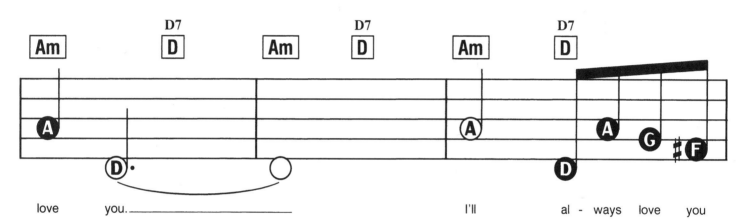

love you._____ I'll al - ways love you

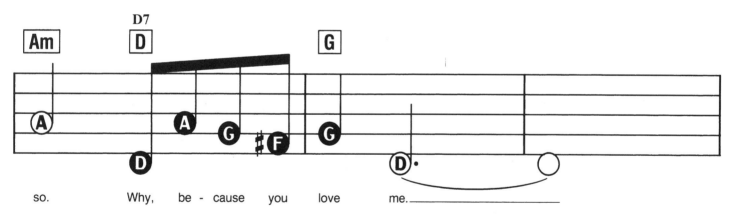

so. Why, be - cause you love me._____

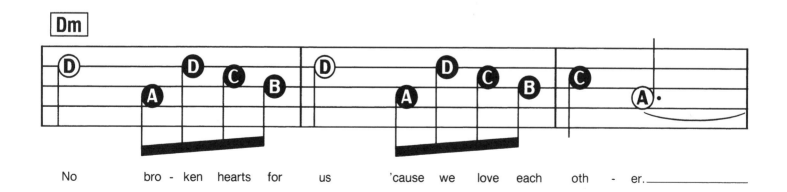

No bro - ken hearts for us 'cause we love each oth - er._____

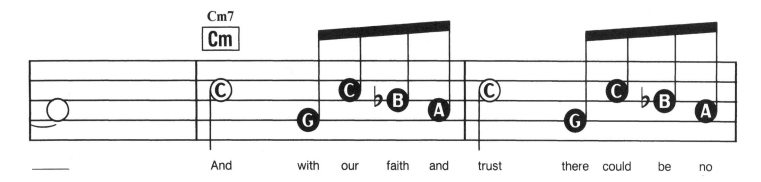

And with our faith and trust there could be no

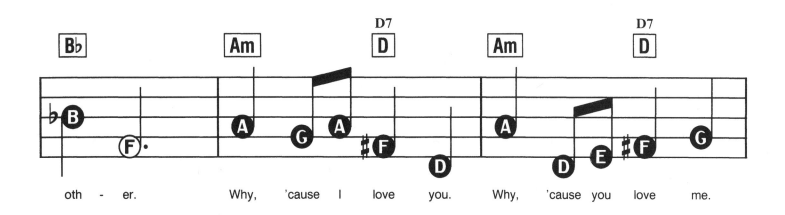

oth - er.   Why, 'cause I love you.   Why, 'cause you love me.

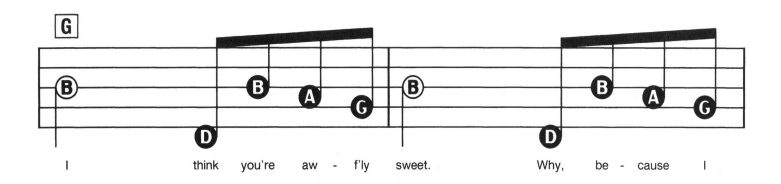

I   think you're aw - f'ly sweet.   Why, be - cause I

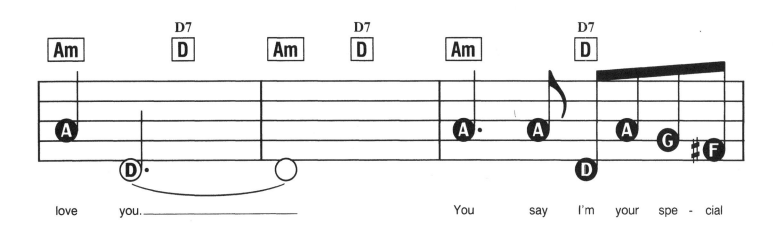

love you.____   You say I'm your spe - cial

252

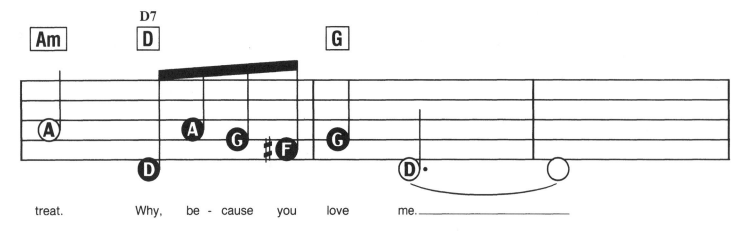

treat.   Why,   be - cause   you   love   me._____

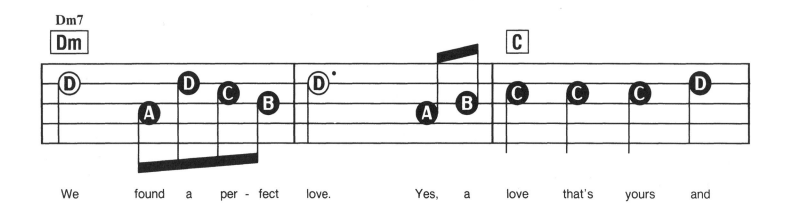

We   found   a   per - fect   love.   Yes,   a   love   that's   yours   and

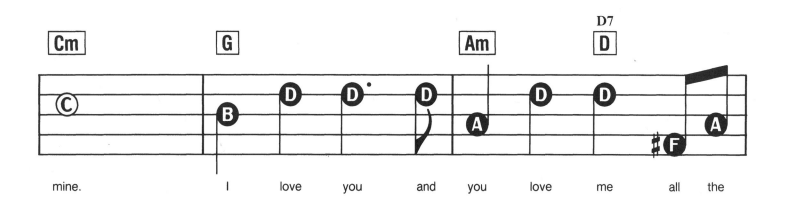

mine.   I   love   you   and   you   love   me   all   the

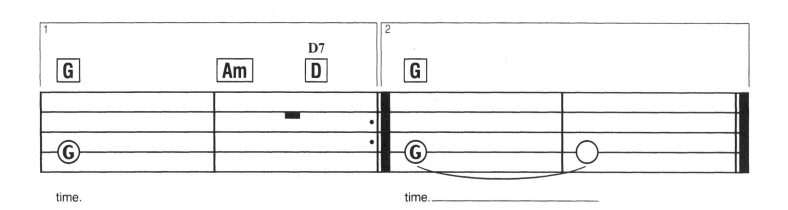

time.   time._____

Young Blood

Registration 9
Rhythm: Rock 'n' Roll or Boogie Woogie

Words and Music by Jerry Leiber,
Mike Stoller and Doc Pomus

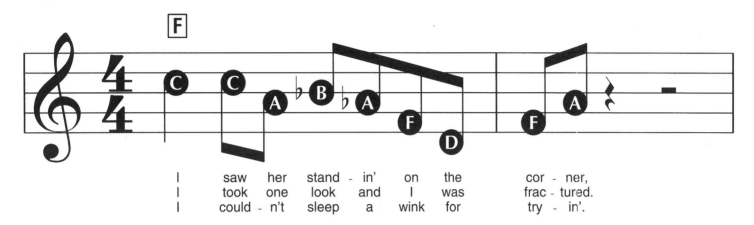

I saw her stand - in' on the cor - ner,
I took one look and I was frac - tured.
I could - n't sleep a wink for try - in'.

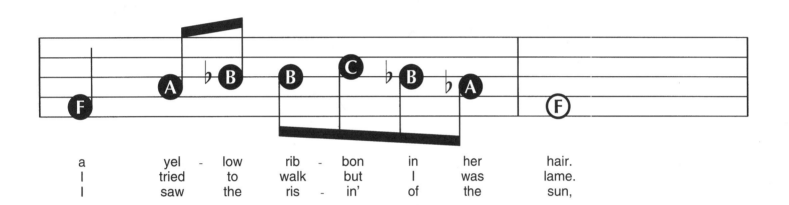

a yel - low rib - bon in her hair.
I tried to walk but I was lame.
I saw the ris - in' of the sun,

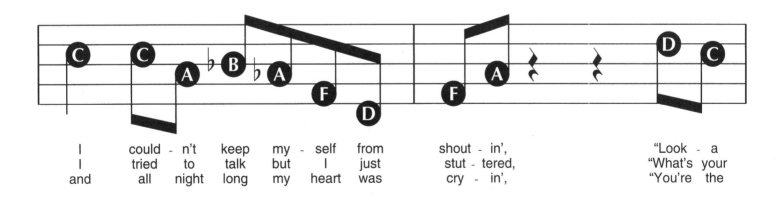

I could - n't keep my - self from shout - in', "Look - a
I tried to talk but I just stut - tered, "What's your
and all night long my heart just was cry - in', "You're the

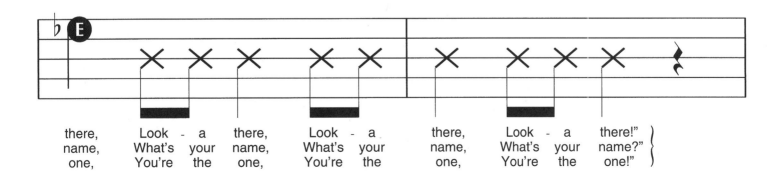

there, Look - a there, Look - a there, Look - a there!")
name, What's your name, What's your name, What's your name?" }
one, You're the one, You're the one, You're the one!")

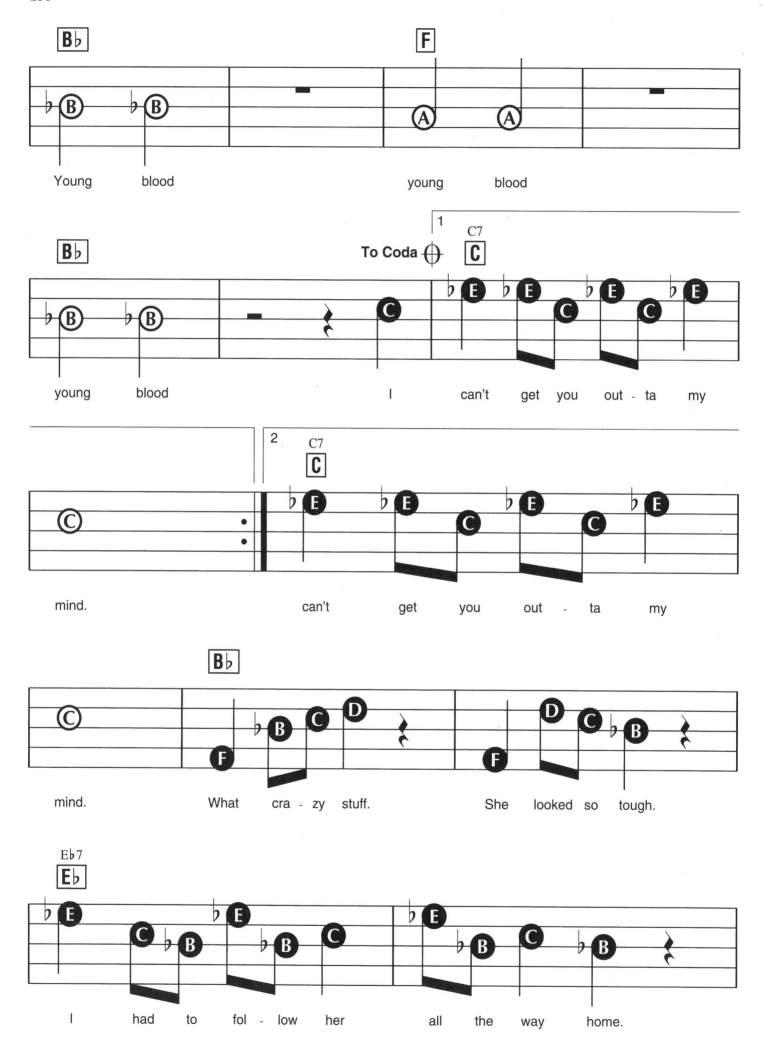

255

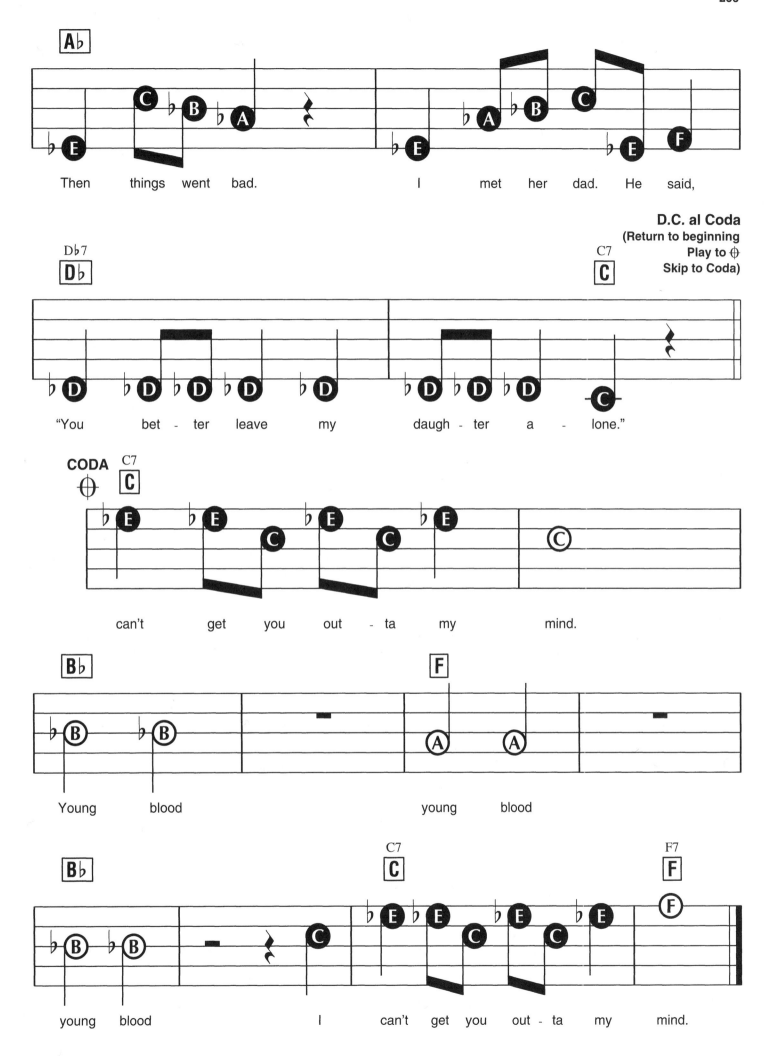

Why Don't You Believe Me

Registration 2
Rhythm: Fox Trot

Words and Music by Lew Douglas,
Luther King Laney and Leroy W. Rodde

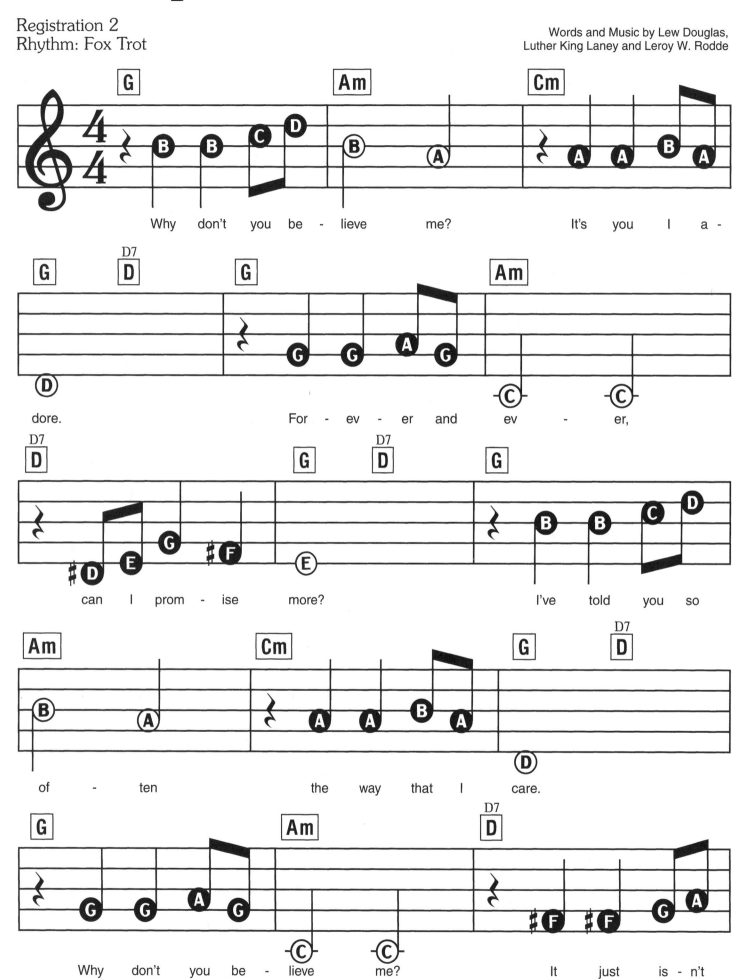

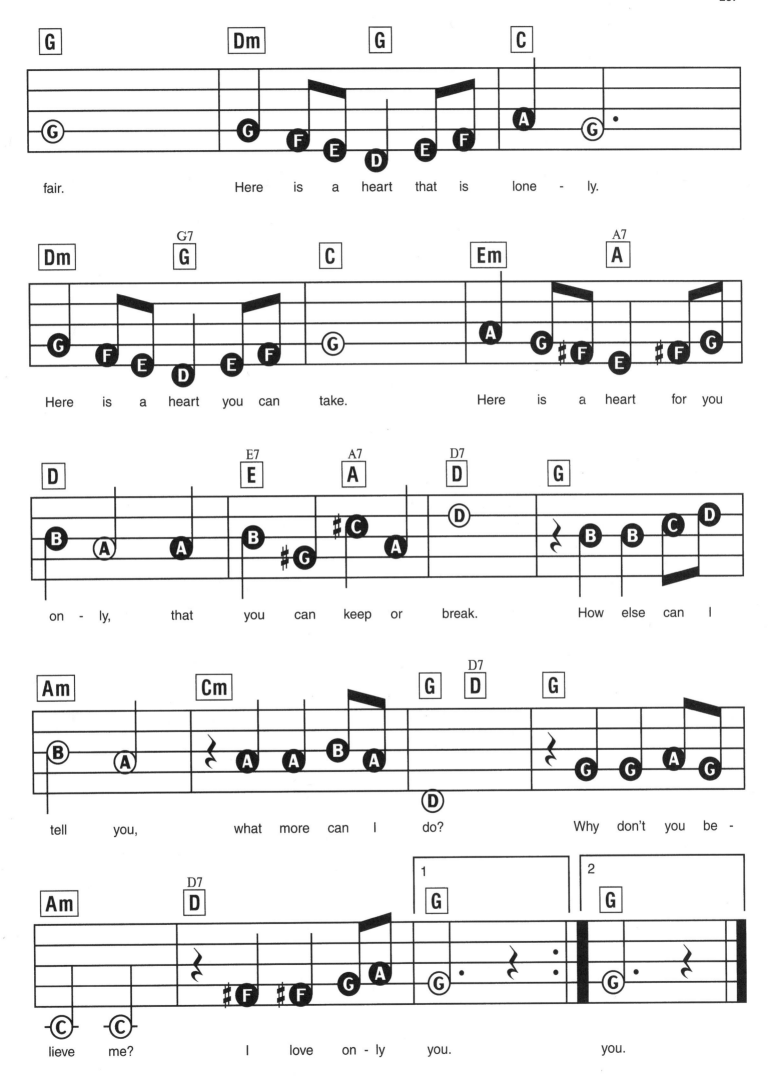

Wonderful! Wonderful!

Registration 10
Rhythm: Ballad or Fox Trot

Words by Ben Raleigh
Music by Sherman Edwards

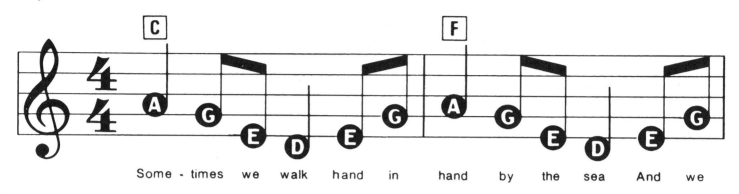

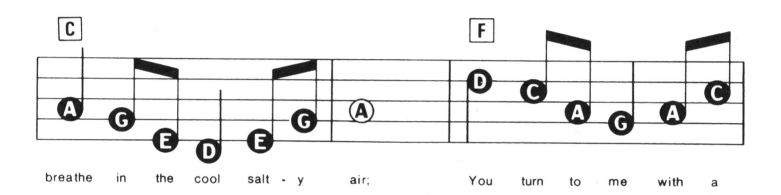

Some - times we walk hand in hand by the sea And we

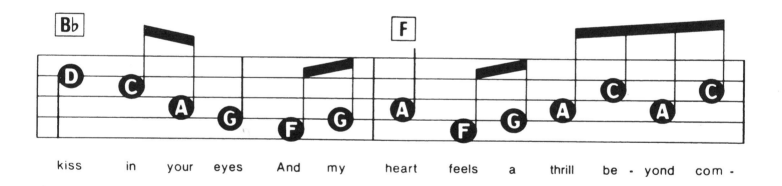

breathe in the cool salt - y air; You turn to me with a

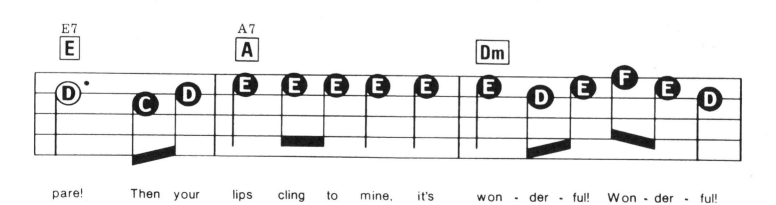

kiss in your eyes And my heart feels a thrill be - yond com -

pare! Then your lips cling to mine, it's won - der - ful! Won - der - ful!

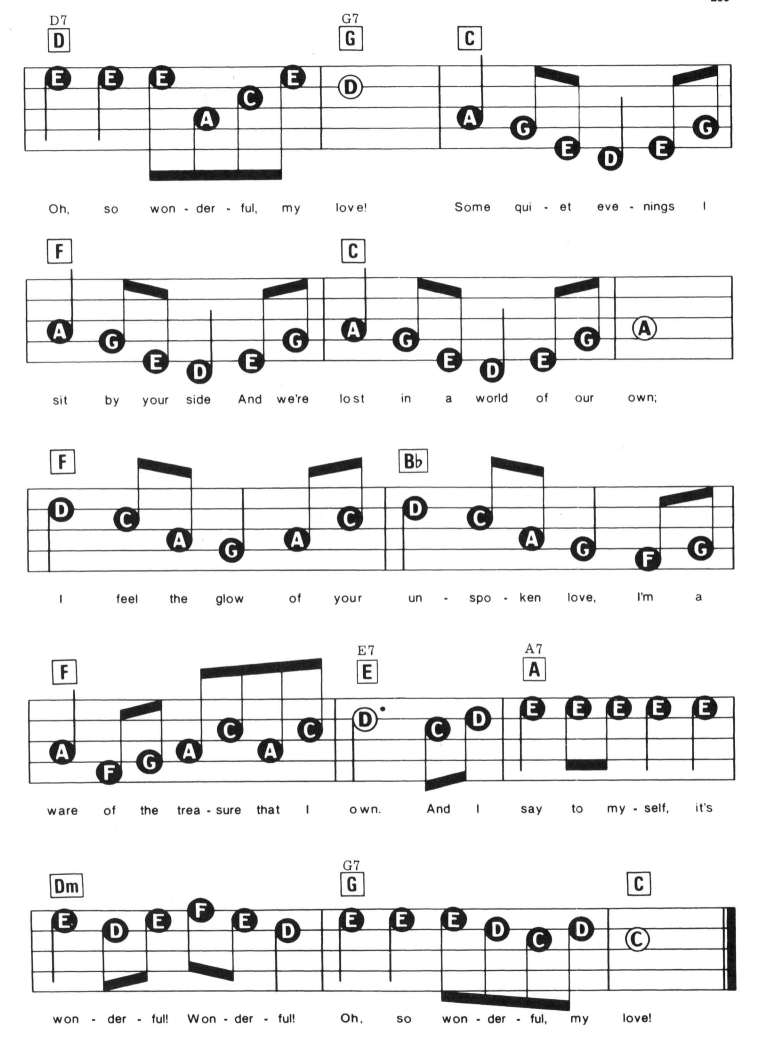

You Belong to Me

Registration 4
Rhythm: Ballad

Words and Music by Pee Wee King,
Redd Stewart and Chilton Price

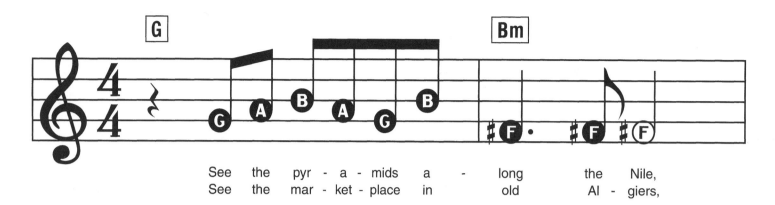

See the pyr - a - mids a - long the Nile,
See the mar - ket - place in old Al - giers,

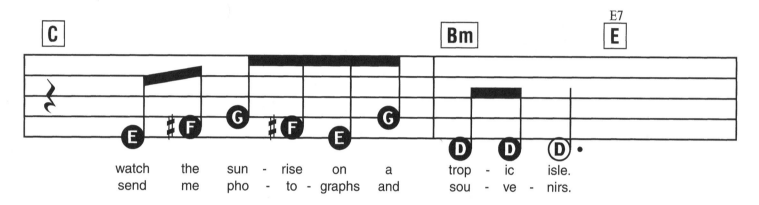

watch the sun - rise on a trop - ic isle.
send me pho - to - graphs and sou - ve - nirs.

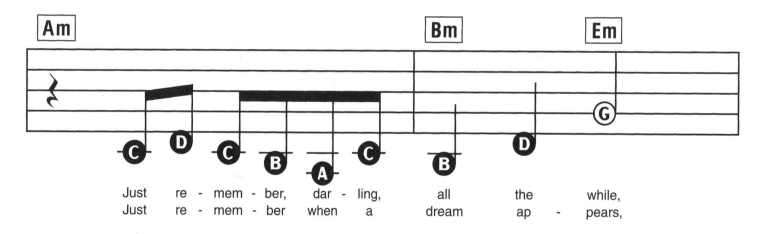

Just re - mem - ber, dar - ling, all the while,
Just re - mem - ber when a dream ap - pears,

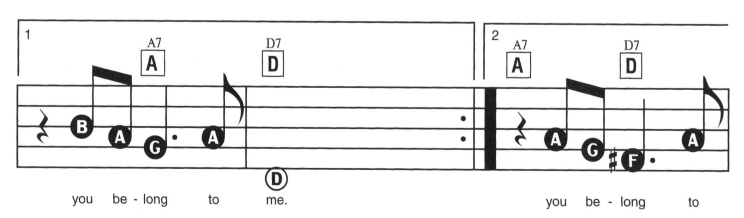

you be - long to me.   you be - long to

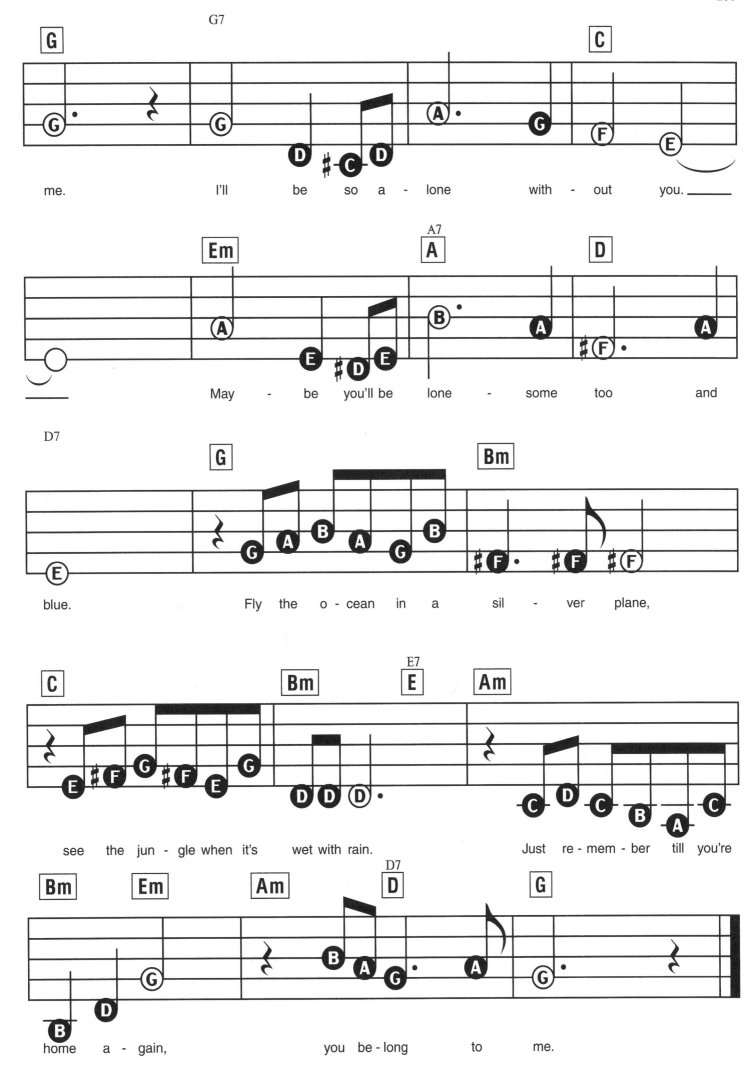

Registration Guide

- Match the Registration number on the song to the corresponding numbered category below. Select and activate an instrumental sound available on your instrument.

- Choose an automatic rhythm appropriate to the mood and style of the song. (Consult your Owner's Guide for proper operation of automatic rhythm features.)

- Adjust the tempo and volume controls to comfortable settings.

Registration

1	Mellow	Flutes, Clarinet, Oboe, Flugel Horn, Trombone, French Horn, Organ Flutes
2	Ensemble	Brass Section, Sax Section, Wind Ensemble, Full Organ, Theater Organ
3	Strings	Violin, Viola, Cello, Fiddle, String Ensemble, Pizzicato, Organ Strings
4	Guitars	Acoustic/Electric Guitars, Banjo, Mandolin, Dulcimer, Ukulele, Hawaiian Guitar
5	Mallets	Vibraphone, Marimba, Xylophone, Steel Drums, Bells, Celesta, Chimes
6	Liturgical	Pipe Organ, Hand Bells, Vocal Ensemble, Choir, Organ Flutes
7	Bright	Saxophones, Trumpet, Mute Trumpet, Synth Leads, Jazz/Gospel Organs
8	Piano	Piano, Electric Piano, Honky Tonk Piano, Harpsichord, Clavi
9	Novelty	Melodic Percussion, Wah Trumpet, Synth, Whistle, Kazoo, Perc. Organ
10	Bellows	Accordion, French Accordion, Mussette, Harmonica, Pump Organ, Bagpipes